Who Cares

Recommendations

'This excellent book is organised and written in a lively and engaging style with illustrations from students, teachers and a range of other sources that bring the narrative to life. The author has had long and significant experience in education and his passionate commitment shines through the text and will greatly appeal to all those who care deeply about the future of education and how they might contribute to present education debates.'

Professor David Woods, CBE.

Who Cares About Education? is a clear, powerful and insightful examination of the state of education in this country. It details the current system, explores its history and, importantly, presents credible, workable solutions. As a political campaigner, I feel better informed and motivated by this book to continue the fight for a better education system for all children in Britain.'

Nick Dineen.

'Eric Macfarlane is unflinching in itemising the way in which the best interests of children, and ultimately of our nation, have been prejudiced by doctrinaire politicians, the tyranny of assessment and distorted notions of what constitutes success. I heartedly wish the philosophy it succinctly and eloquently embodies had set the ethos for governmental thinking throughout the eighteen years I spent as the principal of a sixth-form college.'

Chris Thomson.

'An expert and highly pertinent insight into the nature of the learning and teaching processes and the principles and priorities that currently shape our schools , colleges and universities. It's well-written, very enjoyable and accessible, as well as thought-provoking.'

KCMG.

Some children, be they athletes, artists or scientists, are drawn to their life's work very early. I was such a child and my work as an actor and theatre maker began in the school's theatre department. Eric Macfarlane's new book pleads for a broader curriculum in our schools and I agree.'

Mark Rylance.

'Anyone with a passion for education should read this book. So much recent change has been driven by an overwhelming culture of compliance and accountability where short-term outcomes are pursued at the expense of developmental goals. *Who Cares About Education?* presents a coherent and constructive argument for the changes that are required to deliver the education system that our children deserve.

Gwyn Evans.

Eric Macfarlane has written a sweeping narrative of change and reform in English education covering half a century. He has been a participant and observer in all the key events of the period. It is a fascinating study, not just for the insights he brings to the historical record, but also for the way he shows how this history informs so many of the ideas and decisions being made today.

Professor Bob Moon.

'This is a remarkable work - a book about education that is difficult to put down. It is beautifully written and combines thoughtful analysis with fascinating and entertaining anecdotes. It may make for uncomfortable reading for some, but anyone who believes in true education standards will learn much from its insights. It is essential reading for anyone with responsibility for making education policy decisions.'

David Heaton, OBE.

'This new book exposes the savage inequalities of the English educational system. Eric Macfarlane draws on his extensive and critical scholarship to examine the deep historical roots of a system that systematically reproduces injustice. The arguments are coherent, the style warm but powerful. The book is a tremendous contribution to the struggle to recover teacher professionalism and wholesome education for children.'

Professor Terry Wrigley.

'Eric Macfarlane has a real gut feeling for what education should be about. At a time when discussion is mainly about exam results and giving schools new titles, his forceful arguments provide a timely reminder of what really matters in educating our young people and preparing them for a happy and fulfilled future.'

Chris Green, MBE.

'Education remains political dynamite, with teaching professionalism and autonomy constantly undermined, and school leaders flung aside like football managers in a bad season. That's why we need books like Eric Macfarlane's - restoring perspective, channelling rage, providing historical context, and voicing solutions. It's a book for all who care about real education.'

Geoff Barton.

'Eric Macfarlane describes with insight and clarity the ways in which our education system both reflects and determines the nature of our society. He writes from first-hand experience as an educator who has made a positive difference to so many young people's lives. Eric shares his passion for a broad and balanced curriculum and emphasises the enormous benefits of the arts as a serious part of every child's education and well-being. His book will empower us to ensure accessibility to the arts for future generations - in doing so our power will become our children's legacy.'

Dame Evelyn Glennie.

Published by New Generation Publishing in 2016

Copyright © Eric Macfarlane 2016

First Edition

www.newgeneration-publishing.com

ISBN: 978-1-78719-159-4

 New Generation Publishing

Who Cares About Education?

...going in the wrong direction

Eric Macfarlane

Foreword by Melissa Benn

The Author

Eric Macfarlane has taught in, and been head of, both secondary modern and grammar schools. He was the founding principal of Queen Mary's College, one of Hampshire's pioneering 16+ comprehensive colleges, and has been an LEA adviser, examiner and assessor of several different initiatives to improve the learning and teaching processes in both schools and universities. Whilst Principal of Queen Mary's College, he was seconded to Keble College for a year to assist with the Oxford Department of Education's introduction of a school-based teacher-training course. He worked at the University of Surrey and Birkbeck College promoting the Enterprise in Higher Education initiative, before becoming academic staff adviser in University College, London. Eric has had a long association with out-of-school learning initiatives and was chair of the Governing Council of the Active Training and Education Trust. He received the OBE in the Queen's Birthday Honours List in 1988.

For all who work in education and remain
true to their principles against the odds.

*'Our lives begin to end the day we
become silent about things that matter.'*
Martin Luther King Jr.

Contents

Foreword

This thoughtful book is published just as a fresh set of politicians try once more to overhaul our education system. Young people, says our government (which has, incidentally, no popular mandate for any such reform), should once more be divided into the supposedly academically able and the rest. The only problem with this proposal? It has already proved a failure as was shown, fifty years ago, when educators, parents, politicians and students, from all points on the political spectrum, rejected the binary division of the primary school population into winners and losers. And so our comprehensive system was born.

Yet here come the same old tired and élitist ideas, only this time they are dressed up as diversity not division, a means to promote so-called social mobility rather than suppress the achievements and spirits of the majority and with grammar schools now reframed as 'centres of excellence'. Having been a grammar school pupil, teacher and head teacher himself, Eric Macfarlane is particularly well placed to puncture the discouraging doublespeak of these proposals and he does so with forensic precision.

But this book, which goes to the heart of our current dilemmas, is about so much more. Eric Macfarlane has had an astonishingly varied and interesting life as a teacher, school leader, consultant and examiner, always learning from his many roles (this last is so important). He subtly and gently deploys this long experience to point out how far we have travelled from understanding and developing a profound sense of what education should be about. Instead, succeeding waves of anxious and arrogant politicians have substituted the quick fix for deep thought, the top-down overhaul for organically evolving change, the conventional and the arid for the bold and playful.

Our education system is slowly being strangled by an obeisance to old-fashioned ideas that only the academic route is worth anything, an obsession that not only fails so many of our children but does not even serve the traditionally successful. Every young person, whatever their talents, needs access to a general and more arts-based education and a more exploratory and enjoyable approach to the art of learning itself.

As the head of one of the country's pioneering open access 16-19 comprehensive colleges Eric Macfarlane shows us what such a broad and less specialised educational experience can achieve - indeed, what it *did* achieve - and how much it benefits young people at a point when they are at the height of their creativity and expressiveness. With controlled force, and always resorting to the reasoned, human example, he argues that if we would only stop trying to ape the past and in particular some partial, mythical view of the old public school model we could develop a more original and exciting vision of learning.

At the same time, we need to loosen the grip of centralised political control on our schools. Genuine school and classroom autonomy has been eroded over decades by politicians and policymakers convinced that they, and they alone, know what a good education looks like, sweeping away generations of fruitful experiment and hard-won experience in the process. Now even our primary schools are being robbed of their breadth and vitality in order to become early staging posts on the way to an over-specialised university experience.

Despite his warnings, this is not a pessimistic book. Eric Macfarlane manages to convey the many joys of truly unfettered learning, and acknowledges that there are, and will always remain, many wonderful teachers and heads and pupils in our schools, working against the grain of official policy.

For all that, there beats in this well informed crie de coeur a single powerful message: we are heading in completely the wrong direction.

This wise book will speak to a wide range of audiences. It will surely strike a chord with those lucky enough to have experienced first-hand some of the innovative and intellectually exciting experiments of an earlier era of comprehensive education before obsessive accountability measures and endless testing took over. It will also prove an important resource for a generation of teachers, parents and young people who sense something has gone very wrong in today's system.

This rich mix of memoir, reflection and persuasion will, I hope, act as both tremendous encouragement to their burgeoning rebellions and a guide to shaping an alternative approach.

Melissa Benn
Visit my website at http://melissabenn.com

Chapter 1

Unrealised Potential

" We are all born with immense natural talents but few people discover what they are and even fewer develop them properly. Ironically one of the main reasons for this massive waste of talent is the very process that is meant to develop it: education."

Sir Ken Robinson.

We're having to be on our toes today: our little granddaughter is visiting. We're racking our brains for names for her two butterflies that hatched this morning. Any old names won't do: they must be alliterative, and appropriate for the personality and behaviour of their owners, like the names already chosen for earlier arrivals - Tumbling Tom, who, after emerging from his chrysalis, promptly fell over, and Laura Longlegs who got her limbs tangled up as she struggled to free herself from her cocoon (cue here for question and answer session on human births).

At the moment granddaughter is in the kitchen watching the routines intently and lending a hand. She knows where everything goes and remembers that the cutlery-drawer has to be eased out carefully. We have to explain why there's a new place for the teapot. She's found an unused craft set in the toy cupboard and she closely studies the explanatory diagrams, noting in passing that the colouring of the pictures doesn't precisely match that of the materials to which it relates. Having mastered the processes outlined, she uses them to develop an idea of her own, rather than one of those given in the instructions as an example. At lunch she watches grandpa struggling with a new but refractory salt cellar. Gently taking the offending object out of his hands, she silently demonstrates how it works.

Child prodigy?

I doubt it. Just an alert and watchful child, full of questions and ideas that she wishes to share. Children are born with a sense of wonder and are determinedly inquisitive about the world around them. Confident in their response to their surroundings, they can be remarkably thoughtful, focused and persevering when trying to find out about something they want to understand. And they dare to dream - to imagine what would happen if you apply an established theory to an unknown situation, a process once called intelligence. Children have an obvious potential to become creative thinkers, problem-solvers and innovators. It's easy to forget this, for something happens to that potential as children grow up. Too frequently the sense of wonder and clear-eyed vision become dimmed, even lost. The instinctive interest in everything around them fades. There is a marked falling off in confidence.

Pablo Picasso is said to have believed that all children are artists: the problem was for them to remain so as they grew up. Systems of formal education all too often confine or deny children's potential, rather than develop it. Sir Peter Ustinov's school report stated, "He shows great originality that must be curbed at all costs." Winston Churchill hated school and was consistently bottom of the class at Harrow. Albert Einstein was considered slow as a young child and eventually expelled for his poor attitude: he was alleged to have asked too many questions and to have been a bad example to other pupils. "At school," says Sir Richard Branson, "I was a dyslexic and dunce." Many succeed in spite of the system. Not everyone, however, is so fortunate.

Within a short time of starting their formal education, many children seem reluctant to talk about their experiences, responding to a parental 'What did you do at school today?' with bored and non-committal replies. It's accepted that, by their early teens, children can concentrate their learning on particular aspects of human knowledge and experience and that others areas of human knowledge can be closed off, perhaps forever. Many teenagers are switched off by the whole learning process and just go through the motions to avoid getting into trouble. And by no means all of those who continue with their studies after school do so out of a genuine enthusiasm for learning: there is a significant drift into higher education on the conveyor belt of peer expectations and parental and institutional ambitions. Most university students clearly enjoy the social life, but if you question them closely about their course their response is often an equivocal 'It's all right'.

How does this loss of excitement in the learning process come about? What has happened to the young child's natural curiosity, the insatiable desire to know more about the world? Can we really be unaware how important it is for us to ensure that children hold on to their spirit of wide-ranging enquiry and creative thinking? - important for their own development and the quality of their future life as adults, and indeed vitally important for the survival of our society in a world of unprecedented change and complexity. Or is it that we simply cannot summon up the collective effort to create a new education system fit for this purpose? We are inclined to cling to traditional ideas and ways of doing things well beyond the point when they are effective and relevant. This is particularly true of education. Whilst the need for radical change grows daily, our system is becoming ever more entrenched in the past. We are currently losing what H G Wells called civilisation's "race between education and catastrophe".

The challenges facing the world are multiplying at a bewildering pace. The population explosion, the indiscriminate use of resources and destruction of the environment, climate change, terrorism, stress and mental illness, pandemics and the rapidly-increasing ability of life-threatening diseases to resist antibiotics, an ageing population, mass migration, world-wide economic fluctuations - these are just some of the areas where the rate and magnitude of change are causing immense global problems. Our ability to respond to this situation is seriously impaired by the way in which we have been conditioned to view the human situation compartmentally and parochially. Many of our current difficulties are too complex and inter-related to be resolved by groups of specialists working largely in isolation.

A feature of the regular reports on the economy given by Mark Carney, Governor of the Bank of England, has been his insistence on the need to look at the economy, not as a self-contained problem that has to be sorted out before we tackle issues like education, social welfare, immigration, but as an integral part of a complex pattern of closely-related global problems. Speaking on climate change, Mark Carney has re-iterated the warnings of Pope Francis and President Obama that, unless we take action now, the consequent disaster will be beyond the future generation to rectify. The consequences of inaction on this issue will, he has asserted, not simply be environmental, but will impact on many other global problems and seriously threaten the economic, financial and political stability of the world. Some critics have responded by suggesting that the Governor has stepped outside his brief and should not get involved with things that are not his concern. They could not be more wrong: these problems concern every one of us.

As long as we cling to our compartmentalised view of the human situation we shall struggle to solve global problems. We need to cross traditional disciplines and geographical barriers, consulting, co-operating, sharing information, and working together in a common cause. The paralysis that gripped Europe in the face of the recent waves of refugees escaping from civil war and persecution are a clear indication of western governments' failure to cope with an unforeseen problem. At a domestic level, a series of totally unexpected political developments has completely changed the political scene in ways that no-one fully understands and to which we are struggling to adapt. The key players in both major parties have changed out of all recognition so that many of our new leaders are not only woefully short of relevant experience but appear to be lacking the new ideas and imagination that the current situation requires. The June 2016 referendum on our European Union membership revealed frightening degrees of prejudice and intolerance that show just how fragile our carefully-nurtured democracy is. If the education system is to play a part in seeking to remedy this situation it has to revise its priorities.

Our education system was designed at another time and for another purpose: it is entirely inappropriate to meet current needs. Sir Ken Robinson, a lifelong campaigner for creative thinking, speaks passionately to audiences across the world on the global challenges facing our society and the need for revolutionary changes in the way in which we prepare young people for them. In his book, *Out of Our Minds,* Robinson draws a parallel between our neglect of the environment and our failure to provide young people with an education appropriate to the 21st century:

"... there is a similar calamity in our use of human resources. In the interests of the industrial economies we have subjected generations of people to narrow forms of education that have marginalised some of their most important talents and qualities. In pursuit of higher levels of efficiency and productivity in our organisations, we have overlooked the essentially human factors on which creativity and innovation naturally depend. We have wasted much of what people have to offer because we have not seen the value of it."

Mass education in this country dates back to the latter half of the nineteenth century when it was strongly influenced by the economic needs of the time. A second stage of the industrial revolution required a more skilled labour force and created new kinds of employment which led to a close connection between the education provided by the state and the factory system. The system was based on instruction and repetition with obedience, order and conformity its key features. There has, of course, been enormous progress in education over the last 150 years, but our approach still bears the hallmarks of nineteenth century priorities. Much of what we currently do in schools is inappropriate, even counter-productive.

In the past, change has often been predictable, a gradual variation in an otherwise fairly stable situation, a slowing down or quickening of a trend with which we are broadly familiar. Now change is headlong. We are constantly presented with situations and problems that we haven't previously encountered and that we don't fully understand. They come at us out of the blue - unforgettably so on that cloudless morning of 9/11, which announced an age of global terrorism.

The technological revolution alone is completely changing the way we think and live. We are having to adapt to new ways of working, studying, accessing information and communicating with each other. No aspect of our lives is untouched by the new technology: it has changed our leisure time, our personal relationships, even our sexual behaviour. These changes are not always for the better. Like many of the great scientific discoveries of the past, today's technological developments can be used for good or evil, and we must be concerned that, whilst raising standards of living, technology is also substantially reducing our quality of life. Hackers, criminal gangs, sexual predators, suppliers of lethal drugs, fraudsters preying on the elderly and vulnerable, extremists of every kind - they are all experiencing a bonanza using the internet with impunity. They pose a serious threat to our way of life and we have to learn fast if we are to maintain control of current technology.

In a BBC radio interview on the first day of the 21st century, Sir Martin Rees, the Astronomer Royal, was asked what chance he would give the world of surviving the next millennium. " I'm not sure about the next millennium," he replied," but I think I give us a 50/50 chance of surviving the next 100 years." "Why do you say that?" asked the interviewer. "Well," replied Sir Martin, "I fear that the speed of man's technological discoveries is outpacing our wisdom and ability to control what we have discovered."

Naturally we want to believe that this is an unduly pessimistic view of the dangers we face. But what if these repeated warnings are justified? We have a long history of pursuing scientific and technological research in a vacuum without considering the outcomes, implications and human cost of what we are doing until it is too late - one of the unfortunate consequences of our specialist approach to education. Can we really break that mould? Is there still time for our educational system to be re-invented for the twenty-first century? Are we prepared to turn our practices upside down and nurture rather than stifle children's imagination and creativity? Are there ways in which we can ensure that our children leave the educational system with a better understanding of human needs, combining a spirit of enterprise and innovation with the resilience to respond to fast-changing situations? Will they possess the idealism and moral strength to tackle the manifold problems facing our society? And the empathy and communication skills to work collaboratively to solve them? Charles Darwin stressed that it was those species that were most adaptable to change that stood the best chance of survival.

We have to start educating our young people to think in a wider and more imaginative dimension so that they recognise the connections and transferences between different phenomena and human experiences that many of our compartmentally-trained specialists seem incapable of comprehending. The traditional emphasis on the acquisition, retention and testing of the knowledge of our ancestors has to give way to a skills-based education system in which the next generation learns how to access and evaluate new information and to develop a spirit of enterprise, creativity and entrepreneurship. The CBI's warning that some British schools have become mere 'academic factories' indicates how far away we are from realising this vision. British pupils and students are the most tested in the industrialised world, and the whole paraphernalia of assessing, examining, grading and ranking of schools' exam results in league tables has had a disastrous effect on educational priorities and practices.

There is no sign that our political decision-makers are listening to what is being said or, if they are, that they understand it. Their background - an élitist education, political career and often affluent lifestyle - cocoons many of our leaders from the lives of the ordinary people that they represent. Their interest in educational reform is limited to quick-fix solutions and peripheral adjustments designed to appeal to the self-interest of specific sections of the electorate. They constantly tinker with the system, but remain slaves to it. There is no sense of permanency about the changes that are made: each successive government seeks to cancel out the initiatives introduced by its predecessor and to establish its own limited political agenda. Moreover, there is little consistency, even within the lifetime of a single government: successive Secretaries of State bring their personal ideology to the Education Department and seek to stamp it on the system as a mark of their effectiveness. Since the 1988 Education Reform Act, which introduced the process of political intervention in the curriculum and management of schools, there have been twelve different Secretaries of State for Education with an average tenure of less than two years. Barry Sheerman, a long-serving chair of the House of Commons select committee on education, is quoted as saying: "A school that was changing its leadership as regularly ...would be put in special measures immediately."

As soon as they are appointed, fly-by-night Education Secretaries declare their personal prejudices, announcing, without consultation, that history syllabuses are to have a greater focus on medieval times, or that books by American authors should be removed from English literature courses, or that we should adopt the intensive methods of teaching used by totalitarian states. Having shown their mettle in this way, they often depart, leaving someone else to force through their so-called reforms.

A popular ploy used by Education Secretaries to create the illusion that they are action men or women and up-to-date in their thinking is to alter the name and logo of their Department. Thus the Department for Education and Skills became the Department for Education and Employment, then the Department for Education, followed by the Department for Education and Science, the Department for Children, Schools and Families and back to the Department of Education. These little self-indulgences wouldn't perhaps matter very much if they didn't use up time, energy and money that could be more profitably spent in other ways. The DCSF was known as the Department for Curtains and Soft Furnishings, in recognition of the fact that, when he was Secretary of State for Education, Ed Balls installed a grand staircase made from glass and surgical steel, together with new designer furniture shipped in from Italy - at a total cost alleged to have been £3 million. The Department was having to make £2 billion pounds of savings at the time.

Another more obvious illustration of politicians' extremely limited and superficial view of what constitutes reform is the constant alteration of the system examination boards are required to employ to indicate grades of success and failure in national examinations. My own 16+ School Certificate recorded the result in each of my subject examinations under four headings - very good, credit, pass and fail. Lettered grades were then introduced, initially six (A-F), later reduced to five (A-E). Further differentiation followed with the introduction of a nine-point numerical scale, 1 being the top grade and 9 the lowest. Then a two-level exam system was introduced, with the highest numerical grades of the lower level equating with the lowest grades of the higher level. These two levels were later merged and the recording of results reverted to a letter system, this time with seven categories (A-G). A super grade (A*) was subsequently added to make eight categories. In 2012 the Secretary of State,

Michael Gove, announced yet another resurrection from the past - nine grades designated by numbers, but with 9 this time being the highest grade instead of the lowest. By the time this version of recording exam results is implemented we shall no doubt be due for another turn of the merry-go-round. Teachers are well-used to this scenario: we have all encountered pupils who spend more energy and time on strategies for avoiding their homework assignments than they'd use if they simply got down to doing what was required of them.

The confusion caused by constant re-adjustment of the level of exam achievement denoted by each grade is compounded by the habitual attempts to make success more difficult. So, in the Gove scheme, a 9 grade is to be a 'super grade', an A** in the previous terminology, and reserved for a very small élite of high-fliers. Further refining of the differentiation process takes place as one moves down the scale, with the categories 9-5 representing the old A-C range. Category 5 is tricky, equating with the middle and upper parts of the old grade C, whilst category 4 is equal to the lower part of C and upper part of D. The outcome of all this complex fine-tuning is that in the future it's going to be more difficult to obtain a 5 than it had been to obtain a C. This, of course, is what the tinkering is all about.

Anyone depressed by this latest manifestation of the obsessive desire to establish multiple categories of human success and failure should take heart from the fact that the exam system is becoming increasingly irrelevant to employers, many of whom are seeking to recruit young people with a wide range of experiences and skills, most of which are not revealed by exam results. Exams primarily test knowledge acquisition and retention, the importance of which has steadily declined with the technological revolution. The need now is for the next generation to know how to access, understand, evaluate and use the information that is so readily available to them. In 2014 a survey by the CBI and Pearson, the publisher, indicated that, when they were recruiting school and college leavers, employers considered basic factors such as attitude (85%) and general aptitude (63%) considerably more important than examination performance (38%).

A similar message is coming from graduate employers who are abandoning a longstanding recruitment policy of filtering out candidates on the basis of A level results. PricewaterhouseCoopers, the prestigious accountancy firm, has rejected school exam results as a criterion for determining the potential of their applicants for employment, declaring that they are missing out on able job applicants whose exam results didn't reveal their potential. In a May 2015 BBC interview, Stephen Isherwood, Chief Executive of the Association of Graduate Employers, welcomed this initiative by the country's leading graduate employer and called on all the Association's members to embrace the same policy.

These are small but significant steps forward towards a wider understanding of the limitations of the academic curriculum. Exam results are nowhere near as important as we are led to believe and we need more people to say that openly and emphatically. Judith Carlisle, the Headmistress of Oxford High School, hit the *Daily Mail* headlines in the run-up to the 2014 GCSE exams by asserting that five years after the event 'no-one will give a damn' what results her pupils had received.

It is to be hoped that at least some of the *Daily Mail* 's readers took note of the thinking behind this inflammatory statement. Concerned at the stress that candidates put themselves under in the run-up to public exams, Judith Carlisle urged them to get their exams into perspective. She wanted her sixteen-year-olds to understand that an exam grade is merely a record of something you did on a particular day: it doesn't define you as a person or predict what you will do in the future. Worrying about your performance is likely to be counter-productive.

A similar theme ran through a letter, adapted from an American original, sent by teachers at the Buckton Vale Primary School in Stalybridge to their Year 6 pupils, just before they sat their 2015 Stage 4 National Curriculum Tests, known as SATs:

"Dear Year 6 Pupils,

Next week you will sit your SATs tests for maths, reading, spelling, grammar and punctuation. We know how hard you have worked, but there is something very important you must know:

The SATs test does not assess all of what makes each of you special and unique. The people who create these tests and score them do not know each of you in the way that we do and certainly not in the way your families do.

They do not know that some of you speak two languages or that you love to sing or draw. They have not seen your natural talent for dancing or playing a musical instrument. They do not know that your friends can count on you; that your laughter can brighten the darkest day or that your face turns red when you feel shy. They do not know that you participate in sports, wonder about the future, or sometimes help your little brother or sister after school. They do not know you are kind, trustworthy and thoughtful and that every day you try to be your very best.

The levels that you get from this test will tell you something, but they will not tell you everything. There are many ways of being smart. You are smart! So, while you are preparing for the test and in the midst of it all, remember that there is no way to test all of the amazing and awesome things that make you, YOU!

Sleep, Rest, Believe.

Good luck."

This letter is a poignant reminder of the wider purposes of education that cannot be encapsulated in a fleeting externally-imposed academic assessment. Dedicated primary schoolteachers are keenly aware of their responsibility to hold on to the qualities that young children bring with them into the school system. They recognise the different personalities, interests and skills of their pupils as a precious resource with which to develop the potential each child has to achieve personal fulfilment in adult life and to make a valuable contribution to society. They welcome the diversity that children show in the learning situation and respond by offering a correspondingly wide range of learning experiences. Above all, they see education as a partnership in which children and teachers work together in pursuit of a common goal.

These values and priorities were key features of the influential 1967 publication, *Children and Their Primary Schools*, known as the Plowden Report, after Lady Plowden, Chair of the Central Advisory Council for Education which produced the report. Fifty years on, the insights of this report remain crucial to our education system. The essence of Plowden was its assertion that 'at the heart of the educational process lies the child'. The Council emphasised the need to recognise that any school class, however homogeneous it might seem, should always be treated as a body of children needing individual and different attention.

Crucial roles for the primary school were to build on and strengthen children's intrinsic interest in the world around them and to lead them to learn for themselves rather than out of fear of disapproval or desire for praise. Recurring Plowden themes were: a flexible curriculum determined by teachers' understanding of their pupils' needs and learning through practical experience, discovery and exploring the environment. Whilst the evaluation of children's progress was important, teachers should 'not assume that only what is measurable is valuable'.

In the twenty years following Plowden, almost every document relating to primary education contained references to, or echoes of, the report. A series of government publications stressed the value of building on children's natural enthusiasm and curiosity and the need to respond flexibly not only to individual needs but to the many different stages of children's growth and development.

One of the most interesting endorsements of the Plowden recommendations came more than 20 years after their publication with the 1989 United Nations Convention on the Rights of the Child. This Convention produced a Charter on a range of childhood entitlements - protection, health, welfare and, of course, education. The emphasis was placed on the need to recognise the distinctiveness of the individual child's personality, strengths and potential for adult self-fulfilment. The Charter stresses that if we want children to grow up to respect the rights of other people, including those from other cultures, then we must sow the seeds in our relationships with children, respecting their opinions and recognising the positive contribution that they can make to their own learning:

"Without the active participation of young people there will be no social future. We need to engage in dialogue, to accept children's right to be included, to look actively for their competence, to give them time to express their views in their own way, and to treat them and their views with respect."

Article 12, UNCRC (1989).

The Charter has obvious implications for the curriculum and pedagogy, but it places responsibilities on its member nations that go well beyond formal teaching and learning. The plea for children to have space for their own activities was a key note.

Chapter 2

The Politics of Education

"While we are anxious to see a general system of education adopted, we have no doubt of the impropriety of yielding such an important duty as the education of our children to any government. If ever knavery and hypocrisy succeed in establishing the centralising, state-moulding and knowledge-forcing scheme in England, so assuredly will the people degenerate into passive submission to injustice, and the spirit sink into the pestilential calm of despotism."

William Lovett, 1840.

Many of today's primary school teachers who believe in the principles of Plowden and the UN Convention on the Rights of the Child will never have read the documents concerned. They will, however, have arrived at the same conclusions through their natural respect for children and the understanding of them that comes with teaching and, of course, parenthood. The idea of placing the child at the heart of the education system is not some deep secret that a few perceptive observers have discovered for us. It is no more original than the principle that most doctors and nurses follow in putting the patient at the centre of the health system. You would think that such ideas are too obvious to need constant re-iteration. But you would be wrong. Such fundamental truths are not only constantly challenged but often condemned in the most vitriolic terms.

The Buckton Vale Primary School's celebration of children's many interests and achievements brought the following response from *Daily Mail* readers on the paper's website:

"Yeah, you can sing your way into Medical College to be a doctor!"

"Teaching them properly would be far more useful than stupid PC letters trying to rectify the damage caused by Marxist 'progressive' teaching methods."

"That's right, you are all equal, you can all be rocket scientists ok. God forbid we tell some kids they are just not as smart as others."

"PC rubbish. Yuk."

These sour responses to an attempt by caring teachers to ease the stress of their eleven-year-old pupils before they took their SAT tests indicate all too clearly our divided society and its polarised views on the purposes of education.

Opposition to Plowden approaches to learning has always been fierce and uncompromising. The *Daily Mail* readers' comments on the Buckton teachers' letter are a salutary reminder of how strongly committed a section of our society is to a ruthlessly utilitarian view of education and the priorities of a bygone age. According to this ideology, the over-riding purpose of schooling is to prepare children for their place in society, as determined by their various abilities. Advocates of this view of education focus on the curriculum rather than the child and support a standardised programme that is externally imposed, closely monitored, and not open to variation or manipulation by teachers. It is argued that the teacher's fundamental responsibility is to pass on to children a core body of information and knowledge that has stood the test of time. 'Academic rigour', 'standards', 'hard work' and 'back-to- basics' are much repeated watchwords.

The 'academic standards' lobby believes in early detection and nurturing of 'able' children so that they can be prepared for university and the key roles for which they are destined in society. Those who are academically unsuccessful should be apprised of their limitations earlier rather than later. The theory is that you do children no favours by protecting them from reality: hard as it may seem, we are not born equal and the sooner young people understand and accept the implications of that the better.

Providing a central position for children in the education process, listening to their opinions and giving them a significant say in their learning, involving them in activities like discussion, creative writing and project work, learning through play, discovery and trial and error - these are all, according to this simplistic view of education, largely a waste of time, and, like music, art, drama and other 'fringe' subjects, a hindrance to schools in the unremitting task of 'raising academic standards'. Tight control of schools and university teacher- training faculties is necessary to ensure that the 'progressive' tendencies of educationists are kept in check.

These are, of course, the views of a fascist-inclined minority. But such extremists are dangerous and cannot simply be ignored. They influence, and in turn are influenced by, the politicians and their officers who seek to control our lives. The following comments by Chris Woodhead, HM Chief Inspector of Schools from 1994 to 2000, are disturbingly close, not only to the content, but also to the sneering, contemptuous tone of the *Daily Mail* readers' responses to the Buckton teachers' letter:

" Those who worship at the shrine of 'the child' argue that the primary classroom should be a place of happy spontaneity in which a teacher and child together explore experiences of mutual interest. Children, they suggest, should discover for themselves rather than be told anything by the teachers. One to one, personalised conversations between the teacher and individual are better, therefore, than whole class instruction in which the teacher explains things which, on a different view of education, it might be thought every child within their class needs to know."

When he was appointed in 1994 to lead Ofsted, Chris Woodhead immediately initiated a politicised and campaigning role for the Schools' Inspection service, denouncing 'progressive' methods and equating them with teaching incompetence. Throughout his six years as Chief Inspector, Woodhead pursued a relentless 'back-to-basics' policy with the emphasis on a very limited range of educational objectives and learning experiences. At a time when our education system was crying out for a creative and imaginative change of direction, Woodhead's backward thinking received strong support from both the Major and Blair governments. The Woodhead influence on our education system extended well beyond his disastrous reign as Chief Inspector of Schools: from 2000, when he left Ofsted for a career in journalism, he continued until his death in 2015 to influence government policy and orchestrate media denigration of teachers, educational researchers and teacher trainers. The Woodhead legacy has continued to be a driving force in Ofsted inspections.

In 2010, Michael Gove became the Coalition's Secretary of State for Education thereby giving his previous employer, Rupert Murdoch, a strong influence on the country's education policy. Gove wasted no time in demonstrating his commitment to Woodhead's ideology: further political control of school curricula and pedagogy; more 'academic rigour'; a substantial increase in the already significant role of research-based universities in designing school syllabuses and exams; greater concentration on core academic subjects; more didactic teaching and rote-learning; exam results based on fixed percentages for each grade, rather than on pupil achievement; a further reduction in oral, practical and coursework assessment; a significant devaluing of creative subjects such as drama, art, music and dance, together with a strengthening of their academic content; denigration of 'soft options' such as sociology, media studies, psychology and environmental studies; an insistence on league tables as a tool for state management of schools.

The argument against subjects like sociology is based on their alleged lack of rigour, but another agenda comes into play here. Many of the subjects labelled 'soft options' introduce controversial and topical subject matter and encourage students to challenge the established order, a feature of education that is not on many politicians' agenda. Keith Joseph was so paranoid about the dangers of children being indoctrinated by leftist thinkers that he revised the entry requirements for primary Post Graduate Certificate in Education (PGCE) courses so that only first degree subjects seen as directly relevant to the primary school curriculum were acceptable. This, of course, excluded not only sociologists, but a whole range of graduates with the personal qualities and skills needed in teaching. In fact there are very few degree courses that can be said to be *directly* relevant to the primary school curriculum; you would, for example, have extreme difficulty in finding anything in a maths degree syllabus that had any relevance for a primary school teacher - or indeed to almost any other profession. As many newly-qualified graduates find to their cost when they look for employment, their studies often have little direct application to the world of work. If politicians were to become interested in the need for universities to prepare students adequately for employment they would have a bigger task on their hands than merely closing off career routes to people who hold opposing views to their own.

To what was a familiar stultifying political agenda Gove added a few new suggestions: state schools should work a ten-hour day; testing of children should begin at six; we should return to a wholly traditional method of examining based on externally-marked, timed written tests taken at the end of a course; ex-soldiers could be employed to improve school discipline; teachers don't necessarily need to be trained; school buildings don't affect the quality of learning; social deprivation is not a major cause of low school achievement; consideration might be given to running state schools for profit by commercial bodies.

Like Woodhead, Gove had no compunction in abusing and ridiculing educationists whose views did not conform to his personal ideology. Even in the process of outlining new Government proposals, he could not resist emotive criticism of the Blob, as he called his opponents: " We have stripped out the...piously vapid happy-talk and instead laid out the knowledge that every child is entitled to expect they be taught."

Ofsted is a crucial weapon in furthering the government's education policy and there have been some indications that, post-Gove, not all school inspectors have been punctilious in stamping out Plowden principles of education. This has required a strong rebuttal from the inspectorate and, in launching a 2014 overhaul of Ofsted, Chief Inspector Sir Michael Wilshaw confirmed his unequivocal commitment to formal teaching methods. Sir Michael expressed his determination to root out any vestiges of the "60s' child-centred ideology.... which ruined the lives of generations of children at that time." He stated that inspectors were under instruction to mark down such methods and declared in typical bullish style that anyone advocating them won't " be working for me for very long."

Educationists have learnt not to use terms such as 'child-centred', which has long been categorised as a 'trendy', 'hippy' approach to education. The general public has been brainwashed by politicians and the media into thinking that 'child-centred' refers to a system in which teachers abdicate their responsibility for directing the learning experience, leaving children for long periods engaged in unstructured and desultory activities. Such absence of supervision is associated with time-wasting, disorder, noise and ill-discipline. This is, of course, a travesty of what the good teacher seeks to achieve by treating children as partners in the learning situation, rather than as mere recipients of the teacher's knowledge. Far from being a cop-out, the Plowden approach requires great professionalism from teachers. In Barry Hines' very successful novel, *A Kestrel for a Knave*, there is a memorable classroom scene which admirably demonstrates some basic, early pre-Plowden manifestations of pupil/teacher partnership. The school is a tough 1960s' boys' secondary modern, serving a council estate in a Yorkshire mining community. There's nothing 'progressive' about it, and teachers constantly assert their authority, loudly and sarcastically, to head off any rowdiness or insubordination. Caning is the standard corrective measure. The English teacher is getting his bottom-stream class to think about the difference between 'fact' and 'fiction', and briefly checking that the class remembers the gist of an introduction to the subject in an earlier lesson. He then puts the question, " If I ask Anderson for some facts about himself, what could he tell us?" Thinking back to my own secondary modern teaching days, I admire the way he phrases the question: invited to say what facts *they* would choose to say about Anderson, some of the class would, without doubt, have been tempted to mention something silly or embarrassing about the boy in question. Worded as it is, it elicits numerous sensible suggestions. The teacher accepts these and a picture emerges of Anderson. It is, however, as the teacher points out, rather ordinary, there's nothing really interesting that brings the character alive.

You can see where this is leading. The class is providing the material for the lesson, but the teacher is orchestrating it and determining its direction. Anderson is now asked if he can tell everyone something interesting about himself. The class responds with a suggestive 'Woooo!' which Mr Farthing rides and quickly controls. Anderson can't think of anything, or isn't prepared to put himself on the line. Mr Farthing persists: "Anything that's happened to you or you've seen which sticks in your mind. "Nothing. "What about when you were little? It doesn't have to be fantastic, just something that you've remembered." This is safer ground, the distance likely to make any revelations less embarrassing. Anderson launches into an amusing account of a dare he accepted as a youngster to fill his wellington boots to the brim with tadpoles and then put them back on his feet, and how he'd chased the challenger with the tadpoles spurting out of his boots. The class quickly tunes into this anecdote about their world.

Meanwhile, Billy Casper, the hero of the story, has been sitting quietly inspecting the weals on his hands, under cover of his desk: earlier on he'd had a caning from the head for falling asleep in morning assembly. Billy is a troubled teenager, a failure at school and unhappy at home. He gets up very early each morning to undertake domestic chores, before doing a large paper round. He is constantly upbraided for inattentiveness in class. He is now caught out with no knowledge of what has been going on in the English lesson, and called upon to contribute an account of something interesting that has happened in *his* life. Billy has no ideas and a stand-off occurs, until a member of the class calls out, "Tell him about the hawk, Billy." Billy is initially defensive and un-cooperative and it emerges that his known obsession with a kestrel that he has trained marks him out as a bit of an oddity with the other boys. Mr Farthing perseveres and coaxes reluctant details out of Billy, who gradually warms to his account. He begins to hold his audience by the immediacy of his knowledge and the strength of his passion, the one thing in his life that deviates from the miserable rut he is in. The teacher readily admits his own ignorance of falconry, deferring to Billy, showing a keen interest in everything he says and asking him to explain the specialist terms he's using. These are spelt out on the board for the benefit of the class, who listen attentively to Billy's account. Mr Farthing asks Billy to come out to the front of the class and demonstrate some of the training manoeuvres that he's described. At the end, he draws attention to some familiar features of human expertise that Billy has demonstrated. He then thanks Billy on behalf of the class and Billy returns, flushed, to his seat.

Teacher and class have been introduced to a subject of which they had had no previous knowledge. More importantly, they have learnt something about Billy and gained a little respect for one of their number who has always been dismissed as a no-hoper. Billy has enjoyed a rare moment of recognition and praise, a boost to his very low confidence and self-esteem. The class subsequently moves on to a discussion of the meaning of the word 'fiction' followed by practical work, a piece of creative writing headed *A Tall Story*. Billy writes of an imaginary world where he lives in a large house, has proper meals and to which his absent father has returned to live with the family. At school all the teachers are good to him and pat him on the head and say "Allow Billy, awo you gowing on?"

Literature often features another approach to education. Dickens, for example, abounds in classroom scenes that are the antithesis of that portrayed in Barry Hines' novel. The Lancashire milltown school described in *Hard Times* is the best-known example. A politician is visiting, to bask in the glory of a local manifestation of his educational ideology. However, he encounters a setback, an aberration in the system. He questions a new pupil, who reveals that she comes from 'the horse-riding': the circus is in town. Cissy Jupe is quickly told, "We don't want to hear anything about that here." She is then asked for the definition of a horse, a question that leaves her tongue-tied. Another pupil, Bitzer, is required to provide the correct answer and dutifully recites the comprehensive dictionary definition that everyone but Sissy has presumably had to commit to memory. "Now," Cissy is told, "you know what a horse is."

This 'dictionary-definition style' of education plays a significant part in the current drive to 'raise academic standards'. Success in this process is measured by the number of children that schools can guide through objective tests designed to assess whether they meet 'age-related expectations', the level the government considers children should have reached at different stages of their schooling. There are some serious flaws in this strategy. In order to keep increasing their pupils' success rate in tests and exams, teachers tend to spend more time concentrating on the specific knowledge and procedures that these very limited forms of assessment require - and correspondingly less on the many other educational experiences that are generally thought to constitute a good education.

As teachers help increasing numbers of children to reach their 'age-related expectations', the politicians raise the bar another notch and expect younger children to achieve the level previously expected of an older age-group, thereby enabling the perpetrators of this process to claim that they are 'raising standards'. They haven't of course done anything of the kind: they've merely made the tests more difficult, forcing children to memorise more facts and to follow more difficult procedures, many of which they don't fully understand. The education process is put on hold while schools devote their time and energy to an extremely narrow set of objectives.

Specialist concepts and approaches that were once considered the prerogative of the universities are gradually moving down the system to become part of every child's learning experience, and at an increasingly early age. The universities have always believed that the correct way for students to learn is for experts in a specialist field to give them a thorough grounding in theory before they consider practical applications. This sounds logical, but it's not actually the most effective approach: we learn best when our interest is aroused in a particular human activity or achievement and we are stimulated to find out more about it. Experience something; then access the knowledge that will enable you to understand it more fully. Start with the world you know, and then explore new ground. Practice, then theory. Academia has managed to ignore this basic principle, but is at last having to revise its teaching methods in response to criticism, not least from a student body that is now footing the bill for its higher education. Meanwhile, the old theory-first approach is working its way inexorably down to our primary schools, where its absurdity is plain to see. In English, for example, young children are spending hours learning ancient rules of grammar, distinguishing the difference between the passive and active voice; the functions of different parts of speech; subjunctive, indicative and imperative moods of a verb; main and subordinate clauses.

Primary school children have no need to engage with this kind of dry linguistic analysis. Indeed the vast majority of adults manage their lives quite satisfactorily without it. How many graduates would face the current primary school Key Stage 2 grammar test with equanimity, if they had to do it? The radio interviewer who asked Schools Minister, Nick Gibb, a question from a 2016 Key Stage 2 grammar test paper could hardly contain her glee when he gave the incorrect answer. It would have been interesting to see whether he would have fared any better with the Key Stage 1 requirements of six-year-olds, which include an understanding of the possessive apostrophe. " Mr Gibb, what is the possessive form of Charles Dickens - Dickens', Dicken's, or Dickens's?"

Nick Gibb was unfazed by his failure to distinguish between a preposition and a subordinating conjunction - he didn't seem to think it mattered. Exactly. He moved quickly on to stress the importance of all children learning to write. No-one is likely to disagree with that platitude, but what the Minister seems unable to understand is that children don't learn to write by memorising linguistic jargon and studying fine syntactical points, any more than they learn to speak by memorising the technical vocabulary of professional elocutionists and employing their vocal techniques. Children's natural desire to express themselves, both orally and in writing, is stifled - not encouraged - by their being drilled in academic jargon and specialist concepts. A tennis coach who spends a whole course teaching the theory of tennis strokes and strategies will kill off the enthusiasm of those taking part. Beginners in all games need to experience the enjoyment of playing before they try to master the complex skills that bring success at the higher levels of the game.

Some of our family are visiting for the day and one of the younger members retires to a quiet corner to tackle her

English homework, what sounds like a piece of imaginative writing. She's an academically successful pupil who is remarkably independent over her homework, but after an hour has passed I go to see if she's all right. I find her distressed, still on the first of the six paragraphs she has to write. I'm greeted with the news that she's going to fail her GCSE English: her exams are still two and a half years away, but they dominate the thinking of both staff and children. The class is already working on GCSE question papers. We discuss the incredibly complicated instructions for the homework. The subject set is a narrative essay, with the title *The Assassin,* and the children have been given a detailed plan of the narrative. I later discover that it's based on a model essay used in a web advert posted by a firm supplying off-the-shelf essays for GCSE pupils. The story concerns the aftermath of a murder. The hero of the story is a prime suspect, not charged but strongly suspected of the crime by the community in which he lives. He knows the real culprit and decides that the best way of clearing his name is to take the law into his own hands and 'assassinate' the murderer. The essay has to start with the would-be assassin entering a dark wood where he knows he'll find the murderer's hut; his quarry is apparently a woodcutter. The children have to tell this story, paying special attention to the scene-setting and structure of the narrative. The wood (chapter 1) and the woodcutter's hut (chapter2) are to be described using lots of vivid adjectives. The reader is to be kept in suspense over what's going on, the background to the story being revealed gradually in the form of flashbacks - as in many modern novels. There is another important requirement: the essay is to be a vehicle for demonstrating the children's knowledge of grammar, punctuation etc. Chapter 1, for example, must illustrate the difference between a colon and a semi-colon; chapter 2 must contain an adjectival and an adverbial clause, and so on.

This is what the politicians mean by 'academic rigour'. Michael Morpurgo, multiple literary-award winner and former Children's Laureate, calls it 'rigor mortis'. Politicians are so caught up in the rightness of their schemes for an education system that meets the perceived needs of the state that they lose sight of the human beings that have to be fitted into the equation. So we end up with a system that denies children an active role in their education and, in the process, stifles the individuality, originality and creativity of the next generation whose decisions will determine whether or not the state survives.

It is easy to forget that schools have not always suffered from the kind of political control currently being exerted over the curriculum and the way it's delivered. Churchill was said to have asked Rab Butler, President of the Board of Education during WWII, to ensure that schools demonstrated more patriotism, to which Butler apparently replied: "I have no say in what is done in schools." Just after his two-year term of office as Secretary of State for Education (1965-7), Anthony Crosland made the following observation on the inappropriateness of politicians interfering with the education profession's responsibilities:

"The nearer one comes to the professional content of education, the more indirect the minister's influence is. And I'm sure this is right...generally I didn't regard myself or my officers as in the slightest degree competent to interfere with the curriculum. We are educational politicians and administrators, not professional educators."

This was a widely-held view: government interference with what was taught in schools was unacceptable, a practice associated with the totalitarian regimes of Nazi Germany and the Soviet Union.

However, there were already signs of a shift in politicians' views on this matter. In the 1970s, Plowden principles came under increasing fire from the infamous 'black papers'. In the mid-seventies the spectacular mismanagement of the William Tyndale School in North London provided critics and sections of the media with a prolonged field day in decrying 'progressive methods'. In 1976 Prime Minister James Callaghan gave his famous Ruskin Speech on the state of education, which proved to be particularly influential in paving the way for greater political involvement in education.

When Keith Joseph became Secretary of State in 1981 a succession of measures gave explicit warning of the Thatcher government's determination to shift the balance of power in education. One of Keith Joseph's first symbolic actions was to abolish the Central Advisory Council for Education (CACE), the body responsible for the Plowden Report, which had come to symbolise progressive thinking in education. Another early and significant target was the Schools' Council, an independent body that commissioned educational research and provided a forum for curriculum development and innovation. Various educational interests, including teachers' organisations, were represented on the Council, and much of its work was carried out by practising teachers through a large number of sub-committees. These sub-committees produced a wide range of teaching guides on all aspects of schools' work, initially focusing on secondary education but then embracing the primary sector as well. In 1981 the Council published a working paper on *The Practical Curriculum* which advocated a more relevant curriculum and a more active role for pupils in the learning process. It observed that teachers "too often emphasised the content of subjects instead of their importance as ways of experiencing and knowing the real world". It was one of the Council's last papers before it was replaced by the School Curriculum Development Committee (SCDC), which was constituted to be much more closely under government control.

The loss of the Schools Council was a bitter blow to many who were working in education at the time. I was running a sixth-form college in which several of the senior staff, including the Professional Tutor in charge of staff development, became active members of three of the Council's subject committees. They returned from meetings full of ideas that were then disseminated and debated across the College. We also found the packs of materials that the Council produced to support sixth-form general studies extremely helpful. The emerging colleges broke new ground with their extensive non-examination curriculum and my own college had a particular commitment to this way of providing students with a broad and balanced programme of study. We offered nearly one hundred options from which students chose three each year. They focused on areas of the curriculum frequently sidelined or unavailable in the traditional sixth-form - creative and practical subjects, work experience and community service, outward-bound activities and business projects - but also included a number of resource-based courses of a sociological, philosophical and environmental nature for which Schools' Council materials had been designed.

In 1988 the Thatcher Government passed the 1988 Education Reform Act which reversed a longstanding commitment to the autonomy of schools. The 1988 Act introduced a standardised national curriculum and began the process of loosening the partnership between Local Education Authorities and schools in order to give central government more direct control. A precedent had been created for further intervention and the Education Reform Act is proving to be the most damaging and destructive of all Thatcher's measures to tighten state regulation of our lives. We now have one of the most state-directed education systems in the world.

The steadily increasing government intervention in what goes on in schools has demonstrated just how inappropriate it is for ministers to get involved in the day-to-day management of complex public services of which they have no direct experience. Some ministers have never worked outside politics, having had roles as political party researchers, advisers or speech writers before becoming MPs. Many others started life as journalists or working for marketing firms or publicists. These are all jobs in which ambitious young graduates learn how to promote their own and other people's image and to destroy the reputation of those who hold different views to their own. They rarely involve activities requiring skills of teamwork, project-control or people management. This toxic mix presumably helps to explain why secretaries of state for education fail to understand that it is not a very good idea to denigrate and abuse the very profession that is required to implement their reforms.

Every educationist knows that children respond positively to praise and encouragement and negatively to aggressive fault-finding and condemnation. Good teachers are, on the one hand, quick to recognise their pupils' achievements and efforts to do well and, on the other, to provide the encouragement and support needed when children are experiencing difficulties or falling short of expectations. Genuine belief in human potential is a pre-requisite for teaching - and indeed for all forms of management and leadership. Adults are no different to children in these respects. We all like to have our efforts appreciated but will usually accept advice from someone who, having recognised our achievements, encourages us to look at ways of being more effective. It also helps if criticism is tempered by understanding, and faith in our potential to face up to new challenges.

Obviously neither the increased political control of education nor the systematic return to traditional methods has been welcomed by the teaching profession. But antipathy to these policies has been as nothing compared to the hostility and resentment caused by the manner in which the changes have been introduced. Woodhead and Gove's mocking of those who held views different from their own and the dictatorial way in which they set about imposing their personal ideologies on schools have created a gulf between politicians and educationists that now seems unbridgeable. The familiar House of Commons circus of ministers and shadow ministers trading personal insults and abuse, spurred on by the baying of their leering supporters, may well arouse in us no more than an amused incredulity. However, when we move from the comfortable detachment of television-viewing and find ourselves the actual target of ministers' castigation, we realise just how objectionable and counter-productive this kind of behaviour is.

Politicians are notorious for bypassing the normal procedures that precede decision-making - establishing the relevant facts, listening to expert opinion, considering the views of those most affected by the decisions to be taken, assessing the validity of the evidence used to support different opinions, estimating the likely effect and implications of any action that is to be taken. Woodhead and Gove's attitude to such procedures was particularly cavalier. Their self-importance and unshakeable faith in their personal ideologies enabled them to ignore the loathing their despotic behaviour generated, even at times to appear as if they revelled in it. Woodhead, in particular, saw the extent of the opposition to his policies and methods as a sign of his success. Gove's manner was smoother, more ingratiating - but no-one was fooled.

There is a clue here to the way in which all political policy-makers operate. Woodhead and Gove's methods were merely particularly nasty manifestations of common practices. Political parties come into power with a licence for bringing about changes that their supporters want to see in the way in which the country is run. This applies particularly to the public services, on which they have a significantly different viewpoint from that of the people who provide them. If, for example, you work in Education, the National Health Service or the Police Force you are very aware of the day-to-day demands made of these organisations and the myriad ways in which you and your work colleagues respond to them, trying to do a decent job for children, patients and the public. Your daily routine is an accumulation of small things which go largely unnoticed and unrecognised.

Politicians don't normally have this 'insider' insight: theirs is a much more general perspective representing the view of the electorate that brought them to power and the tax-payer who funds the services. Inevitably, therefore, they tend to focus not on successes but on the negatives, the complaints they receive from their constituents who feel they've been let down by the system, and on the media stories of failures - a mismanaged school or poor set of national exam results, an exceptionally slow response to an emergency call to the police or ambulance service, a neglected hospital patient or a policeman's excessive use of force when seeking to restrain an aggressive offender. Such selected examples of failure will have been repeatedly cited during the run-up to an election and candidates will have declared publicly and vehemently that things will change when they get into power.

Thus, newly-appointed secretaries of state arrive in their Departments committed to strong-arm tactics and a firm corrective agenda that they feel they have a clear mandate to implement. Opposition is quickly rubbished or brushed aside. Requests for proper consultation, weighing of evidence, careful analysis of alternative ways of addressing a problem, discussion of the best ways to implement proposed reforms - these are all seen as delaying tactics. They know that any hint of uncertainty or hesitation is going to be seized upon by their opponents, and indeed by their colleagues, as a sign of weakness and a threat to their party's political credibility. Speed and force are of the essence. Thus, from the outset, the politicians are on a collision course with the professionals who will have to implement their reforms.

Estelle Morris, Baroness Morris of Yardley, has a fascinating perspective on the struggle between the politicians and the teaching profession for control of what goes on in the classroom. She spent 18 years as a PE and humanities teacher in an inner city comprehensive in Coventry and had management experience as a head of sixth-form studies. She entered parliament in 1992, five years later became a minister and then in 2001 was appointed Secretary of State for Education. She talks lucidly about this very unusual combination of the educationist's and politician's views of education. Upon becoming an MP, she quickly discovered that the questions she was asking, for example when visiting schools, were significantly different from those she'd asked in the past: she was already looking at the education process as a representative of the general public, a policy-maker, a politician. At the same time, she never lost her teacher's inside view: the two perspectives existed alongside each other.

Ostensibly an advantage, this 'dual vision' created considerable difficulties for Estelle. Teachers welcomed her appointment but gave her a hard time, wanting more from her than she could deliver. At the same time, her political colleagues were critical of her inclination to take teachers' views into account in her policy-making; they also sensed a certain reluctance to rush proposed changes through. In 2002 she resigned her post as Secretary of State for Education, later becoming Minister of State for the Arts.

As Anthony Crosland explained, the two worlds of politics and education are quite distinct, and they lead to markedly different mindsets and ways of working. This is nowhere more obvious than in teachers' and politicians' contrasting attitudes and approaches to problem-solving. Teaching is a perpetual learning curve. No two days, no two lessons, no two children are the same. Although experience equips the classroom practitioner with instinctive answers to many of the daily challenges, good teachers never let themselves become complacent. They are constantly adapting their approaches and methods to meet changing circumstances and children's different learning needs, all the time adding to their understanding of what works and what doesn't. This habitual learning from experience is one of the reasons why teachers set great store in providing children with opportunities to discover things for themselves and to learn from experimenting. They encourage children not to be afraid of failure, but to turn it to advantage.

"How do you know all this?" I enquire of my young grandson and laptop consultant, after he has coaxed me through a solution to a difficulty I'm having. "Well," he says, "because I know my way around the computer, I suppose. Whenever I have a problem I try to work it out for myself. I try different things till I find the answer. And, because I've found it out for myself, I remember it." Trying alternative approaches to a problem, learning from one's mistakes, starting again - these are endemic in the processes of learning and teaching.

Such procedures don't feature much in the world of politics. Politicians are good at identifying and condemning other people's mistakes and failures, but are extremely loath to admit to any error or incompetence on their own part. In framing and implementing policy, secretaries of state feel they must demonstrate infallibility. Admission to any possible flaws in their argument amounts to political suicide. Thus the standard response to a danger signal that one of their policies isn't working is for the relevant secretary of state to make an aggressive public speech, re-iterating the importance of the policy, expressing dissatisfaction at the rate of progress, naming scapegoats for that situation, demanding more effort from those who are failing to deliver, and threatening punitive action if it is not forthcoming.

The details of MP Jo Cox's selfless service to others that emerged after her murder on 16th June 2016 were a powerful reminder of the altruistic desire to benefit mankind that brings many young people into politics and makes them respected constituency MPs. However, as politicians rise through the ranks and become embroiled in the machinations and power struggles of national politics, this laudable aim isn't so evident to the general public. The wheeling and dealing, the constant trading of insults and the apparent distortion of the truth by key figures - all of this gives politicians a bad name. Because politicians are high profile figures they are closely watched by the media and their every deviation from acceptable behaviour seized upon and widely publicised. Allegations of dodgy financial dealings by individual politicians - 'accepting cash for questions', using tax havens, fiddling expenses - tend to give the general public the impression that politicians as a whole are always 'on the make'. The expenses scandal was particularly damaging in this respect, as the revelations weren't confined to the few bad apples that one finds in all professions, but suggested that a significant number of MPs were habitually making excessive or fraudulent claims on their expense accounts.

A common response to such revelations is that we get the kind of politicians that we deserve, meaning, in this case, that their greed simply reflects that of society as a whole. An abiding memory of the months leading up to the 2015 election is of the two major parties vying with each other in promising that, if elected, they would make sure each and every section of the electorate received the bigger share of the national finances for which it was clamouring. The Liberal Democrats did occasionally mention other possible aspirations for a government - such as building a better, more equitable society - and they were all but annihilated in the election.

It is important for education to have a vision of the future that is more idealistic than the reality of the present. The supreme challenge for all teachers is to promote attitudes and values that will enable the next generation to build a fairer and more just society than the one into which they have been born. Primary schools have taken this ideal particularly seriously, seeking to build harmonious communities whose members behave decently, honestly and respectfully towards each other and take those qualities on with them into adult life. In such a school instances of helpfulness, kindness, compassion and a concern for others are acknowledged just as much as work achievements.

Secondary school teachers have to be rather more pragmatic, preparing their students to survive in the world that actually exists - for example, by ensuring their future economic security and place in society. Nevertheless, they too are concerned to transmit positive attitudes and values, and to help young people to function effectively in their school community and therefore ultimately in the wider society. They teach rights and responsibilities, so that pupils learn to express their opinion, but also to listen and respect the opinions of others. They show children how to work effectively in teams and how to reach a consensus through cooperation and reasoned debate. They are usually quick to deal with negative behaviour - bullying, deceit, unkindness, selfishness.

An ex-teaching colleague of mine recently lost her husband, also an ex-teacher, and a service of thanksgiving was held in Coventry Cathedral. One of the ex-pupils in the congregation of 300 wrote in the book of remembrance: "The man who taught me how to live". The values, attitudes and forms of behaviour that schools try to inculcate are not a reflection of our society as it is, but an attempt to build something better. Politicians frequently seem to have abdicated that responsibility. It's hardly surprising, therefore, if the teaching profession has scant respect for the people who are currently lecturing them incessantly on 'standards' and how they should be doing their job.

Chapter 3

Promoting (and Denigrating) Comprehensive Education

"Comprehensives work. Given an increase in resources and greater political will in relation to school structures, and particularly selection, they could be world-class. And we are simply crazy, as a nation, to permit the dismantling of what has so far been achieved, against all the odds."

Melissa Benn.

The priorities and objectives that our politicians are currently imposing on schools and colleges show little understanding of children, the role of teachers or the qualities of mind, aptitudes and skills that both our young people and our society need for survival in the 21st century. The commitment to a traditional academic curriculum and specialist approach, the obsession with assessment, the emphasis on didactic teaching and a passive role for learners, the suppression of individuality and imagination - these are all taking us back to a bygone age. My own schooldays come vividly to mind.

I attended a prestigious single-sex Royal Grammar School in which the over-riding priority was the grooming of a small élite for Oxbridge. The curriculum was ruthlessly academic: there was no practical work and only two creative subjects, art and music, both of very low status and taught in an unbelievably dry and uncreative way. The RGS was oblivious of the nature of the learning process, of the many and varied experiences that can help young people to develop their potential to meet the challenges of adulthood and to live a full and rewarding life. The staff were academics immersed in their specialist subject. They had received no professional training and simply replicated the teaching method they had experienced in the early 20th century grammar schools they had attended as boys. They spent much of their time instructing or lecturing, not really teaching in the sense of managing and supporting the boys' learning.

The idea of education being a partnership between teachers and pupils never impinged on the RGS and there were few opportunities for pupil participation. Even in language lessons there was little oral work. The staff never stepped outside their specialist knowledge base to take a holistic view of the world or to indicate interesting connections between subjects. We didn't experience any project work or theme-based studies; there were no links with the local community (or the girls' grammar school), no breaks in the relentless academic routine, no chance for a glimpse of the real world by visiting places of interest or having visitors come in to tell us about their lives. As now, the requirements of the exam dictated much of what went on in the classroom and led to some bizarre situations. During my preparation for the School Certificate exams (GCSE equivalent) I spent interminable lessons writing out the whole of a scholarly critical analysis of Hardy's Mayor of Casterbridge dictated by our English teacher.

In the three years leading up to the school certificate exam one English lesson each week was devoted to the précis question. Latinate prose passages had to be reduced to a third or a quarter of their length, in accordance with a long list of rules governing such technicalities as verb tenses, the case of personal pronouns and direct and indirect speech forms. I never properly understood the passages, the mechanical processes involved or the purpose of the exercise. A year or two later, when I was beginning to take an interest in the English language, I realised that these précis lessons had a practical application: they were merely an academic and formalised version of a natural process in which human beings constantly engage , that of summarising something they have heard or read. Our English master was presumably unaware of this or surely he would have tapped into boys' everyday experiences, asking them to give oral and written résumés and summaries of books and articles read, films seen, radio programmes listened to, instructions received, conversations overheard. But, of course, that wasn't what the exam required. The tyranny of the exam. Always restricting the learning experience.

In the sixth form, two masters shared responsibility for our higher school certificate history course. Their approach was identical and never varied: both worked steadily through their university files, dictating and talking from their notes, while the class tried unsuccessfully to record every word. There was no indication that either master had ever reflected on the teaching and learning process. Yet both were conscientious members of staff who seemed concerned that the class should do well. On reflection, it seems strange that neither had even thought of ways of improving his chosen method of teaching, let alone replacing it with something more appropriate. They must have realised how we spent each lesson writing copiously while they lectured.

It would have been a small epiphany for us to have had some guidance on how to take notes, to understand that if we stopped trying to convey all the words of a lecture to our notebooks we could actually listen to what was being said and think about it, perhaps even try to summarise it in a time allowed for that purpose at the end of the lesson, an exercise that would have greatly aided our understanding of the purposes of précis writing. Alternatively, we might have been given some short breaks in the lecture to enable us to jot down what we considered were salient points. As grammar school sixth-formers, we were presumably deemed to be in the top 10% per cent or so of the country's most intelligent youngsters and well able to take an active part in the learning process. As it was, I was in my late twenties before I encountered a lecturer who forbade his audience to write while he was talking - on the grounds that they couldn't experience his lecture if they were busy writing.

It's probably unreasonable to criticise my two history masters for their unswerving commitment to an unimaginative way of teaching. Their own academic success had come via the methods they were using. Their pupils generally passed their exams. They were teaching in a highly-regarded institution that never felt the need to question any of its long-established practices. They simply absorbed and were part of the prevailing culture.

All entrants to the RGS had passed the 11+ selection tests in English, maths and intelligence. They were accustomed to academic success and had no reason to suppose that it wouldn't continue. Many, however, experienced a speedy disillusionment once inside the hothouse grammar school with its intense competition. From the start, boys' lives were dominated by the concept of league tables, with their lauding of the successful and shaming of those who fell short of expectations. Marks gained for classwork and homework were totalled fortnightly and published as a form ranking; each staff specialist published a separate order for his subject. 50% of the boys found themselves in a new situation, competing in the 'less able' half of the table.

After a diagnostic year each grammar school intake was divided into an upper and lower half. The two forms that comprised the top half of the year were 'expressed' into the sixth-form, which they entered a year early in order that potential Oxford and Cambridge candidates could have a third sixth-form year in which to sit the two universities' scholarship exams. One top form studied languages (Latin, French and German), the other the sciences - the two specialist academic programmes that carried most weight in an Oxbridge application. Having had a year as top dogs in the unstreamed classes, 50% of the boys in the express forms now found themselves struggling in the lower section of the league tables, some of them to be discarded in the annual relegation process. The next hurdle was admission to the sixth-form, for which boys had to achieve 'matriculation exemption', consisting of a minimum of 5 credits or distinctions (equivalent to 5 'B' or 'A' grades in current terminology) taken at one sitting and including English language, maths and either science or a foreign language. And so it continued, a constant refining of the classification of boys as successful or expendable until the purpose of the whole exercise was reached - the choosing of a small number of candidates for a shot at the ultimate academic prize, an Oxbridge Scholarship.

My own position within this bizarre form of education was one of mid-table mediocrity. I was fourteenth in the final league table for the first grammar school year and scraped into that half of the cohort selected for the express route to the sixth-form. Some boys showed a definite inclination either towards maths and science or towards English and languages and were allocated to the appropriate express form. The others, of which I was one, were arbitrarily shared between the two specialisms. I lasted two years in the languages form before being demoted. I adjusted to a new range of subjects, including art, but never acquired sufficient knowledge in any of the sciences to achieve a qualification in that part of the curriculum. Nor did I ever learn to speak a foreign language.

Education at the RGS was something that boys had done to them, not an experience that they actively engaged in jointly with teachers. Knowledge was conveyed by staff or learnt from books, and then transmitted back in writing, rarely orally. We were instructed on what to do, but had little guidance on how to do it. We learnt what, but not how, to think. The teaching and learning methods offered few opportunities for boys to get to know the staff who taught them. Very few of the masters showed any interest in the pupils as individuals and we were always addressed by our surnames. There was no care system and I doubt if anyone would have considered sharing a personal problem with a member of staff. In fact, I don't recall even having the courage to ask a master for help with my work. It simply wasn't part of the culture to admit to weakness.

There was a harsh and uncompromising attitude towards failure at the RGS, and blanket condemnation of groups who underperformed. The lower streams were known as 'the snake pits' or just 'the pits'. Sport, like academic work, was fiercely competitive and school teams were expected to win. We had an indifferent cricket season when I was a member of the 1st XI and the member of staff in charge castigated us in his end-of-season school magazine report: "few of the batsmen were capable of staying at the crease", "the bowling lacked fire" and the whole side was "lazy and unintelligent in the field". Lack of intelligence was a cardinal sin, despite the prevailing view of the time that it was an inborn feature that human beings could do nothing to alter.

Occasionally we received a brief glimpse of other educational worlds where things seemed to be handled differently. A few months before my school certificate exam our art master suffered a prolonged illness and arrangements were made for us to receive a weekly art lesson at the town's technical school. Our master had interpreted his rôle minimally - to keep order, set us a task, and then to mark it. He rarely descended from his rostrum to observe how we were getting on, to make suggestions or to offer encouragement. As in our academic studies, we were expected to pick up the requisite skills of the subject by a process of osmosis. At the 'tech' we entered a totally different environment where the serried ranks of desks gave way to a circular arrangement and constant pupil/teacher interaction. We were introduced to the basic skills of drawing and painting and I learnt how to hold a pencil in a way that combined control with flexibility and free-flowing movement. It was, I think, my first intimation that the grammar school was not all that it was cracked up to be.

One day a new member of staff arrived at the RGS who had been teaching in the 7-14 elementary school in the village next to my own. He was a breath of fresh air: a cheery man with a friendly manner and ready smile who quickly acquired a reputation as an excellent teacher. I remember Jim Tucker clearly, although sadly I was never taught by him. I was in the express form at the time and Jim Tucker was only thought capable of teaching the youngest boys and the lower streams - having come from an elementary school he would have been a trained teacher but a non-graduate. One evening he cycled out to the village in which I lived to see the parents of one of his pupils. He was apparently concerned that the boy was having problems at school.

Given the prevailing culture, it was not surprising that the occasional memorable occasion, such as Jim Tucker's arrival, made a big impression. One day in a Lower School history lesson the master let us loose in the school grounds to look for flints that one could shape, by painstakingly chipping and scraping them against other stones, into objects that bore some slight resemblance to Stone Age implements. It was my only experience of fieldwork, but one that may have conditioned my positive response, many years later, to the Nuffield Science project, with its Chinese proverb watchwords: 'to hear is to forget, to see is to remember, to do is to understand'.

In the sixth form a trip was organised to London to a schools' conference at which the speakers included Dr Bronowski, rising maths and science star, and Sir Hartley Shawcross, Attorney General in the post-war labour government and subsequently lead British prosecutor at the Nuremberg Trials. I had never encountered people of this stature before and I remember being surprised that such eminent professionals from the outside world should consider it important to find time to speak to schoolboys. It was a rare insight into what was going on in the real world and how far our normal routine was detached from it.

The RGS, with its arid curriculum, unimaginative teaching and lack of meaningful contact between staff and boys, has served me well as an example of the damage that can be inflicted on children when an educational ideology gets out of control. It has contributed significantly to my understanding of what matters and what doesn't in the way in which we educate our children, and has influenced the principles that have underpinned my work as a teacher, head and university staff trainer.

The pre-war grammar schools were highly regarded for their egalitarian role in challenging the assumption that an academic education, university career, and leadership or management role in adult life were the prerogative of those whose parents could pay for private education. Following the 1944 Education Act's removal of their fee-paying places, the grammar schools' reputation as bastions of the new meritocracy was further enhanced. Few people had the desire or temerity to enquire too closely into what went on within the hallowed walls.

One exception, however, was the scientist and novelist, C.P. Snow, who argued in his famous 1959 Rede lecture that the English obsession with specialisation was producing a two-culture society in which scientists and those educated in the humanities no longer had a common language by which to communicate with each other. In the course of his lecture on The Two Cultures and the Scientific Revolution, Snow exposed the way in which the grammar schools compromised the education of the majority of their pupils by their focus on grooming a very small élite for the Oxbridge Scholarship exam. There was considerable intellectual support for Snow, but his ideas went over the heads of most people. The opposition to the grammar schools that built up in the 1950s, and almost led to their total demise in the second half of the century, came about for reasons other than the inappropriateness and inadequacy of the education they provided.

A country at war inevitably pulls together more than at other times and Britain emerged from World War2 more united and a little less class-conscious than it had been in the 1930s. The landmark 1944 Education Act, master-minded by the Conservative Minister for Education, Rab Butler, symbolised the political will there was to give ordinary people a better deal. And the 1945-51 Attlee government that followed is often cited as the most successful attempt we've ever experienced in this country to unite the nation in search of a fairer and more just society.

The 1944 Act encouraged local education authorities to introduce a tripartite system of secondary education, with children allocated to academic, technical or secondary modern schools. Some LEAs adopted this system but the technical school idea never really caught on and the standard provision became bipartite, in the form of grammar and secondary schools. However, the Act had given the go-ahead to other possible ways of organising secondary education, such as community schools and comprehensives. Comprehensive schools were already on the agenda of some Local Education Authorities (LEAs) and the powerful and influential Inner London Education Authority (ILEA), in particular, had some years previously announced its intention for its schools 'to go comprehensive' as opportunities arose.

Support for the comprehensive ideal increased rapidly in the 1950s. A powerful section of the community still regarded the grammar schools as sacrosanct, but they were a minority: parents of the 80% of children who failed the 11+ were less enamoured by a system that, at the age of eleven, closed so many doors to their sons and daughters. The arbitrary nature of the 11+ selection procedure was too blatantly unfair for it to go unchallenged. How was it possible to make an accurate judgement of a child's potential on the basis of a single day's tests, all employing the same assessment method - written answers? The answer, of course, was that it wasn't, and never will be. We all know that the way in which we perform at a particular point in time is influenced by a whole range of variables. A few marks could separate 11+ successes from failures, marks that on another day or in another situation would have been distributed entirely differently. All exams are a lottery. They should never be used to determine children's whole future to the extent that they were in the 11+.

By the time I became a grammar school head, some LEAs, including Hertfordshire for whom I was to work, had responded to widespread concern about the 11+ exam by replacing it with a system of primary school teacher recommendations. It was a welcome step forward - to ask the teachers who had known children for several years to judge which of their pupils would benefit from a grammar school place. But, of course, when you replace the crude unfairness of objective testing with a subjective judgement you encounter another problem: how to standardise the decisions that different people make.

One of my tasks as a grammar school head was to visit the primary schools in my school's catchment area to meet heads and staff to discuss the selection criteria and to look at the work of pupils on the borderline between selection and rejection. I then encountered a further hazard: I was head of a co-educational school and it was thought to be expedient to keep some sort of balance between the sexes. The boys' work was invariably less well presented than that of the girls and allowances had to be made for this, but how much allowance? The whole process was in fact a minefield and a salutary reminder of the impossibility of categorising and comparing human endeavour, whatever method is used. Why do we do it? The persistent classifying of children as successes or failures and the whole pernicious system of labelling, ranking and grading constantly undermine children's confidence and self-esteem and negate the efforts of teachers to build on children's natural desire to learn.

Both supporters and critics of the 11+ selection system were much influenced by the psychological debate on 'nature and nurture', the perennial argument over whether human potential is determined more by inherited characteristics or by the circumstances of one's birth, upbringing, environment and experiences. The introduction of the 11+ was a triumph for the hereditarians and their assumptions that all the abilities, aptitudes and mental processes with which we are born can be encapsulated in a single quality called 'intelligence' and that this remains more or less constant throughout our life. It was argued that a child's intelligence was measurable and could be given a numerical value, an 'intelligence quotient'. This IQ would than enable LEAs to segregate the superior and inferior intelligences in each grammar school catchment area.

The hereditarian view of human ability and potential took a knock during World War2 from the behaviour of its most infamous disciple. Hitler, of course, believed that the 'inborn nature' theory could be applied to whole races and groups of people and that the superior races' survival depended upon the extermination of those who had been born inferior. The full horror of the holocaust took a surprisingly long time to impinge on the world and there are of course some who still deny that it ever happened. Gradually, though, opponents of the 'inborn nature' theory gained ground after the war and the validity of the static IQ idea was increasingly questioned by psychologists whose research indicated that one's upbringing, education, environment and life experiences could modify inherited characteristics to a much greater degree than that allowed for by the hereditarians.

In the 1950s the rigidity and inaccuracy of the 11+ procedure were also being exposed by a number of secondary modern schools that were refusing to accept their non-academic role and beginning to prepare 11+ failures for the exams that were regarded as the prerogative of the grammar schools and independent sector. Some of the results were spectacularly good and the secondary schools concerned naturally began agitating for an even playing field in the form of a comprehensive intake.

The case against the hereditarians was much strengthened by the 'Burt affair'. Sir Cyril Lodowic Burt was an academic who specialised in eugenics, quantitative testing and inheritance of intelligence. He became President of the British Psychological Society and was the first psychologist to receive a knighthood. Burt was totally committed to the hereditarian view of human ability and was appointed adviser to the committees that decided on the 11+ process. He was much revered and constantly cited by my education lecturers who ran the secondary course at Borough Road Teachers' Training College where I trained. The Borough Road students only ever heard one side of the 'nature v nurture' debate, but then we were being prepared for secondary modern teaching and it was no doubt expedient for the College to produce young teachers who accepted the system. Needless to say, our education lecturers' teaching experience had been in grammar and independent schools. I don't recall our ever challenging what we were told about Burt, but I do remember being a little puzzled by the conclusion he drew from an early piece of research that found that boys in an élite prep school did better than those in an elementary school. Burt attributed this fact to differences in the boys' innate intelligence.

Shortly after I left Borough Road some of the 'pro-nurture ' psychologists began seriously to question Burt's research findings on human intelligence and to suggest that he had succumbed to a familiar temptation for researchers - selecting the evidence that supports their preconceptions and conveniently ignoring that which doesn't. Burt and his supporters retaliated in kind, accusing his detractors of the same malpractice they were attributing to him - the selective use of evidence to prove a case. An unseemly academic debate ensued which rumbled on for years but served a useful purpose in drawing public attention to the dubious methods used by many academic researchers.

Eventually Burt was challenged to produce the data on which his views were based. He failed to do so, claiming that key records had been thrown away and the rest destroyed in a fire at his home. Moreover, some of the research assistants whom he was said to have employed could not be traced. These revelations fuelled suspicions that Burt had not merely been unscrupulously selective in his collection of data, but that he had actually fabricated evidence to support his theories. Eventually the British Psychological Society accepted that the ' father of British psychology ' and key architect of the 11+ had been 'guilty of gross scientific fraud'. The Burt scandal serves as a dire warning of what can happen when theory becomes detached from reality, feeding on itself independently of the context that was its starting point.

It's embarrassing to be taken in by a fraudster and there are still those who cannot accept, or choose to ignore, that the segregation of so-called abilities in the old bipartite system was based on a myth and that the unscrupulous Burt and his school of psychologists were indirectly responsible for denying countless young people the opportunity to make more of their lives. The university department in which Burt was Professor of Psychology and Head of Department was still displaying his photograph in its gallery of distinguished academics well into the 21st century. Moreover, some LEAs have, for half a century, doggedly clung on to the binary system and use of the 11+ exam to segregate children at the age of eleven. Successive governments have turned a blind eye to this situation, presumably not wishing to antagonise those of their number who would dearly love to see a return of the grammar schools. Michael Gove, as Secretary of State for Education, always denied that he was part of the grammar school lobby, but the national curriculum that he introduced is an unmistakable throwback to that of the archetypal grammar school of the past.

The Gove agenda's emphasis on nurturing an élite, its focus on the curriculum rather than the child, its obsession with academic specialisms, its concentration on factual knowledge and historical perspective, on intense competition and narrow assessment criteria - these are all familiar from my own school experience. So, too, are the inevitable consequences: the lower status afforded creative, practical and vocational courses; the over-emphasis on rote-learning and written work at the expense of oral, practical and problem-solving skills; the lack of team initiatives and co-operative group work; the limited opportunities for young people to question the established order and to develop their own ideas. In fact, the whole approach is a defiant refusal to acknowledge the challenges our society currently faces and the sort of educational experiences we ought to be providing for the next generation who will have to sort out the complex problems we are bequeathing to them. Whatever Gove's true feelings on a return to the binary system, David Cameron obviously felt that his party's chance of winning the 2015 general election would not be enhanced by his reactionary Secretary of State's continuing to alienate teachers and Gove was duly demoted in July 2014. Cameron was always watchful of his pro-grammar-school colleagues and their potential threat to party unity.

The most widely-supported argument in favour of introducing a comprehensive system in this country was that it would put an end to the absurd classification of children at the age of eleven as 'academic' or 'non-academic'. It was argued that, in the comprehensive school, decisions concerning children's capability for academic work could be based on a much wider range of assessment criteria than a single day's written exams and, equally important, that they could be adjusted as pupils developed and changed in their response to their studies. Pupils would also be able to undertake different academic workloads and combine academic work with practical and vocational options, a development that might help to raise the status of non-academic courses. It was envisaged that this flexibility would enable many more children to gain academic qualifications.

There were other important comprehensive principles. The new schools would provide all children with a broad general education and a wide range of options. They would recognise and respect different forms of intelligence and approaches to learning. They would seek to nurture every individual's strengths, aptitudes and interests, regardless of their background, social class or money. Educating children from all walks of life in the same school would help the country to create a more understanding, tolerant and cohesive society.

Once comprehensive schools had been formed, it was the first target - the increased access to an academic course - that received most attention.   From the outset, schools were judged by their academic achievements or, more specifically, by their exam results.   Were those pupils who would previously have gone to grammar schools achieving comparable grades in the comprehensives?   And were more children passing academic exams under the new system? The comprehensive schools stood up well to these tests and their success was an important factor in the rapid increase during the latter part of the twentieth century in the number of students undertaking A level work and entering higher education.   Parental and government expectations were, however, increasing all the time and every school's exam performance became a subject for analysis and debate. Schools whose pupils were obtaining comparatively poor grades in their GCSEs and A levels, many of them serving deprived areas, became a cause of genuine concern and a target for increasing denigration and abuse from those who remained opposed to the comprehensive system.

Nevertheless, it was a surprise when four years into his ten-year ministry, Prime Minister Tony Blair announced in 2001 that comprehensive education had in fact failed.   His adviser, Alastair Campbell, journalist turned politician, put it more crudely: "The day of the bog standard comprehensive school is over."   The description stuck and was used repeatedly by ex-public school politicians who knew nothing about the comprehensive school system or its achievements. 'The post comprehensive era', Blair informed us, was to be characterised by diversity, not uniformity.   Each secondary school was to develop ' a distinctive mission, ethos and purpose', an extension of the previous conservative government's 'technology colleges' initiative.   Substantial extra funding was made available to those schools that developed a specialism, a curriculum centre of excellence in, for example, maths, science, languages or sport.   Schools were allowed to offer one or two specialisms, each of which would qualify for additional funding. A stipulation was that the school had to contribute to the cost of the initiative by obtaining private sponsorship of at least £50,000 for each specialism.

Having a practising Catholic as a mother, Tony Blair's children were able to attend prestigious faith schools outside the catchment area of the local standard comprehensive. Blair thought that all parents should have the opportunity to choose their child's school. This, he said, would not only be an important extension to the rights of the individual, but provide keener competition between schools and drive up standards all-round. Other measures were to be taken to further this Thatcherite market policy. In particular, successful schools would be given greater autonomy and extra funding. League tables were drawn up and, from that time onwards, schools have been ranked on the basis of their exam results. The consequence has been constant dissatisfaction with lower performing schools and a determination on the part of parents to ensure that their children gain entry to those schools whose pupils obtain the best results.

Tony Blair's policy for a diverse and competitive secondary school system was masterminded by Andrew Adonis, who came to the Labour Party via the Liberal Democrats and subsequently joined the Conservative government elected in 2015. Adonis was appointed head of New Labour's policy unit in 2001 and then, four years later, was made a life peer, enabling him to take up a position as Minister of Education without his having been elected to parliament. Before entering politics, Lord Adonis had had a short career as an Oxford don and then, like so many of his colleagues, as a journalist. Young, energetic and incredibly dedicated to furthering Blair's vision, he was a very smooth operator in the corridors of power. He believed strongly in momentum politics and clashed with Estelle Morris over her preference for incremental reform.

Adonis worked zealously for seven years interpreting and promoting the concept of autonomous schools, free of LEA control and managed by a private trust. These schools would be top performers in terms of exam results and be appropriately named 'academies'. Much of Adonis's time was spent in obtaining sponsors - wealthy individuals, businesses and a wide variety of other organisations - who were prepared to contribute to the financing of the privately-managed academies. Adonis had a crystal-clear vision of what he wanted. He shared Tony Blair's commitment to faith schools, had an unqualified admiration for the independent sector, particularly the public schools, and a respect that bordered on an obsession with academia. These personal beliefs coloured all that he did and religious groups, public schools and research-based universities became key targets in his quest for sponsors to run the state sector and establish the school ethos that he wanted.

Adonis worked at an impressive pace, admitting that he had "little time to research and think through a subject". He was ruthless in pursuing his personal objectives and seemed unfazed by criticism within his own party at his constant denigration of 'underperforming' comprehensive schools, by which he meant those positioned in the lower half of the league tables. The power he wielded was unusual for an unelected member of government and steadily increased as his efforts bore fruit. Tony Blair allowed him a surprising degree of latitude to develop independently-managed schools in the way that Adonis wished and financial support was provided for various aspects of the new policy. By 2010, when New Labour's term of office finally ended, there were over 200 academies, with many more in the pipeline.

When Cameron's coalition government came to power, one of its first moves was to declare that, despite the considerable sums that New Labour had spent on Tony Blair's specialist school idea, it had not had the desired effect of raising standards. It thus withdrew funding for the project, including the building programme associated with it. Schools were permitted to maintain their specialist role but, without government interest and funding, the initiative quickly lost significance. Parents had, of course, used the specialist designation to support their application for their children to attend a school with good exam results, but had not had to prove conclusively that their commitment to the specialism was genuine. Schools' responses to the specialism idea had been variable: many had spent the associated funding on more general ways of benefiting their pupils and were not too concerned about the initiative's demise.

The academy initiative was, however, a very different matter. In opposition, the Conservative Party had, one assumes, observed Andrew Adonis's activities with approval and not a little incredulity. Certainly Michael Gove, when he was Opposition Education Secretary, didn't attempt to conceal his admiration, indicating that he'd be happy to see Lord Adonis in the Cabinet of a Conservative government. When Gove became Secretary of State for Education in 2010, the academy programme was warmly welcomed and the pace of the development increased spectacularly. The original idea had been for academies to replace failing schools. Now all primary and secondary schools were invited to convert to academies, but with priority given to those designated by Ofsted as 'outstanding' or 'performing well'. These voluntary or 'converter' academies would not be required to have a sponsor, but be established as limited companies with a Board of Directors acting as a Trust and overseeing the running of the school. A big incentive to become an academy has been that, by so doing, schools control all their funds. Local Education Authority schools hand over a proportion of their government grant to the Authority to pay for the various advisory and support services that it provides, services considered by the teacher-abusers to be largely unnecessary. Woodhead, in one of his many derogatory comments on the teaching profession, claimed that the whole idea of support for teachers was 'one of the great contemporary myths'.

All government ministers feel that they have to make their mark on the system that they inherit if they are to move on and upward. Gove's personal contribution to the academy development was the 'free school'. The Coalition Government invited parents and independent groups in England to set up new schools independent of LEA control and run by the founding group itself, or by a company or organisation brought in for that purpose. There are now over 500 free schools, about a third of which are faith schools, and the intention is to double that figure by 2020. Funding, as with all academies, comes directly from central government. The Academies Act of 2010 stipulates that all new schools have to be academies which means that LEAs have lost their power to create new schools, a significant step in the process to transfer control of education away from local to central government.

By 2015 there were nearly 5,000 academies. Most secondary schools, and a rapidly increasing number of primary schools, are now controlled by trusts representing the interests of a bewildering variety of groups and individuals. All academies, including free schools, have more control than other schools do over their policies - for example, the curriculum, teachers' pay and conditions, and the length of school terms and the working day. This greater freedom extends to their admissions policies, although they have not been allowed to select on 'ability'. There have been clear signs, however, that this principle has not always been properly enforced.

The extra funding and autonomy enjoyed by the new schools help them to 'raise standards', that is, to improve their exam results; but this has been achieved at some cost to the system as a whole. The gap between the haves and have-nots has widened significantly, as it has in many other aspects of our society. Meanwhile, league tables have duly achieved their purpose and potential to create fierce competition between schools, competition that has at times become unpleasantly acrimonious and degrading. More complex and flexible admissions criteria have encouraged both schools and parents to look for loopholes that can be exploited to their advantage. The intake of middle-class and high-performing children to schools achieving consistently good exam results is a self-perpetuating process that ensures that the Manchester Uniteds of the educational world dazzle the public with their performances while the league strugglers fight against all the odds for their survival. Fragmentation and market forces are moving us inexorably back to the educationally and socially divisive binary system in the form of 'comprehensive grammar schools' and 'comprehensive secondary moderns'.

On her appointment as Prime Minister in July 2016, Theresa May gave a stirring rendering of the statutory pledge from a new government to represent all its people. Her mission, she said, would be "to make Britain a country that works for everyone" not just in "the interests of the privileged few". Empty rhetoric: the new Prime Minister's first major decision on domestic policy has been to bring her party's pro-grammar-school credentials out into the open and pave the way for a return to a binary system of secondary education. We are now on course to re-establish one of the twentieth century's most pernicious examples of a divided society - the segregation of those children deemed to have ability from the rest of their age-group. Immediately following Theresa May's announcement of a major shift in the government's education policy, David Cameron declared that he had changed his mind over staying in the House of Commons as a back-bench MP. He refuted the suggestion that this surprising u-turn was anything to do with Theresa May's support for grammar schools, but one cannot escape the thought that he didn't want to be around when his successor was promoting her extreme right-wing education policies.

Chapter 4

A Fundamental Error

*"The most fundamental error in the traditional O and A level
system is that each stage is designed to be suited for those
who are going on to the next. Schoolchildren who are not
good enough to go on are regarded as expendable."*

Sir Gordon Higginson, Vice-Chancellor
University of Southampton, 1988.

In the words of a headmaster for whom I once worked, the
English grammar schools provided "an academic education
for able and industrious boys from all social backgrounds",
ensuring that "there may never be wanting a supply of fit
persons to serve God in Church and State". No champion of
the grammar schools could have worked harder than Arthur
Claydon, Head of Maidstone Grammar School from 1940 to
1966, to ensure that 'intelligence', coupled with hard work,
could provide a challenge to the assumption that the natural
routes to academia and public service were privilege, wealth
and influence.

Claydon was an intellectual, a scholar who assumed that
the role of the grammar school was to instil academic
ambition in its pupils. He believed that academic distinction
was unquestionably the highest form of human achievement
and that the greatest honour a pupil could obtain for himself -
and of course for his school - was an Oxford or Cambridge
award. As soon as future star performers had been detected in
the Lower School their reports informed parents of their son's
destiny in the headmaster's portentous words: "a potential
Oxbridge scholar". From that moment these boys were
marked men, the nature and outcome of their studies
prematurely determined by the School, without consultation
either with them or their parents.

In seeking to emulate the academic successes of the public schools, Maidstone copied many of their traditional features, including their Oxbridge-orientated curriculum. Latin was a key subject and provided the school's motto, song and some daily terminology - prefects were, for example, 'praefects' (closer to the original 'praefectus'). The design of the school, like that of many public school buildings, was an imitation of an Oxbridge college, with a quad, cloisters and sacrosanct lawn. The main buildings stood back from the gatehouse and archway entrance and there was a spaciousness and style about the whole place that matched its ambitions.

Watching Claydon from inside Big Hall as he made his be-gowned and dignified way through the cloisters each day to lead Morning Prayers, one felt instinctively that he should have stayed in Oxford, become a don and eventually Master of Balliol, where he had been a student. This surely would have been his true milieu. No doubt that is what he would have wished, but his degree result had let him down - a second, not a first. His class of degree was a source of great regret to Claydon and seemed to fuel his desire to groom boys for academic distinction and the ultimate accolade that had somehow eluded him.

Claydon had packed his staffroom with like-minded academics. During my time at Maidstone, I was the only non-Oxbridge member of my large department. Eight of my departmental colleagues constituted an academic élite within an élite, having been Oxbridge 'scholars' or 'exhibitioners'. This solidity of the Oxbridge aura in the Maidstone English Department obviously owed much to the subject's being Claydon's own specialism, but the weighting of grammar school common rooms in favour of Oxbridge graduates was a deliberate policy in all the more academically ambitious schools. At that time there were numerous Local Authorities that would only shortlist Oxbridge graduates for grammar school headships and, had there been sufficient of the breed to go round, I'm sure there would have been the same stipulation for teaching appointments. Such prejudice was not confined to the world of education: the whole of society was riddled with bizarre examples of this élitist fixation. One of the hop farmers near Maidstone who offered students summer holiday employment as tallymen - measurers of the crops picked by the East End hop pickers - would only entrust the role to undergraduates of the two ancient universities.

The most academically successful Maidstone Grammar School boys were effectively relieved of any responsibility for decision-making concerning their future destination. It simply didn't seem to occur to anyone that these boys might have liked, at some stage, to consider the many options open to them and then to exercise their right to make an informed choice about their career. Even in the mid-twentieth century, school leavers applying to university could choose from a considerable range of HE institutions and courses. Oxbridge didn't have a monopoly of highly-rated departments: some of their rivals had superior strengths in particular areas and also offered courses that weren't available at the two most traditional universities. This applied particularly to the new universities. The early sixties, the period during which I worked at Maidstone, saw the beginning of a great expansion in Higher Education (HE) provision and many of the universities coming on stream - Sussex, Warwick, York, East Anglia, for example - were responding to a changing world and adding exciting new courses to the traditional range of undergraduate options. Some, like Keele, introduced an innovatory approach to the whole curriculum. I don't remember any of these developments being brought to the boys' attention at Maidstone.

Had they been given the chance, it's just possible that some of Claydon's prodigies might even have opted to enter employment after school and follow a professional rather than academic route to a career. Alternatively, they could have gone on to art or music college to become artists or musicians, rather than graduates with an academic qualification in art or music. Or they might have had an out-of-school interest in drama or sport or travel or business, or a hundred and one other fields of human endeavour, that would not be satisfied by prolonged academic study in its purist form.

The paradox of the twentieth century grammar schools was that, whilst purporting to reduce the element of privilege in our society, many of them worked assiduously to groom an élite group for admission to two of the greatest bastions of privilege in the world. As a direct consequence of that policy, generations of young people, identified as key players of the future, were put through a restricted school experience that was, even 50 years ago, manifestly out-of-date. It is much more so now. For the two-thirds of the Maidstone boys who didn't go on to university, the curriculum was even less appropriate - either to their own personal needs or the world of work they would be entering when they left school.

The legacy of the grammar schools' priorities is deeply embedded in our secondary school system and has undermined some of the basic principles of the comprehensive ideal to meet the needs of all children. Comprehensive schools are under constant political pressure to prioritise academic courses, to improve the exam performance of the pupils following them and to increase the number preparing to become undergraduates. 'How many of you want to go to university?' the visiting Secretary of State asks the year 10 class in an inner city comprehensive. And then beams with self-satisfaction when a large majority dutifully, but not necessarily truthfully, give the required answer.

The latest Government initiative to intensify this drive is to return to the 1940s' school certificate, an academic qualification awarded for a particular level of achievement in a defined group of key academic subjects. To obtain the old school certificate, pupils had to pass in all subjects at one sitting - no retaking of separate subjects to accumulate the required number of passes. The newly-introduced English Baccalaureate, or EBacc, is a precise imitation of this, a traditional grouping of academic GCSE subjects that most children are now expected to study. The cohort of children who entered secondary school in September 2015 will all start GCSE courses in 2018 in English, maths, the sciences, a foreign language and either history or geography. Advocates of comprehensive schools could never have envisaged that the principle of equal opportunity would be distorted in this way, by forcing almost every child through a traditional grammar school programme of academic work originally designed as a way of preparing a small selected group of pupils for two specific universities.

All education systems seek to raise pupils' expectations and none of us would quarrel with that. Every child has the potential to achieve fulfilment and economic security in adult life. Our task as educationists is to nurture that potential in every child, to open as many doors as possible so that we cater for all intelligences, aptitudes and interests and explore the full range of possibilities for each child. And, having opened doors, we have to keep them open, so that children leave school still believing in themselves and their potential, not cowed by defeat.

Unfortunately, heavy emphasis on one aspect of the educational process has the effect of *closing* doors rather than opening them. The increasing emphasis on academic courses in secondary schools inevitably reduces the importance and standing of other parts of the curriculum. Creative and practical subjects, together with vocational options, have always fought a losing battle for equal status but, if the present trend continues, it's not beyond possibility that some of them will be fighting, not for equality, but for survival.

The difference in status established between academic courses and the rest of the secondary school curriculum doesn't fully satisfy the current craze for detailed ranking and classification. The academic curriculum has its own hierarchy, with an upper echelon of traditional and self-styled 'rigorous' subjects and a group of poor relations comprising newer areas of study, applied alternatives to the preferred purist and theoretical approaches, and - the bête noire of many politicians - the 'soft' options such as sociology and psychology. This ranking has a very strong influence over the GCSE programmes considered most appropriate for those students deemed to be highfliers: the more successful the students, the greater the pressures upon them to stack their timetable with high status academic courses.

To make the most of their adult lives children need to have experienced a wide range of learning experiences, to be multi-skilled, and generally and broadly well-educated. The world that awaits them is highly complex, fast-changing and challenging: they will not be well-equipped for it by having concentrated mainly on one narrow aspect of the education process, no matter how prestigious that might be. Specialist knowledge and skills are essential to our society, but they need to be developed as part of a much wider range of educational objectives. Our educational system has always encouraged a specialist approach at too young an age and then allowed it to dominate our thinking in the latter stages of the education process. Most other countries achieve a better balance between specialist and general education than we do. We tend to regard curricular breadth and depth as alternatives, rather than as partners in the educational process.

Traditionally, schools have determined the nature of the curriculum they offer and that is still the situation in the independent sector. Since 1988, state schools have been required to follow a standard national curriculum, constantly modified by successive governments in accordance with their political leanings. With the advent of the Adonis academies we are moving back to the situation in which all schools determine what they teach. That at least is the theory. In practice, the curriculum of all schools - private, LEA, academies - is determined largely by the country's academic exam system. The syllabuses and assessment criteria of the A level and GCSE exam courses are designed to meet the perceived needs of the universities, particularly those universities whose primary interest is in their post-graduate work, where the process of specialisation reaches its ultimate goal. The perceived recruitment needs of the research-based universities exert far too strong an influence, not only on the content of secondary school courses, but on their teaching methods and the student learning experience.

Teachers of years 1-6 will tell you that they teach primary school children; those who work in secondary schools will describe themselves as a teacher of physics, geography, art, or whatever else their specialism is. From the moment children enter the secondary school, they are locked into a system in which all human knowledge and experience is compartmentalised and delivered by subject specialists. The largely artificial boundaries between subjects are strengthened, so that specialisms become ring-fenced, their distinctiveness defined not only by a specific body of knowledge, but by a special way of looking at the world and the human situation. They have developed a specialist language and their own mystique. Each subject has its own cult following, together with associations and societies that support its adherents and those who teach it in schools, colleges and universities.

With the exponential growth in human knowledge there are now too many school subjects to squeeze into the timetable and the competition between them has become keener as they vie with each other for recognition, status and time allocation. At those points when students are required to reduce the range of their studies, most subjects are in competition for students. One of the criteria used to measure teachers' success and suitability for promotion is the number of students from their classes who choose to study their subject as part of their GCSE and A level programme.

At A level, each subject syllabus is designed to be a preparation for its honours degree equivalent and has a designated body of knowledge and set of principles and theories that the universities consider students should have learnt if they wish to read that subject at university. GCSE, in turn, provides the background considered necessary for sixth-form work and admission to most A level courses is dependent on students having studied and achieved a specified grade in their GCSE equivalent. New information and ideas are frequently being added to syllabuses and, although some topics are discarded or afforded less time, the overall trend is always one of expansion. The perennial problem of how to 'get through the syllabus' has become a constant anxiety for teachers, comparable to GPs' struggle to cope with the sheer quantity of their daily consultations. One consequence of this situation is to push material down the system and to make an earlier and earlier start on the preparation for undergraduate work.

Academia has always been a powerful influence on the upper stages of our educational system but, since the politicians took control of our schools, it has become an obsession that is skewing the whole system. Our primary schools have, until recently, benefited from a non-compartmentalised approach to education. Apart from a small amount of specialised teaching in areas such as music and PE, the primary sector has sought to deliver a broad, balanced and integrated curriculum taught by a class teacher.

It is important in all schools to have a clear structure to children's learning, but the class teacher system has provided a degree of flexibility that has enabled primary school teachers to adjust the timetable in response to changing circumstances and unexpected opportunities. If children are thoroughly absorbed in a particular topic or activity, they haven't had to stop just because a lesson bell has rung. Learning could be related to their particular environment, to seasonal changes, to news items, national events and local developments and initiatives. Children could be taken out of school regularly to see and experience first-hand the things they've been told about in the classroom. This is how children learn best - by observing and experiencing the world around them and sharing their reactions with an interested adult. Timetabling flexibility is also very helpful when a school wants to engage in large-group or whole-school initiatives - major projects, drama productions, concerts, fund-raising events, and all the many other ways in which schools develop children's practical, creative, social and organisational skills.

All of these things are of course possible in the secondary school, but they are more difficult to organise. The fractured nature of the school day, with its rigid time allocation for each subject, doesn't allow the same flexibility for cross-curricular initiatives and work outside the classroom. In the pressurised exam-preparation culture of the secondary school, staff wishing to organise events such as conferences, visits and joint ventures with other schools, inevitably encounter reluctance on the part of their colleagues to have students withdrawn from their lessons. The sanctity of the exam curriculum is a major threat to invaluable experiences such as foreign exchanges, field courses, school camps and work placements, all of which involve alternative ways of learning and have the potential to open minds and spark fresh interests. These activities introduce children to new situations and environments and often enable them to forge new relationships. Many children who are not motivated by the daily routine in school have their interest in the world around them re-kindled by experiences of this kind.

Teachers work well beyond the call of duty to give children these invaluable experiences, but, as with so much of what they do, they find themselves constantly fighting against the tide. The move to establish a secondary-school- style specialised curriculum on the primary sector is a major setback. The most recent version of the national curriculum requires children to be taught ten separate subjects from the age of 5 or 6, and for a classical or modern foreign language to be added two years later. Parents are already receiving reports on 5 and 6 year-olds implying subject strengths and weaknesses.

The weighting of the new requirements, as always, is heavily in favour of the academic areas of the curriculum; art and music are included, but not drama and dance. The politicians concede that schools may like to teach citizenship and personal, social and health education, but there is no requirement for them to do so. There is no recognition of the excellent work in character training that schools do, both within and outside the curriculum. As always, the new requirements have been imposed without proper consultation or debate. They are accompanied by blanket condemnation of the system they are replacing and politicians' trademark denigration of the teachers who have made it work.

There was an attempt in the 1970s to provide all secondary school students with a course in political education. It never stood a chance of becoming reality and was very quickly stamped out: politicians obviously didn't want the tricks of their trade closely examined in the classroom. Had the initiative been successful, there would have been no shortage of suitable teaching material. Andrew Adonis's book, *Education, Education, Education*, would have been a strong contender as a standard primer for current students. Take, for example, the following passage explaining why, in his opinion, the secondary sector's specialist approach to the curriculum must be extended to the primary sector:

"Excellent teachers and teaching are just as important in primary as in secondary schools. Yet, while secondary teachers have for several decades been expected to have subject honours degrees and deep subject knowledge as well as pedagogic skills and training, primary school teachers mostly come from general education courses - B Eds and equivalents - in university departments which are often the old teacher training colleges amalgamated or renamed. We need to do better than this, both for primary-level teachers themselves and for primary school children who have few - if any - teachers with specialisms in most areas of the curriculum, and few even with graduate-level knowledge in English or maths. In stark contrast to private junior schools, most state primary schools do not systematically employ historians, musicians, geographers, science graduates, drama and PE specialists, and so on. It is time they did so."

This is a clever but utterly duplicitous and specious attempt to get the reader to accept a series of personal prejudices as if they constituted reasoned argument. The passage starts with an irrefutable statement: that excellent teaching and teachers are required in both the secondary and primary sectors. But the platitude is put in such a way that it implies that this isn't what's happening - the primary schools and their staff are falling short of their fundamental duty. The reasons for this are then made clear: primary teachers are academically and pedagogically inadequate. We have to feel sorry for them and their poor pupils who are being let down so badly.

Adonis makes no attempt whatsoever to present a case or to justify his numerous assumptions. There is no basis whatsoever for claiming that

- a specialist primary-sector curriculum would be preferable to an integrated one,
- in-depth knowledge of a single academic subject is a better preparation for primary school teaching than a degree course that focuses on how to provide young children with a good general education,
- the content of maths and English degree courses is especially relevant to the teaching of basic numeracy and literacy skills to young children,
- private junior schools are providing a better education than state schools or, if they are, that this superiority is accounted for by their being staffed by subject specialists, rather than by such advantages as their much more favourable staff/student ratios, superior facilities and stronger parental support,
- university departments whose antecedents were colleges of education are delivering inferior training.

Adonis's desire for every school to become an academic hothouse knows no bounds. He returns to the idea time and time again until eventually disappearing into the stratosphere with a recommendation that funding should be made available to enable primary school subject specialists to have time off to study for Ph Ds. In the Adonis Wonderland applicants for primary headships will presumably need to be Nobel prizewinners.

Anyone amazed at the early start on the academic grooming process now being made in the state sector must have missed a recent trend in the country's independent nursery schools. In the last decade there has been a rapid growth in the idea that parents with big ambitions for their children need to get them on the conveyor belt to academia before they reach school age. This process is very big business in China. In the southern city of Guangzhou parents can enrol their sons and daughters on a £5,700-a-year course designed to train children as young as three in 'leadership abilities' and 'competitiveness'.

A London equivalent has established a chain of nurseries called Young Graduates, the name in large letters on each school's imitation portals. The aim of these establishments is, according to their managers, 'to raise aspirations' and 'to nurture tomorrow's leaders'. They capture the prevailing mood of English education - perpetual motion, a constant striving ever onward and upward, sights trained on the next stage. Much is made of the annual graduation ceremony in the Young Graduate institutions and others like them being developed elsewhere in this country. These occasions introduce the young scholars to all the trappings of the destinations to which their parents aspire for their offspring - parchment certificates, individual prizes, and group photographs of the graduates resplendent in their gowns and mortar-boards before the latter are thrown to the winds in a symbolic gesture of the relief they will feel in 17 years' time when they are finally freed of the yoke of academia. "Parents can sit in the audience," comments one child psychologist, "and laugh and clap at the children performing like monkeys." They are not the only ones laughing: one robing firm in Hampshire claims to have sold over 10,000 gown and mortar-board sets for pre-school children during the summer of 2016.

What a sad reflection on our educational priorities. These nursery school children are emphatically not 'young graduates'. They're three and four-olds with a specific age-related educational agenda to which we ought to be responding. As parents and teachers, we naturally want to do everything in our power to nurture the various aptitudes, interests and skills that children bring with them into the world and to give them the strongest possible chance of an adult life that will be personally fulfilling and economically secure. But we must also recognise their individuality. We don't have the right to take their life-decisions for them and to groom them for roles that we want them to have. In the moving words of Khalil Gibran,

"Your children are not your children,
They are the sons and daughters of Life's longing for itself.
They come through you but not from you.
And though they are with you yet they belong not to you."

Children need, with our help and support, to develop a set of values, a strength of character and a self-awareness that will enable them to make their own independent way in the world. Our schools, colleges and universities should provide the experiences and skills that will prepare young people for the various challenges they will meet as adults and for the decisions they will have to take at key stages of their life.

For longer than anyone can remember, educationists have been lobbying to rid our education system of its preoccupation with specialist forms of study, in order that schools may fulfil their proper purpose - to provide all pupils with a sound general education. The following is the view of an early advocate of a broad, general school education, Sir Frederick Kenyon, Director and Principal Librarian of the British Museum, writing in 1918:

"It seems to me that one wants an examination which will fit in with the ordinary school curriculum, so that a boy can take it without having to prepare specially for it. It will merely show that he has had what we regard as a proper general education, and has reached a sufficient standard in it to justify his going on to University...our object is to reduce the amount of specialised knowledge required ...I want to make it worth his while to keep up his other subjects to some considerable extent until the end of his school career."

That puts our current need in a nutshell: an exam system that is servant, not master, of the curriculum and which gives universities no more than they need to know, that is, whether or not applicants' general level of education suggests they would benefit from higher education. Generations of educationists have sought to persuade our moribund society of this simple truth. Significantly, some of the strongest pleas have come from distinguished academics who have had the vision and courage to deplore the effects of university priorities on the school system. Sir Christopher Ball has been one of the most committed advocates of change. The following observations are taken from a paper written when he was Master of Keble College and Chairman of the Board of the HE National Advisory Body (NAB):

"The pernicious mechanism, the vicious circle, is clear enough. And like many bad things it grows in good soil. Our highly-valued, specialised, academic, research-related honours courses - typical of the university system...impose a narrowing effect on admissions requirements, and lead to an over-valuing of the grades in the required three A levels and a consequent undervaluing of the rest of the school education. And this in turn defeats the good intentions of those who wish to see a broadening of sixth-form studies."

Throughout the 20th century there were innumerable consultation exercises, research projects and pilot schemes leading to proposals and counter proposals for changes in the exam system that would enable sixth-formers to receive a more broadly-based education. All these initiatives were abortive, serving merely to highlight the gulf that existed between the generalists and the specialists. None attempted to address the fundamental problem - the specialist focus of A level courses which limits their value as components of a general education programme. They were all tinkering exercises, trying vainly to provide greater breadth without unduly threatening the traditional character of A levels.

The Higginson Report of 1988 came closest to mounting a significant challenge to the status quo, providing as it did a clear indication of the 'remarkable consensus' that emerged from its very thorough consultation exercise. Gordon Higginson was Vice-Chancellor of Southampton University and a governor of the sixth-form college that I was running at the time. He took a great interest in the College and was very supportive of its efforts to achieve a better balance between the examined curriculum and all the other opportunities a sixth-form education can offer. Gordon was a man of wide interests, with an instinctive understanding of the need for schools to provide a good general education for all their pupils. He and his committee were very impressed by the quantity and quality of the material they received that advocated an entirely new approach to sixth-form education that would achieve this purpose. The Committee didn't pull its punches, highlighting in a preface to its Report the strength of the case against the linear system with its deeply-ingrained assumption that the purpose of each stage of education is to prepare students for the next, the implication being that "schoolchildren who were not good enough to go on were expendable".

Already well outside its brief - which had been a thinly-disguised invitation to endorse the existing A level system - the Committee must have realised it was courting trouble with its direct and honest approach. The immediacy of the reaction, however, took everyone by surprise: before anyone could read the Report - in fact a bare two hours after its launch - Margaret Thatcher announced in no uncertain terms that her Government had complete faith in A levels, the 'gold standard' of the British education system. The speed with which the Higginson Committee's findings were rejected must surely stand as a supreme example of politicians' habitual contempt for the consultative process.

Thomas Arnold of Rugby School claimed that "the first, second and third duty of a schoolmaster is to get rid of unpromising subjects." Current advocates of focusing our educational resources on 'promising subjects' usually avoid expressing their views as crudely as that, at least in public. Nevertheless, Arnold's legacy is still a part of political thinking in this country: our education system is designed primarily to ensure the success of those children deemed to be academic. The gulf in status between academic and vocational school courses is a constant reminder of this ordering of priorities.

In 2004 yet another working group on reform of the upper secondary school curriculum was set up under the chairmanship of Sir Michael Tomlinson. This committee proposed that the GCSE/A level system should be replaced by a new overarching diploma that did away with the class-ridden practice of separating academic study and vocational training. After two years of hearing evidence and sifting through advice, the Tomlinson Committee reached a remarkable consensus in favour of wholesale reform of the examination system. Tony Blair's response was simply a politer version of Margaret Thatcher's reaction to the Higginson proposals 16 years earlier: GCSE and A level would be retained. Mike Baker, the BBC's education correspondent, commented: "It could be an episode from 'Yes, Minister': the government-commissioned enquiry was enthusiastically set up, its recommendations praised, then rejected."

The case for schools to provide a general rather than a specialised education has been repeatedly rejected. In fact, no other important educational reform - equal opportunity for girls, comprehensive schools, raising of the school leaving age - has found it so difficult to make an impression on the established order. C.P.Snow's observation of 50 years ago is every bit as relevant today:

"Nearly everyone will agree that our school education is too specialised. But nearly everyone feels that it is outside the wit of man to alter it."

The gulf between the general education ideal and the educational priorities and practices that militate against it is continually widening.

Academia's instinctive apprehension at the thought of students starting a single honours degree course without undertaking a two-year specialist course of preparation is quite unfounded. If A levels were redesigned to provide sixth-form students with a sound general education, the courses would naturally be very different - in content, perspective and approach. But there is no reason why they should be less demanding or less appropriate for potential university students. Opponents of the idea that sixth-formers should follow a less specialised programme of studies invariably assume that this would entail a dumbing down to benefit 'less able' students, at the expense of those who are 'academic'. That would be just as inappropriate and unfair as the present system, merely swapping the groups who are specially treated and those who are regarded as dispensable. Instead, the aim would be to provide a more interesting, useful and relevant programme of study for all sixth-form students.

Students studying more broadly-based A levels would acquire different, but not inferior, insights into a subject. They might possess less knowledge of a subject's historical development and its established theories, but they would have a better understanding of current applications and the ways in which these were relevant to their own lives. They would have ranged more widely and have a greater awareness of a subject's breadth and how it overlapped with other specialisms. They would, of course, have spent less time being introduced to the specialist ambience of the research-based universities but, as a result of a more student-centred approach, they would presumably have had an opportunity to undertake an in-depth study of a topic that particularly interested them, perhaps a feature of the subject that was manifest in their local environment or a topic of which they already had some experience.

A generalist approach to sixth-form studies would require university staff to adapt to a student intake with different strengths to those of the past. If the attendant reduction in the time students had spent in specialist university-style study was considered a serious loss, universities would have to fill in the gaps themselves. Would that be so disastrous? University staff are nearly all actively engaged in research. If they feel that grooming students to follow in their footsteps should be the focus of undergraduate work - although that, of course, is open to question - then they are well-equipped to undertake full responsibility for that process, far better than most schoolteachers.

We seriously underestimate the speed with which young people learn when they are fully motivated. If universities were to spend more time training their researchers in their teaching rôle they would quickly bring a new intake up to speed in the specific skills and approaches that were regarded as essential. Quite a few academics in fact already have to do this. An increasing number of honours degree courses have no A level equivalent, so that the staff responsible for them cannot assume that their students have any specific background knowledge or expertise. They have to start at the beginning, which isn't actually a bad place for a course to start.

University courses are proliferating and many no longer make rigid stipulations regarding applicants' choice of sixth-form course. For example, bioscience departments offering such options as animal behaviour, conservation and ecology, environmental studies, evolutionary biology, marine biology and zoology frequently accept students from a wide range of subject backgrounds, provided they include either maths or one science in their A level package. The first year of these courses is a foundation year in which students acquire a basic understanding of the new subject and its particular character and importance.

Another reason for increased flexibility over university entrance requirements is that thousands of mature students enrol for honours degree courses every year. For example, most medical courses admit 15-45 mature students a year, some of them graduates in other subjects, others who for various reasons didn't go to university after school. These people come from a range of backgrounds and with various qualifications, some of them very different to the A levels of traditional medical school applicants. Applicants' potential is assessed on a much wider range of criteria than usual. For example, graduates changing direction usually take the Graduate Medical School Admissions Test (GAMSAT) which "assesses the ability to understand and analyse written and graphically presented material" and "measures skills and knowledge acquired over a long period of time, as well as the ability to reason, make logical deductions and form judgements." There are two very demanding tests of candidates' reasoning powers, one assessing the ability to think scientifically, the other a verbal reasoning paper requiring a high level of language interpretation. A third paper requires candidates to write two essays from a range of options that can be on any subject. Candidates testify to the wide range of skills required by the GAMSAT and thus its usefulness as a preparation for a medical career.

If some university courses can accept students who have a general, rather than a specialist, base of knowledge and skills is there any reason why this cannot apply to all courses? Is there any justification for curtailing the breadth of schoolchildren's education so that they can make an early start on their specialist university studies? Do sixth-formers really need to have an in-depth knowledge of a subject to prove that they'll be able to understand it at university? Higher

Education admissions tutors should be looking for potential, evidence of applicants' determination, commitment, adaptability. And, above all, passion. Have they fire in their belly? If so, forget about the preparatory A level and the extent of applicants' specialist knowledge. Accept students on the basis of the qualities they will bring to their studies, and start the course at the beginning.

I recall an occasion when I was a member of a group of head-teachers invited for a day's pampering at Oxford University to hear all about the undergraduate courses on offer and, more particularly from the heads' point of view, to pick up useful hints on how best to play the admissions game for the benefit of their sixth-formers. One member of our party was especially dogged and determined in his quest for detailed information on the policies he should adopt to get the maximum number of his students into Oxford. Notepad at the ready, he asked Jonathan Wordsworth, descendant of the more famous William, what combination of A levels was regarded the best for students wishing to read English. Without hesitation, the don replied, "Maths, physics and chemistry - with a lot of reading of literature in the summer holiday before coming up to university." I got the impression that Jonathan didn't suffer fools gladly, but the head was unabashed and moved on to the entrance exam, which was a feature of the Oxbridge admissions procedure at the time. What was Dr Wordsworth looking for in the essays that applicants wrote? Reply: "A single imaginative adjective." I'm not sure whether the head made a note of what he was told or indeed if he understood what Jonathan was saying.

It's all about potential. The key question is how much of the young child's self-motivation, natural curiosity, spirit of enquiry and enthusiasm for the learning process are still vibrant in the 18-year-old university applicant? There are, of course, many imponderables when trying to assess potential. How well, for example, will the student adapt to the total university experience with its many new challenges and demands - the huge community and more complex environment, the intensifying of the specialist approach, greater responsibility for one's work and life in general, the absence of parental and schoolteacher support, new staff, new friends, the impact of the much vaunted social and sex life? Academic courses simulating research-based learning experiences won't provide many answers to questions like that. And the exam grades that get students into university are notoriously poor predictors of the progress they'll make once they're there. They could hardly be otherwise, for, as they are currently constituted, they reveal so little about those who possess them. We should stop training students to perform a limited number of circus tricks. We could then perhaps concentrate on making sure that they leave school with as wide a range of life skills as possible and with the resilience, imagination and strength of character to adapt to different circumstances and new challenges. The need has never been greater for us to apply the Piaget principle of education: "creating men and women who are capable of doing new things, not simply repeating what other generations have done."

I left my grammar school headship in Hertfordshire to join a group of Hampshire education officers and college principals pioneering a new style of 16-18 education - the open-access sixth-form college. The aim was to concentrate the county's sixth-form provision in a relatively small number of junior colleges catering for all students who wanted to continue with their education beyond the school-leaving age. Students were to be given greater responsibility for their own studies than in a school sixth-form and have the opportunity to select a study programme ranging across all subject areas. The colleges would, however, have strong advisory and support structures - pastoral care, careers service, study facilities and resources. The staff-student ratio would be 1:12.

The Hampshire education officers had a clear idea of the kind of colleges that they wanted to establish, and the principals whom they appointed bought into their vision.

However, once in post, those leading the new initiative were given extensive responsibility for developing their colleges in their own way. I had been very interested, as a grammar school head, in providing sixth-formers with an extensive non-examined general studies programme, but the timetabling logistics with a sixth-form of 130 made this very difficult. A sixth-form destined to be over a thousand strong offered considerably more curricular and timetabling flexibility, which was of course one of the arguments in favour of the new kind of 16-18 provision.

Queen Mary's College effectively reversed the usual sixth-form priorities by reducing A level and other exam programmes to 'minority time' and providing a range of just under 100 non-examined 'Main Studies' which, together with games and private study, occupied most of students' time. A student's timetable normally included three Main Studies, each of a year's duration, but anyone with a light load of exam work was able to take more. Main Studies provided creative, practical and vocational experiences often denied sixth-formers because of pressures to concentrate on academic work. In addition, there were opportunities for working in the community, establishing small businesses, taking on outward bound challenges and a wide range of theme-based studies of a philosophical, sociological, psychological, political and environmental nature. Many of the options involved group projects in which students worked towards a tangible outcome or end-product - a performance, production or presentation; an exhibition or publication; the designing of a piece of equipment or construction of a facility of some kind. Exams concentrate the mind by providing students with a clear goal and aspiration, but there are many alternative ways of giving a course a sense of direction and purpose.

In the College's initial staff recruitment exercise, advertisements asked for applications from those who would like to teach Main Studies, but made it clear that A level work would also be available for those who sought it. Key appointments were the Directors of Study posts - faculty heads charged both with managing the examined curriculum and leading their staff teams in the designing, resourcing and teaching of Main Studies. Traditional criteria used in appointing teaching staff, such as past experience and academic exam results, didn't apply much to these posts. It would have been pointless looking for management experience in huge open-access sixth-forms because they didn't exist. Success in teaching specialist academic sixth-form subjects wouldn't automatically transfer to the task of creating appropriate learning strategies for a Main Study group, particularly one in which a third-year Oxbridge applicant might be working alongside a first-year Down's syndrome youngster (Main Studies were often mixed age as well as mixed 'ability'). Likewise, candidates' A level studies and honours degree subjects weren't particularly relevant to running a wide-ranging general studies programme. Once again, one was looking for potential to respond to a new situation, in this instance a particularly demanding new situation.

The response to the Directors of Study advertisement was encouragingly enthusiastic. I was left to make the selection myself - no governors, no education officers, no politicians. The result was one canon residentiary from Canterbury Cathedral, one history don from York University, one teacher of Russian from Manchester Grammar School and an engineer from Africa. None had had comprehensive school experience. In fact, they were all young, and short of the length of service normally expected of a teacher seeking a senior post. Presumably I noted their academic qualifications, but I don't remember what they were.

The launching of a new venture - in this instance involving a new educational concept - has to be a team effort, a combined operation involving all staff. And that is what it was in Queen Mary's College. If the contribution of the Directors of Study stood out, it was because they were in the forefront of pioneering a new sixth-form curriculum that raised general education to a position of significant importance. The Directors of Study passed the 'potential' test with flying colours and they all made an outstanding contribution to the College's early development. Three years after opening, the subject groupings of the Directors' faculties were re-shuffled, both to accommodate changing priorities and additions to the curriculum and to keep alive the exciting curricular debate of the College's early years. All the Directors were given new responsibilities and one became a Professional Tutor leading the College's extensive in-service training programme for staff.

Another three years and the Directors had moved on to fresh challenges elsewhere, in which they again demonstrated in abundance their adaptability and wide-ranging skills. Three joined the inspectorate at different stages of their careers, two worked as education officers for a time and one became the country's first adviser in political education before establishing a consultancy. Three eventually managed their own colleges, two once more breaking fresh ground by pioneering yet another form of post-16 education, the tertiary college, which combined the roles of both a sixth-form college and an FE institution. At the time, this kind of flexibility and constant role-changing were relatively new to education. The situation in which teachers did virtually the same job for decades, sometimes for a lifetime, is now a thing of the past. In all walks of life people are having to adapt to rapidly-changing situations, different occupations and environments, innovative ways of working, entirely new careers. The linear approach to school education no longer has any relevance.

Chapter 5

Worlds Apart: Independent and State Education

"It is impossible to hope that the classes of this country will ever be united in spirit unless their members cease to be educated in two separate systems of schools, one of which is counted as definitely superior to the other."

Sir Cyril Norwood, Head Master
of Harrow, 1943.

When Tessa Blackstone, former Minister for Higher and Further Education, became Vice-Chancellor of Greenwich University in 2004 she was delighted with the university's site on the banks of the River Thames, once the home of the old naval college. Chair of the Royal Institute of British Architects' Trust, Baroness Blackstone took great pleasure in the many fine old buildings that the former Thames Polytechnic had acquired when it moved to the magnificent Greenwich site. She was said to be less enamoured by a tactless comment from one of her friends who thought it a pity that Greenwich wasn't home to a traditional university, the obvious implication being that her students wouldn't appreciate surroundings that are normally reserved for the privileged and wealthy. There was a similar attitude in the first half of the 20th century with respect to extensive council house provision. Some opponents were of the opinion that it was a waste of money to provide the underclass with quality housing: they would probably keep their coal in the bath.

Despite all the changes that have taken place in higher education in the last fifty years - the explosion of new universities, the changed status of polytechnics and many HE colleges, the ever-widening range of options and opportunities, and the tremendous increase in participation rates - many people's typical image of a university remains rooted in the past. Their instinctive stereotypes are of gleaming spires, immaculate quads enclosed by picturesque old colleges, students reclining languidly on river banks, breathing in the air of learning that wafts by from the ancient begowned professors making their way through the cloisters. There is a sense of a very special quality of life - an air of privilege, a taste of leisure and luxury which we can all enjoy, but most of us only vicariously.

We are fascinated by class, privilege and celebrity status in this country. We love our Royal Family, our pageants, stately homes, Oxbridge colleges, millionaire footballers and pop stars. In many parts of the world inequality is achieved and maintained by totalitarian government and brutal suppression of any dissent. The British way is typically much more civilised and gentlemanly. We simply touch our forelock and bow to what appears to be the inevitability of vast disparity between the haves and the have-nots. Privilege, élitism and the class system thrive on this tolerance and develop exponentially.

Among the many requests for donations I received from charities last year was one seeking funding for an initiative to provide education for children in a part of Africa where many do not go to school. A donation of £9 would apparently provide a child with books and equipment for a year. Another appeal came from the librarian of Oxford University's Bodleian Libraries, one of which had just undergone an "ambitious programme of reorganisation and renovation" with the help of a £25 million gift from a national charity. The University was now seeking funding for the furniture required for the newly-renovated premises and I was being offered "a unique and time-sensitive opportunity" to purchase one of the Bodleian chairs designed by Edward Barber OBE and Jay Osgerby OBE, which had just won the 2014 Icon Award Furniture Design of the Year. The designers' brief had been to combine "a strong sense of craft heritage, sculptural form and complex reader requirements".

The newly-designed icon was intended to be a testament to the Library's "commitment to creating well-designed and highly-considered environments for the most treasured asset, the Reader". There were also new chairs for the lecture theatre which it was anticipated would "be in great demand for those with a thirst for learning". The minimum donation sought was £500, the price of one chair, or I could pay for the superior lecture room version costing £1,000. In return, my name would appear on the chair, together with a dedication message of my choosing. Examples of appropriate inscriptions were enclosed, presumably for those rendered speechless at the prospect of having their support for their alma mater acknowledged in this prestigious way.

My natural inclination is to support any initiative aimed at improving facilities for places of learning and indeed at one stage of my career I was involved in advising Ercol on its range of furniture for colleges. However, the Bodleian library chair seemed to be going somewhat over the top and thus ended up bottom of the heap in my ordering of priorities for charitable giving. According to a supplier of college furniture with whom I have had dealings in the past, an ordinary adult lecture-room chair currently costs £13, or a superior design £20. To spend up to 50 times the going rate in the confident expectation that its alumni would fall over themselves to pick up the tab indicates just how remote the Oxbridge world is from that in which the rest of us live.

I spent a restful and self-indulgent sabbatical year teaching and studying in Oxford and several of my family and extended family have benefited from the Oxbridge experience. I therefore have no personal reason to be critical of the privileged environment that staff and students enjoy at our two most venerable seats of learning. And I appreciate the important contribution these institutions make to our tourist industry. Nevertheless, I feel that our society pays a heavy price for the reverence it has for the Oxbridge way of life and the totally disproportionate influence that it exerts on the rest of higher education and, indeed, on the whole of the education system in this country.

The Oxbridge impact on the school system is, of course, seen at its most extreme in the private sector and particularly in our most famous public schools whose grooming of an élite for Oxford and Cambridge is an important stage in their pupils' preparation for their destined leadership roles in Church and State. The Oxbridge image is, in fact, kept alive as much by its public school imitators as by the two universities themselves. One of the best examples is Winchester, more determinedly Oxbridge in flavour and aura than an actual Oxbridge College.

Winchester College was founded in 1382 and retains many of its original features, including Latin names for the School's numerous special characteristics. There are 670 boys and 85 staff. Boys are labelled Scholars or Commoners, according to their performance in 'Election', the School's specially-designed entrance exam. As the School's superb prospectus explains, the 70 Scholars "live in the original medieval buildings (modernised to a high standard of comfort) combining a tradition of academic excellence unbroken over six centuries." "The Scholars are the academic pace-setters." Although they are taught with the Commoners, "they return to study in Chambers and to take their meals in College Hall." The Commoners live in ten Commoner Houses. The 'dons' are "an exceptionally able group of men and women who are themselves committed to a life of learning."

Scholars and Commoners follow a prescriptive academic programme leading to GCSE, or the International Baccalaureate equivalent, in the separate sciences, maths, English, Latin, German, a third foreign language and three other subjects, which may include further languages. In my Royal Grammar School the highfliers followed an intensive course in *either* sciences *or* languages. Every Wykehamist, whether Scholar or Commoner, faces the intellectual challenge of doing *both,* that is following a specialist academic course in science and the same in languages.

A unique feature of the Winchester curriculum is Division, or Div, the name given to forms. As well as being pastoral care and administrative units, these groups engage in an extensive and demanding study of the history of human knowledge from the Ancient to the Modern World, taught by their Div Don. In 'Sixth Book ' (years 12 and 13), Wykehamists take 3 or 4 subjects from the Cambridge Pre-U, a superior form of A level introduced in 2008. The pre-university course was designed by Cambridge International Exams (CIE), in consultation with 'top public schools', to be a 'more robust' preparation for 'top universities'. Popular subjects are chemistry and physics, history, English, philosophy and theology.

Winchester College's intention is that the young men entrusted to its care should "be carefully and wisely formed in mind, body and spirit". Traditional public school influences have an important role here. There is a 'vigorous sporting programme' coached by specialists, many of whom are 'top-class sportsmen'. The Chapel, which has its own College 'quiristers', is considered to be 'the living expression' of the College's "understanding of the nature of the human person". All boys join the Combined Cadet Force (CCF) for army training in 'Middle Part' (Year 10).

In keeping with all the 'top' public schools, Winchester prides itself on providing excellent preparation for study at a research-based university. The target is, of course, Oxbridge. A third of the cohort, an average of 44 boys a year, are successful, and another 12 or so go on to the most highly-rated universities in the United States. For those who fall short of these intellectual heights the consolation prize is a 'passport' to a 'top British university'. According to the commercially- published Good Schools Guide, Winchester has "arguably the finest tradition of scholarship of any school in the country". It is "uniquely civilised and provides an academically, comradely and architecturally privileged boyhood most Wykehamists treasure throughout their lives."

Most of the young men who enjoy the privileges of an English public school emerge from the experience with a strong belief in their own personal distinctiveness and in the process which instilled that valuable quality. It is not therefore surprising that, in the positions of power and influence that so many of them achieve in later life, they remain loyal and generous supporters of their old school and the system of which it is a part. As with Oxbridge, the wealth that the leading public schools amass from millionaire old boys is staggering. However, probably even more significant is the extent to which alumni in high places are able to maintain society's tolerance of the unacceptable inequalities between private and state education.

The Sutton Trust has scrutinised the backgrounds of nearly 8,000 people who were deemed to be sufficiently important to be mentioned in the birthday lists of the broadsheets. It found that the independent schools, which educate 7% of the country's children, produced nearly half of the people in positions of power and influence. In the diplomatic service, civil service and law approximately 60% of those holding senior posts had been privately-educated. Even more revealing, 12% of the country's most influential people came from an élite group of just 10 boys' public schools.

The Tatler Schools' Guide declares that "the bastions of all-boys, all-boarding tradition are going from strength to strength, secure in the knowledge that so many of their alumni are currently tramping up and down the corridors of power". These figures are worth remembering, for they help to account for many of the anomalies in our society. How else can one explain the habitual difficulty women have in obtaining promotion to key posts in certain key professions, or the government's continuing tolerance of independent schools' charitable status which, it's estimated by critics, costs the tax-payer £700m a year?

The way in which we select, segregate and groom a privileged class for leadership roles in our society is unjust, restrictive and entirely inappropriate for the age in which we live. We instinctively know this, but the tradition is so strong that we feel unable to do anything about it. No-one has demonstrated this strange ambivalence better than Michael Gove during his time as Secretary of State. His condemnation of privilege was unequivocal:

"The sheer scale, the breadth and depth of private school dominance of our society points to a deep problem in our country - one we all acknowledge but have still failed to tackle with anything like the radicalism required...We all live in an unequal society. More than any other developed nation ours is a country in which your parentage dictates your progress."

Michael Gove condemned as 'morally indefensible' the way in which those educated in the independent sector dominate so many positions of wealth, influence, celebrity and power. His examples ranged from the law courts and bank boardrooms to the national cricket team, from medical schools and university science faculties to the field of entertainment.

Never afraid of causing offence, Michael Gove made these remarks on the injustice of the country's two-tier education system to an audience of independent school heads. Some of them must have wondered where all this was leading. They needn't have worried. The future of their schools was not under any threat from the government. The possibility of that unlikely event last occurred seventy years ago when the mood of unity following the second world war added to the widespread hostility to the public schools that had already built up in the 1930s. Winston Churchill and Rab Butler, the driving forces behind the 1944 Education Act, both thought that the days of the private school were numbered, but weren't keen to take a lead in bringing that situation about. A proposed amendment to the 1944 Act, requiring all parents to send their children to a local authority school, was defeated. Not a single member of the Labour opposition voted in its favour.

Michael Gove's radical reforms for tackling the pernicious divide between private and state education are, like Adonis's academies initiative, based on an unquestioning acceptance of the public school as the model to which all schools should aspire. It is the state schools, not those in the independent sector, that have to change. According to Gove and Adonis, our state schools must work much harder to emulate the aims and achievements of the traditional public school.

These pace-setters of our education system seek to inculcate a lifelong love of learning and of intellectual pursuits. They raise the bar of academic study and enter their pupils for exams designed to be more intellectually challenging than GCSE and A level. From an early age, pupils are groomed in the specialist approach to study traditionally required by the research-based universities. By the age of eighteen many are an automatic choice for admission to Oxbridge colleges. Nearly all the others proceed to one of the Russell Group, the self-selected association of research-based universities, named after the Russell Hotel where the group's initial meetings took place.

One of the hallmarks of the English public schools is that they are able to promote an exceptionally high level of academic and intellectual study within the context of an enviable broad and general education. Pupils learn the single-subject specialist approach to study, but don't specialise in the sense of narrowly concentrating on one area of human experience and knowledge. They cross the science/humanities divide, emulating the Renaissance ideal of wide-ranging culture and learning. Moreover, although academic subjects dominate the public school curriculum, there is excellent extra-curricular provision for those with creative and practical interests. Similarly, physical education is taken very seriously. The leading public schools promote competitive sport to energise the whole school culture and strive for the highest standards by employing professional specialists to coach a wide range of games options. At the same time, there are usually other outdoor activities and challenges available as alternatives to competitive sports. The public school experience provides many and varied opportunities for personal fulfilment which helps to explain why those who experience it emerge with a natural self-confidence and awareness of their own worth.

One can understand why Gove, Adonis and like-minded politicians are impressed by what they see when they contemplate the British public schools. But to suggest that state schools model themselves on these highly élitist and richly-endowed institutions is manifestly absurd. Even if such a policy were desirable, no-one could actually believe it were possible. The public school intake is confined to those who can demonstrate a precocious level of academic and intellectual achievement. Most come from privileged home backgrounds and prep schools where many of the qualities that the public schools seek to inculcate have already been nurtured from an early age. The comprehensive school intake comes from the real world.

The other gulf between comprehensive and public schools is of course in the level of educational provision. State schools receive an annual sum of approximately £4,000 to meet the costs of educating each of their pupils. The annual fees for the leading public schools are round the £30,000 mark. State schools have to wait in a long queue for improvements to their facilities; public schools simply tap into their reserves or launch another fund-raising project among prosperous alumni and parents to meet additional needs. The extent of this disparity in resources is evident in every part of the curriculum, the extra-curricular life of the schools, the number of teachers and support staff, the salaries paid, the size of classes, the quality and maintenance of buildings and grounds and the range of facilities and equipment.

A 2014 Ofsted report on *Going the Extra Mile: Excellence in Competitive School Sport* draws attention to the disproportionate number of our most successful sportsmen and women who have had an independent school education.

The report attributes this situation to a marked difference between the attitude taken towards competitive sport in the independent and state sectors. It stresses the importance that independent schools attach to the competitiveness that is bred on the sports field:

"The drive to compete and excel in sport shapes a youngster's character, binds the school together and reinforces the drive to compete and excel academically.... Children are expected to compete, train and practise secure in the knowledge that teachers will go the extra mile to help them."

In contrast, most state schools, according to the Report, don't recognise the importance of sport in the education process, regarding it as 'an optional extra' or failing "to offer it in any meaningful way: they get on the bus but fail to turn up on the pitch."

No doubt some PE staff in inner city comprehensives will have pointed out that they would be happy to turn up on the pitch if only they had one. However, the Chief Inspector, Sir Michael Wilshaw, completely discounts differences in facilities as a factor in the independent /state school comparison:

"As this report makes clear, it is not resource that is the key to independent school success, but attitude."

This, of course, accords with the Government's view on all aspects of the independent/state school divide: if state school teachers were to get off their backsides and put their minds to it, their pupils could outperform the independent schools, irrespective of the enormous disparity in resources and learning environment between the two sectors. There is, apparently, no reason to assume that the prestigious public schools have a head start over state schools on account of their sports provision - their acres of immaculately maintained pitches, state-of-the-art sports complexes and teams of professional coaches. But, if Ofsted is right in its claim that facilities aren't important, why exactly do the famous public schools bother to make such extensive provision? Surely their income isn't so enormous that they can waste millions of pounds on initiatives that will have no effect on the quality of their pupils' education.

Marlborough College, near to where I live, illustrates the kind of sports facilities on offer in the public schools. It's a 13-18 co-educational school of just over 900 pupils. The playing fields are set in lovely grounds and include 11 rugby pitches, 8 cricket squares, 14 artificial grass cricket nets, 7 soccer pitches, 6 hockey pitches, 2 volleyball courts, 4 lacrosse pitches and a golf-driving range. In addition, there are extensive hard court areas for netball (10 courts) and tennis (12 courts), two all-weather astro-pitches (one floodlit) for hockey, and a further 10 all-weather tennis courts. There are local facilities for canoeing and polo and a choice of two golf courses. According to the College prospectus,"fishermen can try their luck in the River Kennet or in the College's own trout ponds". "Under the lee of Granham Hill, stands an all-weather, porous rubber, athletics track ... fully equipped to international standards." The indoor facilities match the outdoor provision: gymnasium, fencing salle and a sports complex providing facilities for indoor tennis, netball, basketball, volleyball, badminton and cricket practice. There are 2 rackets courts, 5 squash courts, 6 fives courts and an activities centre with indoor climbing wall. Next to the Parade Ground there is a ·22 rifle range. The recently-built 'state of the art, 25-metre, competition, indoor swimming pool' has eight lanes and an haudraulic system which alters the depth of the pool from ·8 to 3 metres, thus providing the different conditions required for squad training, water polo, sub-aqua , canoeing and recreational swimming.

Of course, no-one believes the government's mantra that teaching conditions and facilities are unimportant factors in a school's success, not even their front-line spokesmen on the subject. Another place, another time and they are busy pointing out to the most privileged independent schools that it is very much in their interest to justify their charitable status more fully by sharing their generous staffing and lavish facilities with state schools. The response to this idea has been decidedly lukewarm. There are a few exceptions: 3% of independent schools were persuaded by the indefatigable Adonis to become sponsors of his academies and 5 % lend teaching staff to state schools. However, as the Chief Inspector for Schools, Sir Michael Wilshaw, has pointed out, the vast majority of the independent sector has made only a token gesture - 'a bit of coaching for A level students; the occasional loan of a playing field'. When Headmaster of Wellington School, Sir Anthony Seldon, now Vice-Chancellor of Buckingham University, was an active supporter of closer co-operation between the independent and state sectors, but he found the role extremely difficult:

"The pace of change...has been agonisingly slow. (David) Cameron charged a small group of us ...to encourage independent schools down the academy sponsorship path. It has been the most frustrating challenge of my career. The reality is that governing bodies don't want to bond with state schools. They put up spurious reasons such as parental objections for masterly inactivity."

Parents of privately-educated children pay heavily to ensure that their sons and daughters receive a privileged education that will give them a better start in life than other children. It is therefore not very surprising if they object to their children's school diverting some of its funds to subsidise other schools. The harsh reality is that our society has become too governed by market forces to expect competing organisations to engage in genuine cooperation. Sir Michael Wilshaw cites a prominent member of the Independent Schools Bursars ' Association who issued a blunt warning to private school heads to have nothing to do with such schemes, pointing out that the state and private sectors were competitors and, the more successful state schools became, the more difficult life would be for independent schools.

The idea that staffing inadequacies and vacancies in the state sector can be rectified by private schools lending their teachers to neighbouring comprehensives is not a long-term solution to the underfunding of state education. 1,400 teachers move out of the state sector into private schools every year. Many of them haven't been able to cope with the demands of teaching in state schools; others are disillusioned by the incessant interference of politicians in their work; some simply want an easier life. Whatever the reason for their leaving the state sector, they aren't going to be unduly receptive to returning, however minimally or briefly. As for those who've never given the state sector a chance, what incentive do they have for a slumming stint? How long are most of them going to last in the totally different world of the comprehensive school? And what sort of messages does it send out to parents and the general public if a comprehensive school has to relinquish some of its key examination work to staff brought in from elsewhere? The prospect of the private sector working in a long-term partnership with the state sector to raise standards in comprehensive schools is as likely as Tony and Cherie Blair deciding to make one of the three-dozen or so houses and flats in their property empire available to some of London's cardboard-box street dwellers.

State and public schools inhabit different worlds, but they have very similar aspirations. Schools of all kinds strive to build an harmonious community in which individuals feel respected, are at ease and able to express themselves, and are able to work together with a common purpose and shared set of values. They seek to provide a varied learning experience, a broad and balanced curriculum and a wide range of extra-curricular activities. The aim is to give every child a well-rounded education, but at the same time to encourage individual enthusiasms, interests and aptitudes and to find a context for every child to taste success and therefore to develop confidence and self-esteem. Much importance is attached to providing an effective care system that supports children in their work and school life, informs them of the full range of higher education and career opportunities, and obtains professional guidance and help for those with special educational needs and personal problems.

Graduates do not enter teaching for the money. They are attracted by the enjoyment and job-satisfaction of working with children and seeing them develop and grow. They want to help young people to enjoy learning, to feed their natural curiosity, to open their minds to the world around them, to enrich their lives and to equip them with the various skills they will need in a complex society. Teachers live for those eureka moments of understanding and practical accomplishment that fill pupils with enthusiasm and self-belief. To this end, the imaginative teacher is ever searching for new ways of arousing interest and making the learning experience meaningful and relevant. The fundamental difference between the public and the state school is that the former provides an excellent context for furthering these manifold aspirations, and the latter doesn't. Teachers in state schools are continually struggling to achieve their aims and objectives in the face of inferior facilities, over-large classes and, most damagingly, a stultifying political ideology.

Although Ofsted ostensibly continues to judge the success of a school against a wide range of educational objectives, its political masters have become increasingly focused on those few academic routines that can be most readily measured by standard objective tests. The more educationists and psychologists learn about the complexity of the learning process and the exciting range of children's potential, the more limited and unimaginative the politicians' agenda appears to be. The greater society's need for people with original ideas, multiple skills and creative energy the more entrenched our educational system becomes in outdated early academic specialisation.

Influential politicians such as Gove and Adonis share Arthur Claydon's absolute faith in academic study as the supreme human achievement and have the same vision of the maintained sector's exam successes surpassing those of the public schools. All Gove's reactionary reforms of the curriculum were designed to strengthen academic studies and processes at the expense of every other facet of education. In a sad distortion of the 'equal opportunity' ideal, all children are being required to get on the academic conveyor belt, regardless of how inappropriate this may be for them. By means of a crude carrot and stick policy, schools are being bullied into concentrating their efforts and resources into one narrow educational target - academic success measured by written exams and tests. In the process, state schools are finding it increasingly difficult to achieve the basic educational aim of developing each and everyone's potential, in order that their pupils might leave school able to face the future with the same confidence and self-assurance that is bred into their public school counterparts. The contrasting levels of investment in private and state education in this country are a constant reminder of our deeply-rooted class system.

Chapter 6

Obsession with Academia

"We insist on sustaining an education that is narrow, partial, entirely inappropriate for the 21st century and deeply destructive of human potential."

Wally Olins, Founder Wolff-Olins,
Business Consultants.

The strongest objection to the bipartite system of grammar schools and secondary moderns, introduced in 1944, was that it denied over three-quarters of the country's children an opportunity to undertake academic study. That situation has been rectified so thoroughly that, not only do all children now have the opportunity to follow academic courses, but almost all of them are actually expected, and indeed pressurised, into doing so. Whether or not they bear the title 'academy', all secondary schools are now academic, some just more so than others. Those comprehensive schools with a solidly middle-class intake and a large number of students classified as academic are able, if they so wish, to create a grammar school ethos and groom the 'able and talented' for Oxford, Cambridge and other Russell Group universities. The rest vie with each other for places at the lower status or 'rubbish' universities, as Nick Gibb reportedly called them on his first day as an education minister. We have a new binary system of grammar school comprehensives and ordinary comprehensives. As Sir Tim Brighouse commented on the problems facing London schools in 2007, "There is more selection now in London than before it went comprehensive."

The Russell Group Universities are a powerful ally of politicians committed to academic education. The Group established itself in 1994 as a select association of the best universities in the country. The basis of this self-assessed appraisal of their importance was that the institutions concerned were all intensively research-based: their primary interest is in post-graduate work and together they receive 80% of the research funding provided by the Higher Education Funding Council for England (HEFCE). They work extremely hard to attract those students from home and abroad who have achieved the highest grades in their IB, Cambridge Pre-University and A level exams, the most successful of whom will eventually be in a position to proceed to post-graduate work and so help maintain their university's research reputation. The linear nature of our education system doesn't end when students enter university. In the same way that GCSE/EBacc courses have been designed specifically to prepare students for A level, and A level courses designed to prepare students for university study, so most of the undergraduate courses in research-based universities are devised with postgraduate work in mind. The Russell Group attach great importance to undergraduates being taught by staff who are 'at the cutting edge of research' and able to pass on their research expertise to those who will follow in their footsteps.

Throughout our education system we have been conditioned to concentrate on those we consider 'able', and to leave the rest to get by as best they can. Most university students, of course, don't see their undergraduate studies as a preparation for further study, but as a step to obtaining an interesting and well-paid job. Some view their course as an end in itself, a chance to pursue their interest in a particular aspect of human experience and knowledge. Courses designed to provide these groups with a relevant, meaningful and enjoyable undergraduate experience have not been a priority in the research-based universities. Even seemingly vocational courses, such as Law and Medicine, have often been determinedly academic in their approach.

When it was formed in 1994, the Russell Group was a fairly informal and low-key body. That is certainly not the situation now. In 2006 the Group created a new Director

General and Chief Executive post, to which it appointed Wendy Platt, Deputy Director of the Prime Minister's Strategy Unit. Under her leadership, the organisation became increasingly politicised and aggressive in its marketing. In the process it drove a wedge between its members and the rest of Higher Education. The Russell Group's promotional literature consistently implied that its teaching was better than that of other universities because it was enhanced by the staff's research: "Excellence in research supports the teaching process"; "It's much more interesting to be taught by staff who are writing research articles in their discipline." This kind of thinly-veiled denigration of other universities not surprisingly caused considerable offence and the Group's marketing strategies have had to be modified.

The reality of the relationship between research and teaching is very different from the rhetoric. Anyone thinking that the articles produced by researchers for their specialist academic journals are likely to be of interest to undergraduates has only to glance at the pages of obscurity in one of these publications to be disillusioned on that score. Most researchers are concentrating on a highly specific aspect of their specialist subject which provides very limited material for their teaching. I worked for eight years in higher education, observing lectures, interviewing undergraduates to obtain feedback on their learning experiences, running training courses and discussing with departments ways in which they could improve their courses and teaching. I don't recall anything during that time that justified the sweeping claim that researchers are better teachers than staff who devote all their time to the teaching role. There was, however, plenty of evidence to the contrary.

The dual responsibility of research and teaching brings together two extremely demanding activities and there is often a conflict of interests between them. Staff in a Russell Group university are left in no doubt by their department's grandees that their overriding priority has to be their research: they are under constant pressure to justify their share of funding by producing a regular flow of scholarly articles. Newly-appointed lecturers working enthusiastically to give their students a better deal than they felt they'd had themselves during their time as undergraduates are quietly taken aside and told a few home-truths on how they should be ordering their priorities. Promotion prospects are traditionally closely allied to the number of published articles that staff are able to churn out. It is not a situation that automatically leads to the high quality teaching implied in the Russell Group's recruitment literature.

There is an enormous gulf between the best and worst university teaching, far greater than in any other part of the education system. At the top end there are researchers who are extremely enthusiastic and committed teachers who, despite traditional ordering of priorities, ensure that their undergraduates always get a fair share of their time and expertise. They work extremely hard, they are good organisers, and they are prepared to ease off their research during the short teaching terms. Others, however, struggle to accommodate the teaching role. Regrettably, some clearly regard it as an irksome chore that they would much rather be without.

In 2013 the Russell Group established an Academic Board to advise the British examinations watchdog on the content of A levels and Michael Gove moved quickly to give this body a role that was more directive than advisory. He based most of his changes to A level syllabuses on the views of the Board, explaining that "by placing responsibility for the content of A levels in the hands of university academics, we hope that these new exams will be more rigorous and will provide students with the skills and knowledge needed for progression to undergraduate study." Boosted by their strong political backing, the Russell Group intensified its recruitment campaign, constantly stressing the importance of traditional academic A levels - English, maths, physics, chemistry, biology, classical and modern foreign languages, history and geography. The Group designated these A levels 'facilitating subjects', by which it means subjects that its member universities regard as academically sound and to which they therefore attach particular importance when considering student applications. Anyone hoping to obtain a place in a 'good university' is urged to think very carefully about their choice of A levels in the light of this advice.

The Russell Group has adopted Gove's contemptuous term, 'soft subjects', for what they regard as non-facilitating A level courses. Teachers and students are informed that these subjects lack rigour and so are not a good preparation for university. As part of this drive to increase the sixth-form's already heavy emphasis on the grammar school curriculum of the 1940s, some research-based universities have underlined their association's policy statement by circulating blacklists of 'soft' A levels that are best avoided by their applicants. At the moment, academia's marketing material is careful to avoid explicitly stating that students should not include *any* 'soft subject' in their study programme. However, given the terminology used, there is no likelihood of any prospective university candidate misunderstanding the basic message - that to maximise your chances of getting into a Russell Group university you need to study traditional academic A levels.

In flirting with the politicians' trademark ploy of denigrating the opposition, the Russell group made some enemies, but was very successful in achieving its aim. Figures currently published by the exam boards show a marked increase in recent years in the number of A level candidates studying traditional academic courses, with, of course, a corresponding decline in those subjects on the research-based universities' blacklists. Academia has succeeded in establishing a two-tier higher education system in this country with an élite group of Oxbridge-style universities setting themselves apart from the rest. Backed by the politicians, it is now well on its way to replicating this situation in the school sixth-form by promoting the idea that any A level that doesn't conform to its idea of what constitutes a worthwhile course is an inferior option. This false dichotomy in our school curriculum is being established at a time when we should be seeking a more integrated and interdisciplinary approach. We need to take an holistic view of human knowledge and experience, not regress into yet more ring-fencing.

Generations of educationists have argued the case for updating the sixth-form curriculum, and their efforts are reflected in the much wider range of A level subjects that have gradually become available. There are now a number of well-established interdisciplinary subjects that break the specialist mould, for example, communication studies, citizenship and environmental studies. Numerous vocational options have been introduced, including business studies, law, health and social care, accounting and media studies, As an alternative to A level, sixth-form colleges and large school sixth-forms have been able to develop very successful Business and Technology Education Council (BTEC) courses which, as one college prospectus puts it, 'provide a practical, real world approach to learning without sacrificing any of the essential subject theory'. Assessment on BTEC programmes is largely through coursework, allowing students to gauge their progress and performance on a continuing basis, which is what they will, of course, do as adults in employment.

Educationists have sought to reform the sixth-form curriculum not only by introducing new subjects, but also by persuading the exam boards to offer alternative syllabuses within a subject, syllabuses that respond to the priorities of the twenty-first century and provide more imaginative, interesting and varied learning opportunities than their traditional counterparts. These new syllabuses nearly always envisage an active role for students - in discussion, in creative and practical work, in experiment and investigation, in individual and team projects. This kind of reform often has its source in an innovative and pioneering school or college and gathers momentum in local and county consortia and/or working groups set up by teaching associations or other national bodies with an interest in education.

It was in this way that a sea-change was brought about in sixth-form foreign language studies. In the 1970s, taking a foreign language at A level meant studying a country's literary classics, because that was what students would do if they proceeded to a university honours degree course in a foreign language. I once heard an Oxford don justify the absence of any opportunity for his students of French to spend time abroad by explaining how it would distract them from their studies. In pandering to tradition, schools seemed to lose sight of the fact that the large majority of students who followed an A level language course did so in the hope that they would actually learn to speak the language competently - either for vocational purposes or simply as a useful accomplishment when travelling abroad.

That scenario has changed radically. Initially boards were persuaded to offer alternative language and literature syllabuses. They now provide broadly-based foreign language A level syllabuses within which students can study different pathways to meet their particular interests and needs. A typical French A level now involves studying the language via a wide range of topics, such as 'lifestyles', 'family relationships' and 'contemporary issues'. In addition, two cultural topics have to be selected from a long list of options. A student combining A level French and geography might choose to study a region of France; likewise, someone studying A level history and French has the opportunity to learn about a period of modern French history. Someone interested in literature can study a French novel and/or the work of a French poet. Other options include the study of a French architect, film director, musician or painter.

Most universities have kept pace with these changes and offer interesting, broadly-based foreign language courses. The foreign language scene is one that must be highly satisfying to all those who have been involved in creating it. They will, however, have taken note that a recent Government drive to return to traditional practices includes a requirement for the exam boards to re-instate a compulsory literature component in foreign language A level syllabuses.

Those who have argued the case for extending the range of options in our sixth-forms have had to fight hard against the weight of tradition and vested interest to establish the credibility and relevance of new syllabuses. In the process, some of the character and principles of their original proposals have had to be sacrificed to satisfy demands for greater adherence to the purist and traditional approach. In order to combat the purists' assumptions that new subjects will by definition lack rigour, innovators have to ensure that the content of any newly-proposed A level syllabus is manifestly substantial and academically challenging. As a result, far from being soft options, some new additions to the sixth-form curriculum deter students from taking them because of the extra-heavy demands they make.

A level reformers can never rest. Once a new option has been accepted, the staff promoting and teaching it have to build up numbers and maintain its viability as an acceptable alternative to the well-established and prestigious subjects. The greater the pressure for students to conform to traditional priorities and the more the alternatives are branded as 'soft options', obviously the harder this task becomes. Schools play safe and, no matter how attractive and relevant new A level syllabuses may be for their students, they are inclined to stay with the traditional approaches that they know the prestigious universities much prefer. Boards are very watchful of their academic standing with the Russell Group and don't want to be seen championing a lost cause. In this climate, all innovation remains vulnerable.

In a linear system, any changes to one stage of the education process inevitably have a significant knock-on effect elsewhere and the Russell Group's crude division of the sixth-form into academically respectable subjects and 'soft options' is proving to be a significant factor in the re-ordering of priorities lower down the secondary school - and indeed beyond, even in the primary sector. The pressure to concentrate on a traditional academic curriculum is coming at schools from all directions. Academic exam results have become the crucial criterion for judging the quality of a school's work, the EBacc encapsulates the grammar school curriculum of the first half of the twentieth century, and academia's domination of the sixth-form curriculum completes a three-pronged attack on non-academic courses.

Early specialisation is widely condemned as the most damaging feature of our education system. In a recent BBC radio programme Lord David Willetts, who was an Education Minister in the Coalition Government, called it 'the English disease'. Yet the prevailing trend is to exacerbate, not alleviate, this unacceptable situation. In response to the English Baccalaureate, schools have begun to narrow pupils' programmes of study a year earlier than previously - at the beginning of year 9 instead of year 10. We are rapidly moving towards a situation in which the norm will be for pupils to spend three years on their specialist EBacc group of courses, instead of the two years previously taken for GCSE. Nearly all secondary school children now follow a predominately academic programme and, as soon as the EBacc options have to be considered, all potential university applicants are under pressure to commit themselves totally to this narrow form of education. A thirteen-year-old told me recently that at the beginning of year 9 she had dropped four of the subjects that she had been studying during her first two years of secondary schooling. They were drama, art, music and design.

What struck me forcibly in my conversation with this teenager was how matter-of-fact she was concerning what seemed to me a very significant, even potentially life-changing, decision. She was sorry that she'd had to discontinue her art and design because she'd found them very interesting and enjoyable subjects, but she didn't question the system that required her to specialise at such a young age and discontinue all her contact with creative and practical subjects: she was hoping to go to university, so naturally she had to concentrate on her academic work. That was the way of the world. But then, I never questioned any of the curricular decisions that my RGS took for me: it wasn't until later in life that I came to realise how much my education, and indeed subsequent quality of life, had been impoverished by the lack of a creative and practical dimension to my schooling.

Art, music, dance, drama, design - these are invariably the first casualties of early specialisation. Always battling for parity of esteem, these subjects currently face a significant drop in status if their secondary school place in the curriculum is confined to years 7 and 8. The advent of the English Baccalaureate, with its enlarged core of academic studies, is already reducing the number of pupils opting for 'soft subjects' and smaller schools have begun discarding options that are no longer viable. As early as 2012 a DfE report on *The Effects of the English Baccalaureate* noted that the most commonly withdrawn subjects were drama and performing arts, followed by art and design technology. Vocational studies were the other significant casualty - BTECs were dropped in 20% of schools where subjects had had to be withdrawn.

Sixth-form colleges face a particular problem. Education has been one of the areas of government expenditure protected from the recent series of cost-cutting exercises but, oddly, the post-16 age group has not been included in this protection. As a consequence, schools have seen a steady reduction of funding for their senior students which has had a marked effect on those with a large sixth-form. The impact on the sixth-form colleges, whose students are of course all in the 16+ category, has been particularly serious. Repeated reductions in funding have forced the colleges to shed staff and cut back on their course provision. 'Enrichment programmes' have inevitably been the first to suffer, but some colleges are now reporting that they are having to limit students' A level work and curtail their extra-curricular activities and student-care services. If this trend is not quickly reversed there is a real prospect of sixth-form college education becoming part-time, and limited to the mere acquisition of a narrow range of academic qualifications.

Our present priority in schools and colleges is clearly to prepare young people for the academic way of life. In the process we are failing to develop the variety of skills and personalities required by our diverse twenty-first century society. We have long since lost sight of the educational ideal that seeks to respect and nurture every child's potential to find personal fulfilment in adult life. We clearly now have a two-tier curriculum throughout the secondary school with the academic subjects in the top half and the 'inferior' non-academic subjects in the lower. The implications for the status, confidence and self-esteem of the teachers and children whose interests, enthusiasms and aptitudes lie outside academia are obvious. A recent Ipsos poll of young people aged 20-22 found that 21% agreed with the statement that 'people like me don't stand a chance in life'. It will be interesting, but no doubt depressing, to see what the percentage is in a few years' time when the intensified focus on one section of the school population has taken full effect.

Leading musicians, artists, singers, dancers, actors - and the organisations that represent them - have been outraged by the Gove agenda and vociferous in condemning the marginalising of creative subjects in secondary schools that has taken place in recent years. In a public letter the influential Schools Music Association expressed the fear that the new curricular policy would "effectively mean the end of the teaching of creative subjects". Representatives of Britain's creative industries have been equally concerned: on 6th January, 2016, the *Times* published a letter signed by over 70 chief executives and directors pointing out the economic implications of the decline in the arts in British schools:

"In 2010-2015 we have already seen a 14 per cent drop in creative and technical qualifications being taken. The UK's creative industries are world-leading in their own right, contribute more than £76 billion to the UK economy and employ more than 1· 7 million people (more than 1 in 20 UK jobs). To continue to build a thriving creative economy, the arts must be given equal visibility in our schools...it makes no sense for the government to implement an educational strategy which is narrowing a skills base in an area so integral to our economy's success."

The creative industries have a very specific reason for being alarmed at the Government's ever-narrowing view of educational objectives. But the whole of the business world should be up in arms at the current extent to which children are being denied opportunities to develop their imagination, creativity and originality. Business today functions in a fast-paced, innovation-hungry market-place. As Britain's vote to leave the European Union dramatically demonstrated, the ground rules can change significantly overnight. To meet new challenges, firms must be able to fuse scientific and technical knowledge with a creative, design-led approach.

We are fast losing our position as a world leader in the arts. Julian Lloyd Webber, speaking about the 'boiling point' reached in the crisis in musical education, recalls how music education in this country was something to be proud of when he began his studies at the Royal College of Music in 1959. It was the benchmark embraced and adopted by other nations. At College, Julian was one of a small number of ex-public-school students in a department that was '90% per cent from state schools'. All this has changed dramatically, he says:

"Look at the make-up of something like the National Youth Orchestra. It's a brilliant orchestra, but its members are very much from privileged backgrounds, not from the state system."

There is, Julian explains, a pronounced increase in the number of international students at British music schools and a shrinking pool of British musicians. Learning a musical instrument, once a commonplace, is becoming a 'curiosity' and British orchestras are increasingly reliant on international musicians. Meanwhile, he says, the audience for classical music is collapsing as generations of children leave school knowing nothing about composers who have been responsible for some of "the greatest achievements of mankind". A £1 million feasibility study is expected to recommend the building of a new show-piece concert hall in London at an estimated cost of £500m. The scheme has high-profile backers including senior members of the Government. Julian says of this "grand gesture concert hall": "I wouldn't build a brick of it. The (London) halls are already adequate and it's about music, not buildings. We are going to build this fantastic hall and who is going to fill it?"

Representatives of the performing arts and creative industries have repeatedly lobbied the Government over the marginalising of their subjects in schools, but with little or no success. Their frustration is familiar to educationists who are weary of trying to get the Department for Education to listen to informed opinion. On the basis of a personal whim or prejudice, individual politicians are able to push through measures that can suddenly undermine years of progress in our schools. Unconsulted and sidelined, experts in the field and the bodies that represent them are left to fume and protest - to no significant effect. Their representations to government, their petitions, speeches, letters to the press are brushed aside by government spokesmen well trained in the tactics of evasion. If the outcry is loud enough, governments may sometimes make some conciliatory gestures or token adjustments that give the impression of their being reasonable people, but, however strong the protesters' case, once a government has made its decision, it's very unlikely to risk the political consequences of admitting a major mistake in policy. The prospect of legislation ever being based on factual information and sound evidence is remote, but, if educationists are to retain any control over what happens in schools, they must make a concerted effort to establish a procedure by which they are consulted at the planning stage of major changes to the system. Even that modest step forward will be some challenge.

The current plight of drama education is a very good illustration of the power the Department of Education has to cancel out years of successful curriculum reform and development in pursuit of one person's outdated ideology. In the three schools in which I worked in the 1960s, the term 'drama', if used at all, referred to the reading and academic study of plays, mostly those written by Shakespeare. One of the schools provided an opportunity for a hand-picked group of boys to perform in an annual Shakespearian production. This scenario has changed significantly in the past 40 years. Drama as a creative subject became an invaluable part of both the primary and secondary curriculum in most schools and established itself as a valid examination option at both GCSE and A level. The transferable skills that the subject develops were considered so important that drama was increasingly used as a learning method in other subjects. In its document, *Drama in Schools,* in 2003, the Arts Council felt able to declare that it was "an exhilarating time to be involved in teaching the arts in schools. Government understands the importance of creativity in education and this is demonstrated in a range of recent policies and initiatives."

Yet, within a few years, a new government introduced a raft of measures to intensify the heavy academic bias of the school curriculum with the inevitable effect of sidelining the arts and severely limiting many children's opportunities to develop their creative and practical skills. The Gove curriculum is so governed by a fixation with knowledge acquisition that, by definition, a subject such as drama has no status as a school subject. The following observation was made by the Department of Education following a 'review' of the primary school curriculum in 2012: "Ministers do not consider drama to be core knowledge, as it is more a question of pedagogy and therefore outside the remit of the curriculum review....Where drama features in the (new) primary English programme of study it is in relation to pupils studying great works of great dramatists, including Shakespeare." Thus the time-honoured English honours degree ritual of reading and studying play scripts written 400 years ago is now assured of a place in the primary school curriculum, but there is no room for creative drama, an immensely enjoyable and valuable experience through which children learn to act out their thoughts and ideas in speech, movement and body language.

The plight of school music and art is in some ways worse than that of drama, which does at least have a slight foothold in the curriculum as part of the academic study of literature. Art and music also have strong academic credentials and, if a way could be found to include the historical development of these subjects in the core history syllabus, the politicians and purist academics would no doubt be delighted. What they can't stomach is the emphasis that is now placed on music-making and artistic expression: it's the creative and practical experiences that lie at the heart of these subjects that have condemned them to second class status. This ordering of priorities, in which pure academic study is revered as the supreme human achievement and everything else is considered of secondary importance, underpins so much that is wrong and inappropriate in our traditional education system. It is a false dichotomy that is deeply damaging.

Educationists who have devoted their lives to establishing artistic and creative subjects as a vital part of the school curriculum are bewildered by the recent undermining of all that they have achieved. They are appalled at a political agenda so in tune with the *Daily Mail* readers who sneered at the primary school teachers who wanted their pupils to get the SATs ritual into perspective. The politicians' unwillingness to consult with practitioners, to find out how arts education has changed since their own schooldays and, above all, to try to understand the important contribution that creative and practical subjects make to children's development and general education - these features of the present situation have caused widespread frustration and bitterness in the arts world.

Patrice Baldwin, Chair of National Drama, a professional association for drama and theatre educators, has an impressive record in arts education as a head-teacher, Ofsted inspector, LEA adviser and school improvement partner. Yet her repeated requests during the Government's 2012 review of the primary school curriculum to meet someone from the Department for Education to represent the views of her Association's members were all rejected. Her despair at what is happening to school drama matches Julian Lloyd Webber's for music. She takes little comfort from ministers' assurance that drama is adequately represented in the new primary school curriculum by the inclusion of Shakespearian studies in the English programmes of study:

"Ministers like Shakespeare. They experienced it in their own education so it must exist and it must be good. It's recognisable to ministers (not like this new-fangled drama that they have never personally 'studied' and so don't understand and don't want to). Ministers are probably privileged to see Shakespeare's plays performed brilliantly by the Royal Shakespeare Company. They might ask themselves how many great actors entered the profession because of good drama teachers in schools introducing them to drama. Ironically, reading and testing children's knowledge of Shakespeare will probably survive in schools, even if drama as a subject doesn't. Shakespeare would turn in his grave. He wrote for performance, not for tests. Maybe children in future will just read Shakespeare. After all, performing it would run the risk of acknowledging it as drama."

In theory a two-tier curriculum caters for everyone. The 'able' children can improve their chances of going to university by focusing on academic routines, such as the study of Shakespeare, and the rest can follow a 'softer' programme, including options such as drama. But of course it doesn't work like that. The prestigious hard core academic programme is an attractive target even for those for whom it is manifestly unsuitable and it becomes the norm in schools positioned in the upper reaches of the league tables. 'Soft' subjects decline steadily in status and eventually struggle to survive.

Any overt division of human activity into 'superior' and 'inferior' categories results in a devaluation of one category and an over-valuing of the other. The bipartite system of secondary schooling distorted the curriculum in both types of school. 80% of children were denied the opportunity to take academic courses and the other 20% were forced to follow an unnecessarily concentrated programme of study. Having taught in and managed both grammar and secondary modern schools, I am convinced that the bi-partite system of secondary schooling was as damaging to the grammar school pupils as it was to those in the secondary moderns - possibly more so. Similarly, I believe that the current two-tier school curriculum is detrimental to everyone - not least the 'academic' students for whom it is designed most to benefit.

Arts subjects, and indeed many other so-called 'soft' options, offer a wide range of learning experiences that are not given regular attention in academic courses, but which are, nevertheless, invaluable to those who will be seeking a university place and aspiring to a career requiring multiple skills. The exclusion of these experiences from the programmes of many potential university students leaves a significant gap in their general education. For those students who can spare the time from their studies, the extra-curricular life of a school offers a way of addressing this situation, but with the increasing funding problems that schools are facing that is another area that is retracting.

It was my good fortune to live and work in Hampshire when Local Education Authorities had significant control over the way in which education was organised. No LEA could now initiate a major re-organisation equivalent to Hampshire's county-wide introduction of pioneering open-access 16-18 colleges. Authorities also had a strong influence in the last decades of the twentieth century over the quality of the education their schools provided. Hampshire, for example, believed in a broad and balanced school curriculum and appointed a large team of professional advisers who supported teachers in the full range of subjects. Those responsible for the arts were particularly prominent and the Authority's commitment to creative and practical subjects was unequivocal. All three of my children studied music to A level and, throughout their secondary schooling, had tuition in two musical instruments which enabled them to play in a variety of orchestras and bands. The cost of these activities - the instrumental tuition and the management of the various district and county orchestras and bands - was met by the LEA.

Music-making didn't dominate my children's lives and none of them intended to make it a career. It was, however, an important part of their general education and one that gave them much enjoyment and a really good social life. They were not exceptions: many of their friends shared their experience, and the sixth-form college in which I worked benefited greatly from all this music-making coming together in one place in a 16-18 college serving a borough with a population approaching 100,000. The most advanced musicians were already playing at a high standard when they arrived in the sixth-form college and in one five-year period we had five students in the National Youth Orchestra and two in the European Youth Orchestra. More importantly, music became a shared college experience through day-time concerts and recitals that everyone attended, staff and students. Up-and-coming professionals were often prepared to perform for a modest fee and the College obtained sponsorship from local businesses and charitable trusts for more expensive initiatives.

This situation wasn't confined to music. Numerous subjects that were side-lined or non-existent in the traditional sixth-form thrived in the Hampshire sixth-form colleges, which offered an unprecedented variety and flexibility of student programme. We had a huge drama department, with a third of the college - some 400 students eventually - taking its courses. There was a sustained programme of student and professional performances some of which were, like the concerts and recitals, whole-college events. Visiting theatre and dance companies ran workshops in a wide range of performance skills. Inevitably these opportunities led to some students proceeding to higher education drama courses or going to work in the theatre, in television or arts centres. Some formed their own small companies bringing drama to schools, streets and festivals. But, again, the main purpose wasn't to groom potential specialists. The drama department's view was that they didn't teach their subject to produce actors, any more than the English department taught English to produce novelists.

The aim of the college drama courses was simple: to give as many students as possible an enjoyable learning experience that would enhance their quality of life, and to develop skills that would help them to meet the challenges of adulthood, including those of the workplace, whatever form that took. For the large majority of drama students, the subject was a natural part of their general education - but often a very important part. This emphasis on general, rather than specialist, education accords very well with the principles of the performing arts, in which you learn the importance of the group and of every individual within it. In a dance or drama class, a choir or orchestra, you work together, respecting everyone's contribution. The teacher or conductor doesn't focus on the most successful members and regard the rest as dispensable.

Many of the students who immersed themselves in the College's drama courses were destined for the traditional academic route to professional jobs. I am confident that they were better equipped for their specialist honours degree courses and eventual leadership and management roles as a result of the width of their learning experiences and the quality of their general education. I recently tracked down an ex-student who had been heavily involved in drama courses whilst at college, someone who would certainly have had a much narrower sixth-form experience had he been following the current hard-core academic curriculum. I wanted to find out what his memories of the drama component of his sixth-form studies had been and whether it had been helpful to him.

Because of their size, sixth-form colleges have the timetabling flexibility to enable students to take virtually any combination of A level subjects and we encouraged entrants to exploit that opportunity if it appealed to them. Richard decided to continue with two of his GCSE subjects, maths and French, to which he added two entirely new courses of which he had no experience - Russian and economics. He was with us for two years and a term, staying on after A levels to take the Cambridge entrance exam. During his seven terms he had experience of three different non-examined drama courses - improvisation, theatre arts and technical workshop. I asked him what they had contributed to his education. This is what he wrote in response to my enquiry:

"Participation in theatre studies during my sixth-form years had a profound impact on my growth and development and fostered in me skills that I have made use of across the range of my work and leisure activities.

Through improvisation workshops, I developed awareness of the subtle interactions, verbal and non-verbal, that occur among people in a group and of the methods we use to communicate with, support or manipulate others. Taking part in theatrical performances helped me to develop team-working skills and the various competences required for public speaking. These have proved invaluable in my role as an economic consultant, working in teams and engaging with clients. Similarly, an appreciation of what 'works' in writing and performance has enabled me to communicate much more effectively in writing and in meetings and conferences. Theatre studies developed in me an understanding of the role of ritual and convention in social interactions and helped me to notice and interpret differences between cultures, both within the UK and between the UK and other countries. This understanding has supported me in study and work abroad, in voluntary youth work and, most recently, in my commitment to preaching in local churches.

Theatre studies also gave me entry into a rich cultural heritage which has nourished me throughout my life, exposing me to new ideas and widening the breadth of my experience. I remain a fan of live theatre, whether the RSC, student productions or the local amateurs. From time to time I contribute to drama work with young people or adult volunteers, in writing or production, and get huge satisfaction from seeing the impact that the experience has on the self-confidence of participants and the special moments of exhilaration that can happen for them."

I like the phrase 'special moments of exhilaration': they were what I most missed when I traded my teaching role for one in management.

Richard won an open scholarship to Sidney Sussex College where he gained a first-class degree in economics. Following his graduation, he was awarded a Fulbright Scholarship to study at the University of Massachusetts for his Master's degree. He then worked as an economist for the Botswana Government before joining Cambridge Econometrics, a project-based consultancy firm providing economic analysis to support strategic planners and policy-makers. Clients include public and private sector organisations in the UK, the European Commission and national governments within and outside Europe. At the age of 37 Richard was appointed to his present post as managing director of the firm.

Cambridge Econometrics is the trading subsidiary of a charitable trust of which Richard is a trustee. The charity seeks to advance education in the field of economics, with special regard for the following principles: that economic behaviour is primarily social rather than individual, that it is influenced by aesthetic and ethical - as well as economic - values; and that the pursuit of self-interest in economic behaviour can impact adversely on both society and the environment. The charity aims to increase public awareness and understanding of these principles and also of the policies and practices that are required to redress the adverse effects of disregarding them. Richard's project experience ranges across major problems associated with energy, employment, population, environmental pollution and climate change.

Cambridge Econometrics and its governing charity provide a model response to twenty-first century needs. Their staff teams have academic knowledge, research skills, creative energy, and intellectual and moral integrity, coupled with an understanding of people and their organisations. We need many more organisations like these that can combine expertise in a particular field with a holistic view of the human situation and its current challenges.

How our education system could do with an independent, multi-skilled body capable of raising public awareness of its present plight and the decisive measures that need to be taken if our society, as we know it, is to survive.

Chapter 7

Knowledge Is Not Understanding

"The principal goal of education in schools should be creating men and women who are capable of doing new things, not simply repeating what other generations have done; men and women who are creative, inventive and discoverers, who can be critical and verify, and not accept everything they are offered."

Jean Piaget, 1953.

The relentless pressure on schools and colleges to prioritise traditional A level courses has wide-ranging implications for the whole education system - not least for those universities that have moved with the times and developed a range of interesting and imaginative responses to students' and society's current needs. Their practical and vocational courses are, however, not well-served by the kind of preparation for higher education that schools are now being expected to provide.

Julia King, the Baroness Brown of Cambridge, who was Vice-Chancellor of Aston University from 2006 to 2016, describes the 'backward-looking sixth-form curriculum' as 'a nightmare scenario'. She wants students 'to be creative, practically-skilled and with minds that have been allowed to wander'. Too many traditional A level academic subject combinations don't develop qualities of that kind. Julia would like to see much more flexibility in sixth-form study programmes. A combination of A level maths and a BTEC course would, for example, be a very good preparation for engineering at Aston University. Maths, design/technology and psychology or English language would be another equally valid sixth-form package for a prospective engineer. Engineers have to be able to draw and to communicate well.

They spend their time designing things to improve our lives; it helps, therefore, if they know how people think and behave. These aspects of engineering studies don't receive much attention in the traditional school routes to university engineering. Julia King feels that the really vital areas of competence for university entrants are mathematics and English. Preparation of students for university focuses too much on content. If students develop the essential skills required for their chosen university course, the rest of their sixth-form programme doesn't need to be as narrowly prescribed as it is at present.

Anyone who becomes involved in the perennial battle to reform A level and undergraduate courses soon becomes aware that they are immersed in a major battle of ideologies. The aims and objectives of A level reformers are closely in line with the thinking that has inspired many of the most exciting developments in the newer universities: to provide students with more interesting, challenging , and, above all, more useful learning experiences that are directly relevant to the world in which we live. There is no lack of support among educationists for learning experiences in which students have to work out solutions to real-life problems, instead of merely memorising and regurgitating facts in order to pass exams. However, efforts to develop such approaches are constantly undermined by those who have a vested interest in maintaining the status quo. And the traditionalists have loud voices: they are extremely effective in extolling the virtues of long-established syllabuses and the institutions that prioritise them. Thus reformers find themselves championing sixth-form and university courses that many of the public have been brainwashed into believing are second-rate.

The Salters A level syllabuses provide a good example of what reformers are up against. Salters alternatives to traditional science A levels are the result of a collaborative effort by educationists and employers to provide sixth-form students with academically challenging, but essentially practical, courses in which students learn the scientific theory of a subject within the context of its modern applications. The original specifications for these alternative A levels were sponsored and written in the 1990s by two London livery companies, the Worshipful Company of Salters and the Worshipful Company of Horners, in association with the Nuffield Foundation. The initiative was supported by various educational, charitable and industrial organisations, including British Telecom and Esso UK. The resulting courses are based on a simple principle - that science is happening all around us and the best way for students to find out about it is to set their learning within the context of current social and industrial developments. Syllabuses consist of a range of context-based studies which introduce students to scientific ideas and principles through their applications in the modern world.

The Salters courses are planned so that students learn, stage by stage, all that they need to know to gain a full understanding of the scientific concepts relevant to each contextual study. Students have the opportunity to consolidate their previous learning before moving on to the next section of the scientific content. The teams of educationists working on the Salter A level initiative provide extensive materials designed to support teachers and students as a coherent whole. These resources help students to connect and integrate the concepts introduced in the different study units.

The Salters approach to sixth-form science was first developed in chemistry and the course has become a well-established A level option. It is very highly regarded by the staff and students who teach and study it. The most recent chemistry specification includes 10 contexts and associated units of chemical concepts that range from drug synthesis to dentistry, from the use of alternative fuels to the chemistry of colours in spices. The educationists responsible for designing the course maintain that it conveys the excitement of contemporary chemistry. The introductory and support materials, with their accounts of, for example, the content of the medicines we take, the materials used in replacements for parts of the body, DNA testing, organic farming, nylon machine parts, amply justify that claim.

The chemistry materials are truly seductive. The text that traces the enquiry or storyline behind each contextual study is a model of clarity, and beautifully presented. I once contributed to a review of school text books and found many of the science texts, in particular, depressingly inadequate for their purpose. The turgid and inaccessible prose was a barrier rather than an aid to understanding the concepts being explained. In contrast, the style of the Salters texts is mature but uncomplicated, the tone supportive but not patronising. The prose is broken up with photos, diagrams, tables, and coloured panels with bullet points, a method of presentation that can sometimes become distractingly busy and fragmented, but here the balance is just right: variety but also coherence.

In addition to the text books that tell the story behind the contextual studies and explain the chemical principles that relate to them, the Salters team sends out a regular newsletter to schools and colleges, maintains a website with up-to-date information and a bank of teacher-produced materials, runs a free helpline and organises group networks and regular training workshops for teachers and technicians. This kind of professional support for teachers from fellow educationists has been sadly lacking since the Schools Council was closed down.

Further services that the Salters chemistry team provide for teachers include planning overviews for each teaching unit and a wide range of suggestions for student activities. The course places a strong emphasis on the student's active role in the learning process. A distinctive feature has been for all students to undertake an individual project through which they develop a range of investigative and problem-solving skills. The 'individual investigation' is crucial to the principles of the course and accounts for 15% of the marks awarded in the first year and 30% in the second. Along with other practical components of the course, the investigation is internally assessed and externally moderated by the exam board.

The feedback on the Salters' chemistry course is precisely what you would expect from any learning experience that actively engages students in experiences that are clearly seen to be relevant to the world around them. It arouses and holds their interest and they understand the point of what they are doing. Staff enjoyment and job satisfaction are summed up in one comment in particular: "We find ourselves saying 'Wow' quite a lot." I tracked down a university professor responsible for admissions to his chemistry department and asked about Salters sixth-formers and how they shaped up as undergraduates. This is what he said:

"Salters students have a key advantage over their peers from a different A level background because of their preparedness for practical work. The Salters practical investigation has been the main factor here as other students have only had the experience of completing overly simplistic and prescriptive practical assessments during their A level studies. The fact that Salters students have had to think for themselves in planning their experiment and to draw conclusions from their analysed data leads to a much more meaningful learning experience than the 'hoop-jumping' that other students experience. The difference between Salters students and other undergraduates is still evident in their practical work at the third year stage of their course."

The Government has now put a stop to internally assessed elements of A level courses and in the process ripped the heart out of the Salters chemistry course. Consistent with the Government's 1940s' view of education, all assessment is reverting to the linear model with a single set of written exams at the end of each course. The Salters team find themselves in a position all too familiar to pioneering and reforming educationists - experiencing the thoughtless and peremptory destruction of years of patient building of a highly successful initiative that has given satisfaction to thousands of students and their teachers. In their initial despair, they'll probably contemplate giving up - opening a teashop or becoming sheep farmers in the Welsh hills - but then, if they're true to type, they'll re-group, pick up the pieces and re-build their course round its remaining distinctive features. Reformers are resilient and determined. They need to be.

The Government's official line - in so far as it has sought to justify its commitment to the ancient linear approach to course assessment - is that internal assessment, even with external moderation, is unreliable. In other words, teachers cheat to get their students better results. Cheating is one of the unfortunate side-effects of intense competition and not confined to any one system of assessing human achievement. The more obsessed a society becomes with paper qualifications and the whole paraphernalia of tests, marks, grading, certification and the classification of young people and their schools as successes or failures, then the more sophisticated and prevalent cheating becomes.

The various ways in which students cheat in traditional written tests and exams is legendary and has reached new heights of ingenuity with advances in technology. The web offers advice on an extensive range of high-tech gadgets that enable parents and friends to supply information to examinees in the examination room. Amazon openly advertises a 'student smartwatch' specifically designed with special programmed software to enable candidates to cheat in exams and tests. It is a sophisticated piece of technology that enables, and of course encourages, students to store and access extensive exam crib sheets, including pictures and diagrams. Candidates can communicate with friends within and outside the exam hall. Researchers agree that these devices are extensively used and very difficult to detect. The smartwatch has an emergency button that changes the screen from text to normal watchface in order to avoid detection.

In China, a country where the pressure on children to pass prestigious state exams is, incredibly, even more intense than here, the use of these devices has apparently reached such a level that the police are having to use drones to patrol the skies over exam centres to intercept messages being passed to the candidates inside. There is something very wrong with a society in which competitive intensity has got out of hand to this extent. We need to scrap the whole examination farce and find other ways of assessing learning and achievement.

Politicians' innate distrust of teachers certainly lies at the heart of the UK government's ban on continuous and internal assessment, but the decision is also influenced by a longstanding prejudice against modular courses and the kind of learning experiences they encourage. With its context-based units, the Salters' chemistry A level has done well to survive as long as it has. Some of its predecessors had a much shorter shelf-life. The excellent Wessex A levels that preceded Salters lasted only a few years. There were twelve of these courses, all designed by a consortium of west country LEAs in the late 80s. They retained the traditional core curriculum delivered in a traditional way, but teaching of the core was suspended at regular intervals to enable students to work intensively on a series of practical projects which they chose themselves from a bank of modules. Students had to complete four modules over the two-year A level course and together they accounted for 40% of the marks. The variation in learning situations and types of task that were set widened the normal demands made of students and revealed their different strengths. Once again, staff and student response was enthusiastic. An independent survey established that the Wessex courses were considered more accessible, relevant and interesting than traditional A levels. However, in the face of increasing government antipathy, the examination board that had agreed to trial them withdrew its support.

The politicians and academics who now maintain tight control of the sixth-form curriculum keep a careful watch on any attempt to transfer responsibility for learning from the teacher to the student. Thus practical and experimental work, learning by trial and error, encouraging students to question and think for themselves, allowing them to choose study topics in which they are personally interested - these experiences - valuable as they may be - mustn't be allowed to figure too prominently. The priority is always knowledge acquisition, in a form that can be recalled in the all-important A level exams. The irony is that this emphasis undermines the traditionalists' own avowed aim of preparing students well for the demands of university. Undergraduates must be able to think for themselves so that they acquire understanding as well as knowledge.

I was once invited to play a small part in interviewing applicants for a place on the BA English Honours course at York University. One of the young men we saw posed a nice problem. Impeccably qualified, with top grades in all of his A levels, he was also extremely knowledgeable, in fact staggeringly so. He was a mine of detailed information on authors' lives and works, literary genres and movements. But it was all clinical, drily encyclopaedic, pretentious. He was 'academic' to a fault, a sad justification of the Chambers English Dictionary definition of the term: 'scholarly, formal, theoretical only, of no practical importance or consequence.' There was no life or passion in him, no personal response to anything he'd studied, in fact no real understanding of what he was talking about. We could have been interviewing Dickens' Bitzer, or CJ de Mooi, who was a regular panellist on the popular BBC2 quiz show Eggheads and had an almost flawless 'knowledge' of literature - works, authors, situations, background etc - but appeared not to have read a single literary work. The York lecturers were adamant that this interviewee would be wholly unsuited to the York course and, notwithstanding expectations of a backlash from his school, they rejected him.

There is growing concern among university admission tutors at the number of applicants entering university with an Egghead's facility for recalling a vast body of memorised facts and academic rhetoric, but little genuine feeling for their subject or understanding of the skills required to study it effectively at undergraduate level. The tremendous pressure that schools are under to get their students through their exams at all costs is responsible for some extremely unimaginative teaching and arid learning routines, narrowly focused on the limited range of competences that can be assessed by terminal written tests. The more we teach to exams, the poorer our children's education.

The increase in university applicants who are well-qualified, but lacking in genuine understanding of their subject, is exacerbated for Russell Group universities because of their global aspirations. A third of the intake to some of our best-known universities now comes from abroad. Many of these students are from countries where the government's control of what goes on in the classroom is a situation that totalitarian-inclined politicians in this country can only salivate over. The success of these schools in getting their pupils through public exams is something that our government would dearly love British schools to emulate.

As we are often told, the Chinese have greater respect for education than we do, or at least they are keener to obtain academic qualifications. And this is a feature of all classes of their society. The reasons for this are not difficult to understand. The different levels of social standing in China are much more clearly defined than in our class system - more akin to the Indian caste system. The degree of deprivation is far greater. You move up the social scale and improve your standard of living through education, and that means acquiring academic qualifications. There are very few other options and failing the all-important gaokao exams, which equate with our A levels, more or less puts an end to any aspirations of a worthwhile job and a better life. Thus parents and children are totally compliant to an education system that indoctrinates them in the Chinese way of life and is heavily committed to didactic teaching and rote learning. There is a concentration on maths and science and meticulous preparation for the tests that children have to take at various stages of the system.

One of the successes of the Chinese system told me her story. Like many of her contemporaries, Chun Xiao went to a state boarding school. She experienced much less family life than her British counterparts and didn't have a close relationship with her parents. The State controlled people's lives, determined their work and where they lived. Chun Xiao's parents were low-level civil servants, both graduates, but poorly paid and subject to the government's wishes with regard to where they worked. They saw little of each other, being posted to very different parts of the country and unable to afford to travel long distances in order to meet.

Chun Xiao entered a state boarding nursery school at the age of 3 and was a weekly boarder for most of her school life, returning home at weekends often to live with grandparents, teachers or other parent substitutes. At one stage, at the age of seven, she looked after herself and her younger brother in a flat. Chun Xiao's school day began at 7.30 am with a flag-raising ceremony and physical exercises. Classes started at 8am and, with a break for lunch, continued until 4.30 pm. Children then had a period of free time when they could attend to their own personal needs, washing their clothes etc. The period from 7.00 pm till 10.00pm was taken up with compulsory private study. Through this intensive system, Chun Xiao and her classmates acquired an impressive body of knowledge. Even those who found learning difficult became knowledgeable, by virtue of the sheer time devoted to the process. Chun Xiao loathed the regimentation and wasn't responsive to the methods used. She suffered a great deal of anxiety over her work. She was a sensitive child and would, she thinks, have been receptive to the arts, but these were sidelined and of low status. However, she did well in her academic work, proceeded to university and became a university lecturer in English.

I asked Chun Xiao how her educators would have responded to the idea of education as a process of ascertaining and developing each individual's interests, enthusiasms and talents to ensure that all children develop their potential to live a fulfilling life. She looked at me very seriously and said, "They'd have absolutely no idea what you were talking about. Chinese children don't discover their passion. And they don't develop creative, problem-solving or innovative skills. The country doesn't seem to produce many inventors. Its computer experts are committed and skilful, but they aren't often innovators."

Many of the politically-imposed features of our present education system - the increasing emphasis on the academic curriculum and exam success, on competition and league tables - stem from the politicians' resolve to emulate those countries that consistently occupy the top positions in international league tables that purport to show which peoples of the world are the best educated. When Michael Gove introduced his changes to the curriculum, he said he wanted his own children "to have the sort of curriculum that children in other countries have, which are doing better than our own...because when my son and daughter graduate from school and then either go on to university or into the workplace, they're competing for college places and jobs with folk from across the globe, and I want my children to receive an education as rigorous as any country's."

We all have aspirations for our children and most of us want our country to be able to compete economically with the rest of the world, but that doesn't mean that we have to buy into a curriculum from a totalitarian state with a culture completely different to our own. If we really think that other countries' education systems look as if they could be embedded in UK schools, we need to consider the evidence and implications in some detail. In other words, we have to do some homework, something politicians rarely undertake. For a start, we need to analyse precisely what the league tables can and can't tell us about the quality of education they purport to measure. We know that the grooming for exams that takes place in a country like China leads to students achieving levels of exam success that cannot be matched by most of their British counterparts. But we don't know whether or not this means that the students concerned are actually better educated in terms of understanding the material they've learnt. Another area of uncertainty concerns the price that young people in China pay for the intensity of their exam preparation. The anecdotal evidence concerning the country's child suicide rates is extremely disturbing, but the truth is elusive, just as it is concerning the number of Chinese athletes whose achievements are attributable to taking performance-enhancing drugs or, more importantly, concerning the full extent of the country's human rights abuses.

Recent statistics indicate that a large number of Chinese children share Chun Xiao's experience of living apart from their parents - in boarding schools and orphanages, or with grandparents or unrelated parent substitutes, or simply alone. A particular cause of concern is the extent to which rural children are being left behind by parents who have migrated to the cities to improve their standard of living and contribute to the country's economic success. Some estimates suggest that the number of children that fall into this category may be in excess of 60 million, almost equivalent to the total population of the UK. These are not official figures but, significantly, China hasn't denied them. Surely this isn't what Michael Gove wants for his children.

Another area of concern is the whole question of how genuine and accurate the international league tables are. The table that carries most weight when making comparisons between countries' exam results is that based on the Programme for International Student Assessment (PISA), which reveals a number of inconsistencies and contradictions. Of greater concern is the question of how genuine and accurate such tables are. China 's PISA test results are based solely on Shanghai and Hong Kong. How representative are they of the education provided for the peasant population in the vast rural tracts of the country? The UK PISA results would certainly present a different picture if we were to select a specific area of the UK to represent the whole of the country - the city of Winchester, for example, where the private and state sectors between them achieve almost 100% success at A level and an annual Oxbridge entry of over 100 students a year. But what would those statistics tell us, other than that Winchester is the most sought-after residential area in the country, has one of the most prestigious of all public schools and a state sixth-form college that attracts many of the most academically successful students from across the whole of Hampshire? Would the Secretary of State then announce that all schools in the country should emulate Winchester and Peter Symonds Colleges? Probably.

All arguments concerning the reliability and validity of league tables are really an irrelevance, an anachronism. These tables, national and international, are based on tests and exams that focus on the facility to recall memorised information and to use techniques that have been repeated over and over again in the weeks leading up to the exam. But the world has moved on. We are currently requiring teachers to drill children in procedures that can now readily be digitalised, automated and outsourced. In so doing, we are training the future generation for a labour market that is rapidly disappearing. Andreas Schleicher, Special Adviser to the Organization of Economic Cooperation and Development (OECD), oversees the administration of the PISA tests and admits that they have passed their sell-by date:

"Skills have become the single most important driver of the success of individuals and nations...The knowledge economy no longer pays you for what you know... The knowledge economy pays you for what you can do with what you know."

One of the more inexplicable hang-ups of the politicians who cling to past priorities is their blinkered interpretation of the concept of 'rigour'. The present school curriculum has been devised by people who seem to believe that rigour is the prerogative of academia, a distinctive quality that only traditional academic subjects possess. These subjects are therefore given a special status that distinguishes them from the rest of the curriculum. They are the subjects that all 'able' students are advised to study, as they provide a passport to a traditional research-based university and further immersion in the prestigious academic way of life.

According to this view, all other fields of human endeavour lack rigour. Thus creative, practical, vocational and general or interdisciplinary studies are all classified 'soft subjects', inferior options to be avoided by anyone with 'ability' or potential. But the term 'rigour' applies to attitudes and procedures, routines, ways of doing things. It implies commitment, determination and self-discipline. It's not an automatic feature of some areas of human experience and activity that isn't applicable to others. Learning a musical instrument or singing in a choir, perfecting team strategies on the training ground, designing a mural or piece of equipment, choreographing a dance routine, preparing a meal - these can all be extremely rigorous and demanding experiences, not soft options. It's an insult to children who 'find their passion' in such activities to label their achievements second-rate.

The term 'academic rigour' is normally understood by educationists to refer to educational experiences that are academically, intellectually and personally challenging. Rigorous learning enables students to understand complex concepts, encourages them to think critically, creatively and more flexibly, and provides them with the technical, practical and communication skills that they will need to pursue their interests and careers effectively. This interpretation of rigour has significant implications for the tasks that teachers set their students. Lessons need to encourage students to question and think about what they learn, not merely to memorise and recall. A rigorous history lesson for young children, for example, might be one in which they have to suggest ways in which information they've gathered from the inscriptions on graves in a local churchyard adds to their understanding of a particular period of history. A less rigorous activity would be memorising a list of dates and then completing a multiple choice test. At university level, a history course based on lectures and note-taking would be less rigorous than one in which students had to learn how to interpret and analyse historical data, make connections between historical periods and current events, use both primary and secondary sources to support an argument or position, and arrive at their own interpretation of an historical event after thorough research of the topic.

Rigorous learning challenges and engages students, requiring them to find things out for themselves, either working on their own or in a group. With good teacher support it creates the opportunity for students to experience a sense of achievement, thus motivating them to further and deeper learning. Conversely, passive learning, in which students are presented with a huge body of knowledge for memorising and recall, can overwhelm students and lead to tedium and disengagement.

'Politician speak' occasionally pays respect to a broadly-based, imaginative interpretation of the concept of rigour, but the reality of the current curriculum is that it promotes precisely the opposite approach. The paramount demands on today's teachers are to 'get through' content-heavy syllabuses and to drill children in glib answers for tests and exams that are designed to assess a very limited range of skills. These requirements lessen the opportunities teachers have to respond imaginatively to children's natural desire to learn and understand the world they live in. The emphasis is on pumping in information. 'Filling the little pitchers', Dickens called it.

Dickens' genius for caricature tends to obscure, for modern readers, the accuracy of his presentation of the most pernicious features of nineteenth century life. For example, Sissy Jupe's Coketown school,with its dictionary definition approach to education is no allegory or comic fantasy dreamt up by the novelist: it is almost a straight copy of the utilitarian and mechanical teaching system, derived from the

Catechism, that was employed during the early part of the nineteenth century in schools for the poor. There were two rival but similar versions of this system, one the brainchild of a Quaker called John Lancaster, who claimed to have invented it under the blessing of Divine Providence, the other put forward by an Anglican, Andrew Bell, and called the Steam Engine of the Modern World. Lancaster and Bell advocated a regimen of pure fact. Dickens had only to add the pompous, politically- motivated Thomas Gradgrind to nineteenth century reality to provide his picture of urban education:

" ' Now, what I want is, Facts. Teach these boys and girls nothing but Facts. Facts alone are wanted in life.' The speaker, and the schoolmaster, and the third grown person present, all backed a little, and swept with their eyes the inclined plane of little vessels then and there arranged in order, ready to have imperial gallons of facts poured into them until they were full to the brim."

This strictly utilitarian education system was developed across the country and greatly admired by the ruling classes, who saw it as an excellent preparation for the tight discipline imposed on the workforce in the mills and factories of industrialised Britain. The schooling of the working class had more to do with subjugation than education. Schools turned out a standard employee, regulated, indoctrinated and totally submissive to routine. What impressed the governing classes was the orderliness that prevailed. Order and uniformity are key indicators of a government's control of its people. In a totalitarian state the ultimate symbol of power and subjection is the bizarre goosestepping precision of the troops in the parades held to celebrate the country's achievements and military might.

Although the methods used to achieve orderly uniformity have mercifully changed, it is still the acme of good education for many politicians. The following is an extract from an expansive eulogy of the 'remarkable headteacher' of an 'outstanding primary school in a highly deprived part of Lambeth in South London' which is cited as a model by Andrew Adonis in his book *Education, Education, Education*:

" 'Structure and Routine, ' he says, as he gestures at a class of immaculately uniformed children lining up for class. 'Routine, Structure, Routine, Structure,' he chants as we witness room after room of kids, heads bowed intently as they write in neatly drilled cursive."

Adonis quotes this iconic head's explanation of his obsession with orderly uniformity:

"That's what parents want. Those people shouting 'don't put them in a sausage factory' are the very ones who can pay for their children to have structure at home. They make them have ballet, they have to learn the violin whether they like it or not. And then they go private at secondary because they do want a sausage factory really."

The exciting challenge of education: to produce a standard product immaculately turned out and thoroughly drilled in compliance.

All organisations require clear structures, routines, procedures, in order to function. A school has the added responsibility of developing children's understanding of why these features of our society are so necessary. The better children's understanding of the reasons why they have to conform to their organisation's requirements, the more natural and genuine their cooperation. The ideal classroom situation is one in which children share the teacher's understanding of how learning is facilitated by certain established procedures and routines. Teachers who have a good relationship with their pupils, and who can rely on them to adhere to set principles and formalities, can free up the learning and teaching process. They can be more imaginative and adventurous in the activities and experiences they provide for their classes. Pupils can be fully involved and have a wider range of opportunities to develop personal interests and approaches, and to work in the ways that they find most productive. They can confer and learn how to work productively in a group. Learning becomes more personalised, enjoyable and rewarding. More children are likely to savour success and seek to extend their knowledge and understanding of a topic or subject.

Structures, procedures, routines are essential tools for teachers in managing their pupils' learning. They are a means to an end. What schools have to guard against is letting these aids become an end in themselves, a symbol of adult control and pupil obedience, a shop-window for inspectors, politicians and parents. We don't want to institutionalise children to the extent that they are governed by routine, and so dependent on it that they stop thinking for themselves. If we are afraid of doing anything that hints at disorder - allowing children to discuss their work with each other, to get out of their desks, to move freely around the school - then we are in danger of creating a modern version of Lancaster and Bell's nineteenth century utilitarian schooling.

One of my younger acquaintances was telling me about the new acting head of her primary school where she's a year 4 pupil. It's a happy place and she has enjoyed her time there. I know the school quite well and the frequent musical, dramatic and sporting activities that I've attended have always given a clear impression of a community that is well-run and well-ordered, but relaxed and at ease with itself. The head had young children of his own and was very much in tune with the primary age-group. The pupils obviously approved of him. I asked some of them what it was they liked about him and the first answer was 'everything'. Specific points were that he was kind and always had a smile, that, although he was firm over school rules, he didn't shout when he told someone off - 'he never made anyone cry'. The children particularly appreciated the support he gave them in their sport and games and the way in which he'd once unexpectedly suspended the daily routine for the whole school to build snowmen on the playing field. He was apparently a very good story-teller and made assemblies interesting - and sometimes amusing, as on a particular Shrove Tuesday when his pancake-tossing attempts had proved a disaster. It was reassuring to learn that their head wasn't perfect. On another occasion, one of the school governors summed up the qualities that the children had catalogued: 'he was good at the things you can't measure'. He was also presumably good at the things that are measured, ad nauseam: the school's Ofsted rating was 'outstanding' and it also does very well in the more significant, but less publicised, 'value-added' tables that purport to show rates of progress.

It came as a considerable surprise that in mid-career, and only his fourth year of headship, he resigned and joined the flow of successful teachers currently leaving the profession. He was relaxed about discussing his decision with me, talking enthusiastically about the job satisfaction he'd always obtained from his life in education and indicating briefly why things hadn't worked out as he'd hoped. The anecdotal version of the situation in a close community that usually knows what is going on was that there had been ongoing differences of opinion between head and chair of governors over the way the school should be run. I deduced that this was probably accurate, an unfortunate personality clash that was no-one's fault. But there were no recriminations and we quickly moved on to his own future and, more particularly, his concern for the school he was leaving. He'd been the only applicant when he'd been appointed four years ago and he wasn't optimistic about the chances of the governors filling the vacancy. I appreciated the problem: in the present climate, very few of the small number of teachers prepared to take on the rigours of headship wish to do so with a school that is manifestly already successful and can only go in one direction in the lottery of the league tables.

More than a year later and after two temporary appointments, the governors are no nearer to filling the vacancy. The first temporary head arrived appearing to have been briefed that, despite the inspectors' report, the school required more discipline. Her first demonstration of 'new broom ' tactics was to announce that, from the moment they came into the school, all children were to keep their hands clasped behind their back. When they entered the hall for assembly they were to lower themselves onto the floor with their hands remaining clasped. Similarly when getting up. No doubt lissom youngsters could manage these requirements easily enough, but I found it quite difficult when I tried them. My informant on the new regime had been bawled out for breaking the rule when she was about to enter her classroom. Not being a shrinking violet, she explained to the acting head that she'd wanted to open the door. 'Open it with your foot, then!' was the reply.' 'What did you do?' I asked incredulously, to which she responded with a very entertaining Charlie-Chaplin-style sequence demonstrating the procedure she'd adopted.

If only adults, when they've lost the plot, could see themselves as children see them.

Good teachers don't seek to dominate children. Rather the opposite. They look to wean them off their dependence on adult control, gradually increasing opportunities for them to take decisions for themselves. Teachers' ultimate role in managing the learning process is to make their students self-sufficient and themselves redundant. This is, of course, an extremely challenging task. Managing students' learning is a totally different concept to the traditional classroom process of informing, instructing, lecturing. The moment you actually involve children in the learning process you release energy and significantly change the dynamics of the classroom. When teaching formally, you alone determine the content, direction and pace of the lesson. As a manager of students' learning, you are responding to what others are thinking, saying and doing. You are constantly building on your pupils' contributions to the lesson and exploiting the opportunities that arise from them. You have to be a multi-tasker, alert to everything that's going on, sensitive to individual needs, constantly answering questions and dealing with problems, trying to ensure that everyone is engaged and that the total experience is productive.

One of the most obvious benefits of giving students a major role in the learning process is that it greatly increases the opportunities that children have to develop their powers of oral communication. The ability to express oneself orally is arguably one of the most important of all learning experiences and the most marketable of skills for students to take from their formal education into the workplace. Yet traditionally our education system has restricted pupils' spoken contributions to supplying factual answers to direct questions from the teacher. Classroom talk and discussion in which pupils exchange information, speak of their interests and problems, develop their own ideas, sustain a reasoned argument - these haven't been given anything like the attention they deserve. In fact they have often been dismissed by traditionalists as yet another trendy idea out of the progressive stable that leads to disorder and a waste of valuable time, time that ought to be spent on knowledge transmission. There is now a much greater awareness of the importance of talk in children's development, but the rhetoric of the national curriculum runs well ahead of the reality in most state schools. And that will be inevitable as long as the education system continues to be driven by objective tests and exams that rely so heavily on written answers.

Pauline Gibbons, a specialist in classroom talk who works at the University of New South Wales, believes that it is the most important component of the learning process:

"It is not an exaggeration to suggest that classroom talk determines whether or not children learn, and their ultimate feelings of self-worth as learners. Talk is how education happens."

Some leading US independent boarding schools and colleges make extensive use of a modern version of the Socratic method of fostering critical thinking, pioneered by Phillips Exeter Academy in Boston, USA. Students participate in seminar or conference-style dialogue seated round an oval 'Harkness table', named after a philanthropic oil magnate who donated funds to Phillips Exeter Academy to develop this approach to learning. The aim is to engage all students fully in dialogue - actively listening, reflecting, evaluating and, of course, contributing to discussion. It's a co-operative exercise in which students share ideas rather than compete for attention. It builds up reticent students' confidence to express themselves and teaches talkative students to listen to other people's ideas. Students discover *how* to learn, not just *what* to learn. The teacher's role is to support each student's development as a critical thinker and, without getting too involved in the interaction, to keep the group on task.

Humanities teachers in this country have for decades experimented with various forms of student discussion in which the teacher assumes a role as a neutral chair-person. What makes the Harkness approach distinctive is the way in which the schools committed to it have embedded it as a key learning method right across the curriculum. It also manifestly passes the 'academic rigour' test: Harkness discussion is a highly principled and demanding process. Students have a clear obligation to come to sessions well-prepared, having read and thought about the subject that is going to be discussed. The whole process is designed to develop students' reasoning powers and communication skills. They must therefore be able to contribute fully.

This method of learning has a downside: in order to be effective, it requires small groups, and therefore much more generous staffing than a UK state school can provide on a regular basis. One school that is attempting to overcome this problem by carefully modifying the Phillips Exeter model is Isaac Newton Academy in Ilford. For Harkness lessons, the school divides classes into two, creating discussion groups of about 14, which have proved small enough for everyone to participate. A co-teacher or learning assistant facilitates discussion in one group and the class teacher in the other. Alternatively, the class teacher takes responsibility for both groups simultaneously, sitting or moving between the two of them. Staff have also experimented with an inner and outer circle. Half the class sits round a Harkness table, or small tables arranged in a similar oval shape. The other half forms an outer ring and listens to the discussion and makes notes. A variation on this arrangement is for the students not participating in the discussion each to observe a specific member of the inner group and subsequently provide feedback on the contribution he or she makes to the discussion.

Isaac Newton Academy is fully committed to providing maximum opportunities for students to develop their leadership potential, and discussion-based learning provides an ideal context for furthering that policy. Each year, six Year-8 students are awarded a bursary to attend a five-week summer school at Phillips Exeter Academy, where they are immersed in the Harkness approach. They meet students from all over the world and have an experience they'll never forget. They return prepared for a role as champions of their new way of learning:

"Exeter Academy was an excellent opportunity which has allowed us all to enhance our academic skills and acquire new friends. Risk-taking and independence were a vital part of Exeter. This entire opportunity has taught us all what it is like to be Harkness champions as well as independent students. In our lessons at the Phillips Exeter summer school we were taught using the Harkness method, which means that the students take over their own learning, rather than the teacher giving all the information. "

On their return to Isaac Newton, each year's 'Harkness champions' have a responsibility for promoting the principles of Harkness learning. Each champion is linked to a subject area and supports staff in planning schemes of learning and by facilitating discussion with one half of a class. The students lead year assemblies and talk to visitors about the Harkness method and the impact of their summer school experience.

Ongoing staff training is essential for the successful development of a new and challenging approach to learning and all newly-appointed staff at Isaac Newton have to be inducted into the Harkness method. Each year two members of staff spend time at Phillips Exeter Academy and, upon their return, are able to contribute to the training of Isaac Newton staff. One of the first teachers to do this is now in charge of the Isaac Newton initiative and returns to Phillips Exeter each year to teach on the summer school. This close connection with the school that first developed the Harkness method has been invaluable. In addition, Isaac Newton staff have attended joint training sessions with staff from the public school, Wellington College, which has also adopted the Harkness approach.

Isaac Newton Academy's strategies for modifying the Harkness approaches have enabled the school to go a long way towards embedding the approach, without too high a cost in terms of staffing. However, the links with Phillips Exeter Academy are a significant financial commitment for which the school requires annual sponsorship. This is a familiar story: imaginative and innovative approaches to learning are not only more demanding of teachers: they are invariably more expensive to implement. Didactic instruction of large groups of passive learners is by far the cheapest way of delivering education. That is, of course, a major reason why the alternatives are so frequently derided by politicians: MPs know full well that, despite all the 'education, education, education' rhetoric, the electorate will not be prepared to fund state schools for what are unfortunately often regarded as fringe activities. In the independent sector, schemes like the Harkness learning initiative have ideal conditions in which to thrive. In a state school they encounter constant obstacles and objections. Exceptional staff commitment and ingenuity are required to get them off the ground and then to realise their full potential.

Current educational priorities are unfortunately a strong disincentive to good teaching. The heavy emphasis on standard procedures and uniformity of outcome, the preference for traditional syllabus content and, above all, the tedious routine of preparing students for narrowly-focused exams - all combine, with lack of funding, to discourage teachers from using a full range of experiences that enable children to become effective learners and well-educated adults. We have not yet quite reached the stage where schools' teaching methods have to conform wholly to political prescription, but we are moving in that direction with curricular priorities that are increasingly associated with a traditional, formal style of pedagogy. And yet, despite all the disincentives, dedicated and determined teachers continue to provide imaginative and innovative learning situations for their students. They find ways to get round or subvert the system: they show their pupils how to jump through the regulation hoops, whilst focusing on more important educational experiences as much as they can. They take on two jobs: the one they came into the profession to do and the one that's subsequently been imposed on them. They're inspirational teachers, *despite* the system. Society owes them a big debt.

Chapter 8

University Learning and Teaching under Scrutiny

"Those offering us evidence commented on the irony that, in institutions devoted to learning and teaching and to the advancement of knowledge and understanding , so little attention is paid to equipping staff with advanced knowledge and understanding of the processes of learning and teaching."
Sir Ronald Dearing, National Committee of
Enquiry into Higher Education, 1997.

My transition from the school sector to the world of Higher Education came about as a consequence of a chance phone call. I'd just completed a review and evaluation of the effect of the Technical and Vocational Education Initiative (TVEI) in Hampshire schools and was asked if I'd be interested in a similar task in relation to the HE equivalent, Enterprise in Higher Education. EHE was a typical highly publicised/low impact government initiative designed to show that politicians were aware of a problem and doing something about it: in this instance, the failure of HE to modernise its teaching methods, particularly in response to advances in technology.

The first EHE unit that I visited consisted of a director, an administrator and a secretary, plus a temporary research assistant who appeared to have spent three months analysing the meagre returns from a questionnaire distributed to all students on the penultimate day of the Christmas term. There was a high-powered management board of businessmen and local dignitaries overseeing the unit's work. The basic procedure was for the director of the unit to persuade subject departments of the university to think of a mini-project to improve the teaching and learning process and then for them to make a bid for EHE funding to support their 'initiative'. Bids were then assessed, accepted and pursued, with varying degrees of willingness or reluctance. The unit monitored and evaluated progress and reported to the management board.

The whole exercise was absurdly top-heavy with accountability procedures. Even before my arrival with a further layer of evaluation, a wholly disproportionate amount of the EHE unit's income was being swallowed up in the administration of the scheme rather than on the actual initiatives that it was supposed to introduce and support. Ironically, the EHE unit's preoccupation with the paraphernalia of window-dressing, evaluation, recording and reporting meant that there was little time actually to engage with departmental initiatives and provide advice and support for the staff trying to initiate change. Direct contact with some of the mini-projects was minimal. The reports that departments were required to provide were high on rhetoric, but short on convincing evidence of the ways in which the taxpayers' money was actually changing hearts and minds in relation to learning and teaching. I suspected that more than one department was doing what many of Tony Blair's specialist schools did with their extra funding: spending it in accordance with their own priorities and traditional practices.

I spent several years involved in various ways with the EHE project. It wasn't a very edifying experience, but it led to a more challenging and rewarding university post with responsibility for the training and development of several thousand academic staff in their teaching role. It was a new post, one of the first of its kind. University vice-chancellors were becoming sufficiently alarmed at some of the public criticisms of university teaching to feel that it would be expedient to put their house in order before someone suggested doing it for them. After all, preparatory training is the norm for all other teachers. Why should university lecturers be assumed not to require it?

I arrived on the university staff developer/trainer scene just before an extensive inquiry into the future of Higher Education in the UK, led by Sir Ron Dearing, the Chancellor of the University of Nottingham. The subsequent series of reports made 93 recommendations. Among those that it singled out for urgent action were:

- that all institutions of higher education should give high priority to developing and implementing learning and teaching strategies that focused on the promotion of students' learning;

- that all institutions should begin to develop or seek access to programmes for teacher training of their staff;

- that a professional Institute for Learning and Teaching in Higher Education (ILTHE) should be established to accredit the training programmes that institutions designed, to undertake research into good practice and to stimulate innovation.

Most post-1992 universities had already made a start on addressing the manifest weaknesses in the system to which the 1997 Dearing Report drew sharp attention. But for the Russell Group implementation of the Dearing recommendations called for a seismic shift in attitude and policy. I came to the university world with no illusions about the standard of much of the teaching in research-based universities but, even so, I was surprised at the gulf in status that existed between research and teaching and at just how little the latter featured in everyday conversation. For eighteen years I'd worked in an institution where curricular and pedagogical issues had been a daily preoccupation, where sharp minds had constantly discussed, debated and argued about course content and the best ways of helping students to access it, where staff were busy modernising courses and methods, designing new syllabuses and learning experiences, researching best practice and adapting it to their context, producing packs of study materials and trying out innovatory approaches. Student conferences, workshops, simulation exercises, visiting speakers and offsite activities provided a constant stimulus and talking point. It was a basic assumption that successful teaching entailed constant dialogue about classroom practice. It was, therefore, a considerable culture shock to work in educational establishments in which the quality of students' learning experiences was rarely on the agenda and where one had to make a considerable effort to interest some people in it.

Part of the difficulty was linguistic. Dearing used terms that were unfamiliar to many academics. Staff didn't refer to themselves as teachers: they were lecturers. The concept of academics as managers of student learning was quite alien: it was generally assumed that students came to university knowing how to study or 'read' their subject. Putting the terms 'teaching' and 'learning' together seemed to confuse some people; it was almost as if they needed time to unpack them separately. Adopting Dearing's order of priority - 'learning and teaching' - was particularly counter-productive, only serving to increase people's irritation with what, for them, was provocative jargon.

The biggest stumbling block to engaging academics in discussion and debate about teaching is that many of them aren't very sure what there is to talk about. Teaching has tended to be regarded as a matter of common sense, a natural process of passing on academic enthusiasm and knowledge to students. It's acknowledged that some staff aren't terribly good at it, but generally considered unlikely that that situation can be rectified by forcing poor performers to attend staff development courses: either you can teach or you can't. Skills teaching is regarded as a less intellectual, and therefore inferior, activity to the transmission of knowledge, and the prevalence of this view explains the difficulty that practical and vocational courses have in gaining status in the older universities. The negative reactions to Dearing were far more than the grumblings of a few crusty old professors hoping for a quiet life before retirement: they were indicative of a deeply embedded culture inimical to any initiative focusing on skills acquisition.

A few years ago Oxford University introduced a two-year, part-time Master's course in Creative Writing. It was a very modest innovation, combining traditional 'academic rigour', in the form of the usual critical analysis of literature, with the development of creative writing skills. Nonetheless, there was strong opposition to the move, illustrated by the following letter to the *Oxford Today* magazine:

"A Master's degree in Creative Writing? At Oxford? In 50 years, a latter-day Gibbon will note this nonsense as a milestone in the Decline and Fall of Oxford. Writing is a craft well within the normal compass of every Oxford student, indeed it is a *sine qua non* of scholarship....It is absurd to argue that writing is a craft worthy of scholarly study and a university degree ....These craft degrees debase the credibility of all other degrees and bring the university into disrepute."

The critical analysis of literature is one of the most well-established of university practices: no-one would dream of challenging it as a bona fide academic pursuit. Yet the idea of potential authors studying creative writing as an artistic activity in order to develop their own writing skills is anathema.

Sir Ken Robinson recalls another example of this peculiar attitude from his days as head of a university English department and member of a professorial promotions committee. He had put a colleague's name forward for promotion and had to wait outside the room while the committee deliberated on his recommendation. After half an hour, he was called back into the room.

"The vice-chancellor said, 'We've had a few problems with this one. We're going to hold him back for a year,' meaning that they were not approving his promotion. Members of the committee are not meant to question decisions that concern their own recommendations, but I was taken aback. I asked why, and was told there was a problem with his research. I wasn't prepared for this and asked what was wrong with it. I was told there was so little of it.

They were talking about an English lecturer who, in the period under review, had published three novels, two of which had won national literary awards; who had written two television series, both of which had been broadcast nationally and one of which had won a national award. He had also published two papers in conventional research journals on nineteenth century popular fiction. 'But there is all of this,' I said, pointing to the novels and the plays. 'We're sure it's very interesting,' said one of the committee, 'but it's his research we're worried about, ' pointing to the journal papers. 'But this is his research too,' I said, pointing to the novels and plays. This led to a good bit of shuffling of papers.

By research, most universities mean papers in academic journals or scholarly books. The idea that novels and plays could count as research clearly hadn't entered the debate....In universities, research is defined as a systematic enquiry for new knowledge. So I asked the committee whether they thought that novels and plays, as original works of art, could be a source of new knowledge. If so, does the same apply to music, to art and to poetry? Are we really saying that knowledge is only to be found in research journals and in academic papers? "

The purpose of our endless search for new knowledge and deeper understanding of the world is presumably to enhance the quality of our life in some way. Thus research can lead to a cure for extending the life expectancy of a cancer patient, or to increased enjoyment of reading literature or going to the theatre, or to improving police detection of a particular kind of crime, or to discovering a means of reducing carbon emission from cars. Unfortunately, academics' perversely narrow perception of what constitutes intellectually respectable research sometimes suggests an entirely different view: that the more esoteric and obscure the process, and the less capable it is of practical application, the more highly it should be regarded. Recent research projects announced by Oxford University include "a new review of Mark Stoyle's historical account of the black legend of Prince Rupert's dog" and the grand-daughter of one of my neighbours has just obtained a higher degree in breast-feeding in Biblical times. No doubt these undertakings are intensely interesting to those engaged in them and to like minds in the academic community, and it may be that they have something to add to the world's store of knowledge, but there must be more urgent issues requiring researchers' attention. And where do these obscure studies lead for the young academics involved in them? Many graduates lack marketable skills, but can usually figure out some way, no matter how tenuous, of translating what they've learnt at university into the workplace. It must be particularly difficult for those who have spent several years obtaining a doctorate in some field of study that has virtually no relevance whatsoever outside academia.

I have always been puzzled by a paradox in our education system - that the most interesting, enjoyable and seemingly relevant parts of syllabuses are often regarded as the least important. At school, I very much enjoyed my study of social history and human geography and felt cheated when I discovered that the syllabuses of my sixth-form history and geography courses relegated these interests to a very minor role, in order to accommodate what was considered more academic material appropriate for potential university applicants. At Borough Road Teachers' Training College, my English course required students to undertake an extended dissertation. I decided I'd like to write on the subject of journalese, analysing and comparing the various styles favoured by different newspapers and assessing their impact. The choice of topic was normally left to the student, but the assumption was that it would be a literary study, yet another critical appreciation of a particular text or author's works. My preference for a linguistic topic caused obvious concern and, although I was allowed to go ahead, it was clear that my tutor felt the university marker would not be impressed. The training colleges relied on university approval of their courses and were desperate to demonstrate that the academic aspects of teacher-training reflected standard university practices, however irrelevant they might be.

Some years later I encountered a similar obstacle when starting post-graduate work. Upon completion of my degree I was encouraged to enrol for Ph D research. It hadn't been something I'd been expecting, or indeed contemplating, but I suppose I was flattered and the tutor was someone I respected and liked. The thought of further study under his supervision was tempting and I knew what I'd like to submit as my subject. I'd thoroughly enjoyed the Restoration comedy component of my course and particularly the plays of William Congreve, whose masterpiece, *The Way of the World*, had been one of our set texts. My supervising tutor, Dr Brookes, was a recognised authority on the restoration dramatists.

Our undergraduate study of set texts had been greatly assisted by the scholarly editions of the plays, poems and novels that were recommended to us. These normally contained well-researched introductions, background notes on the period in which the works had been written, and detailed contextual information. The *Way of the World* was an exception, in that there was no scholarly edition available: we simply had the text of the play. My plan was to rectify this surprising deficiency and to produce a scholarly but accessible text for undergraduates, and possibly sixth-formers.

Dr Brookes was delighted with my choice of Congreve as a subject. However, when I began to detail my plans for editing the most famous of the playwright's works, a similar worried frown appeared on his face to that I'd experienced some years earlier with my Borough Road English tutor. Editing a play was (just about) acceptable as a Ph D undertaking, but it would have to be carried out according to time-honoured procedures. The requirement was for the textual minutiae to be subjected to a degree of anal scrutiny that would be of no interest to anyone other than members of the academic community researching in the same area. Dr Brookes was the kindest and gentlest of men and it was too painful for him to say outright that there was no common ground between us. We co-existed for a few weeks as he tried to show me the precise routines that I had to follow and I searched for a compromise that would enable me to go at least some way towards achieving my objective. But it was hopeless and I terminated my studies, apologising for having misunderstood the nature of research.

The rituals and mystique that academia attaches to much research creates an unfortunate image of an esoteric fraternity divorced from the real world. And yet the process of increasing existing knowledge and understanding of the human situation - in order to find better solutions to the challenges and problems that we all face - this concerns every one of us. Research and development are crucial to the survival of many businesses and organisations. As individuals, we all need to know how to access, analyse and evaluate information if we are to make informed choices and decisions in our complicated lives. An understanding of research processes is crucial to the education of our children at all stages of their development.

Teachers have a double obligation to master the skills of research. They need to pass them on to their students, but they have also to use them constantly themselves to ensure that their own professional practice remains effective and fully responsive to changing needs. Educationists need to challenge decisions in education made on the basis of the personal ideologies of politicians who have little understanding of the issues involved. It is useful in that situation if they are able to demonstrate that the principles they've established as a result of their own direct experiences are confirmed by reliable research evidence.

The Hampshire open-access 16+ colleges presented sixth-form staff with the phenomenon of the 'new sixth-former', a term applied to students who would not previously have continued at school beyond the age of 16. Some of the comprehensive colleges had several hundred of these students and their needs were extremely varied. There was intense debate over the content of their courses and the best ways of delivering it. I became involved with a discussion group drawn from more than one college that became interested in undertaking a major piece of classroom action research that involved some of us in registering for a Master's degree in Education with the Council for National Academic Awards (CNAA). My particular study was on the subject of *sixth-formers' organisation and management of independent learning, with particular reference to one-year students.* It involved teaching an experimental course on study methods and evaluating its effectiveness. The proposal was accepted and all went well until the point at which my supervisors suggested that I seek to transfer my registration for a Master's degree to that for a Ph D. That application was rejected.

I was considerably more streetwise than I'd been over 20 years previously when I had meekly accepted that my plan to edit Congreve's *Way of the World* had too practical an outcome to qualify as proper research. I challenged the CNAA's decision and did so repeatedly. In the course of a protracted exchange, I gleaned that my study was sufficiently weighty to merit Ph D registration and also met the 'breaking fresh ground' criterion. Even the practical nature of the study - the classroom action research aspect of my project - was apparently tolerated. What, then, was the problem? It was simply that the CNAA had no precedent for awarding a PhD for research on an education topic; in other words, education as a discipline lacked the academic respectability to justify its study beyond Master's degree level. Accompanied by Dr Silver, the Principal of my sponsoring institution, I was eventually given an audience with the CNAA hierarchy who finally capitulated and accepted their first ever Ph D (Education) registration.

Academia's comparative lack of interest in the education process and the university teaching role is demonstrated most clearly by the research-based universities' traditional policy with regard to staff recruitment. Russell group universities are always looking for academics who will enhance their research reputation and increase their research funding. They are the academic equivalent of football's premier league teams, seeking and attracting the big names from throughout the world. At the time of Dearing, the research reputation or potential of applicants was not merely the most important factor when staff appointments were made, but often the only one. Some newly-appointed staff actually arrived thinking they weren't going to have a lecturing commitment, as it hadn't been mentioned at their interview.

This failure to acknowledge the teaching role at interview had some dire consequences. Shortly before the start of a new academic year a mature gentleman came to see me for some advice. He was Chinese and could speak no English at the time he'd been appointed in April. I was very impressed by the progress he'd made in learning the language during the summer, but I fully understood his concern that he and his students were going to find life very difficult when he started lecturing in September.

If you are charged with bringing about some changes in the culture of an organisation, you need to know what the person at the top has in mind. I therefore sought an early meeting with the Provost, an approachable and down-to-earth engineer, to find out how he personally hoped his university would benefit from appointing a training officer for academic staff. He strongly advised that I started by working with the converted: "Don't bang your head against a brick wall." It was a less ambitious approach than I'd envisaged, but he clearly understood the size of the challenge and it proved wise advice.

The response of most of the Russell Group to the Dearing Report was to interpret its clarion call for an urgent re-ordering of priorities as a mild suggestion "that teaching staff receive some amount of training in teaching during their probationary period". Interestingly, it is in that much diluted form that his clear recommendations on learning, teaching and staff training now tend to be reported and remembered. Most universities introduced at least a modicum of lecturer training and advised departments that this was to be part of the requirements of the two-year probation that staff in their first post were expected to complete. In the past, successful completion of probation had, as with promotion, been judged on research progress. Some departments were very reluctant to change that policy and gave little or no encouragement to new members of staff to participate in the training programmes that were being introduced. The traditional autonomy of university departments makes it very difficult to introduce new procedures that everyone is expected to follow.

Most probationary lecturers were quite amenable to a certain amount of training and were in fact pleased to receive some help with their early teaching responsibilities. In schools, new entrants to the teaching profession are usually broken in gently; not so in the university world. Departmental support and guidance in the teaching role are generally very limited. Young lecturers can feel isolated and weighed down with their combined research and teaching responsibilities. Equal workloads are normally the stated policy. The reality, however, can be very different. New and inexperienced staff not infrequently find that they had the heaviest timetables, largest student groups, least popular aspects of the course, most uncongenial timetable slots and the more tedious administrative tasks. You don't, for example, find many of the professorial staff teaching elementary maths to economists or English as a second language, late on a Friday afternoon.

There are, of course, complaints procedures in place for victims of particularly dirty tricks, but these are notoriously weighted in favour of the status quo and, in a strongly hierarchical environment, young lecturers aren't inclined to take on the Establishment so early in their careers. In fact, they often contribute to their difficulties by being too ready to assume responsibilities that more seasoned campaigners have learnt to avoid. A particular hazard for popular young lecturers is the acquisition of additional students for personal tutoring. Most students who find that their personal tutor is ineffective or non-existent seem to accept the situation as a well-established feature of university life. Some, however, make their own arrangements to obtain the advice and guidance that they need.

I am constantly surprised that students aren't inclined to take more initiatives of this kind. As a learning and teaching trainer and adviser, my work in universities was naturally mostly with staff, but I had a good deal of contact with students through various surveys of student experience that I devised and administered. Most of these involved face-to-face meetings. That's by far the best way of finding out what people really think about an experience: get them talking about it. I found that students were usually very willing to speak frankly about their disappointments and difficulties and any obvious ways in which their course might have been improved. But all student feedback needs to be treated with caution. Students aren't really in a position to make an accurate assessment of the genuine quality of course content or to compare the standard of teaching they are receiving with that elsewhere in higher education. For a start, one person's idea of a good teacher may not be another's. In watching a teacher or lecturer, a staff trainer will be looking for more than single-minded spoon-feeding for the exam, but, given the importance our society attaches to levels of certification, some students may well settle for that limited educational objective. Students' response to university depends a great deal on their own expectations. It is also clearly strongly influenced by their previous experiences and their own personal comfort zones in the learning process.

A second-year student was recently telling me about her undergraduate course. It was obviously a revelation to her. Based on case studies and problem-solving scenarios, it required constant student initiative and practical work, and regular involvement in the workplace. She was obviously thriving on what was to her a totally new and exciting experience. She mentioned that she'd just come back from a weekend with a friend who was studying at another university on a course that, as sixth-formers, they'd both put down as their first choice.   The friend was experiencing a very different education, based almost entirely on traditional lectures and note-taking. I asked her what her friend thought of that. "Oh, she's loving it," was the reply. " And what would you have thought of it?" "Oh, I'd have loved it too," she replied, "because I wouldn't have known anything different."

Students are resilient.   They take what they can from a situation and are good at making the most of a bad job. They're remarkably tolerant and will sometimes attribute a poor experience to their own inadequacy rather than blame the institution or the course they're on. A common admission of students whom I interviewed was that they'd made their decision over choice of university on the basis of its reputation, which, although they didn't realise it, was, of course, research reputation.   They had not often probed beneath the surface of brochure summaries to brief themselves thoroughly on their chosen course, let alone the methods by which it would be delivered. Thus it was not surprising if someone whose desire to study English was based on their enjoyment of current novelists was disappointed to find how much of their time was devoted to learning sufficient Old English to translate Beowulf and other Anglo-Saxon texts. Many tedious and out-dated university syllabuses survive through inertia - and not only the inertia of staff. There are plenty of more interesting and relevant alternatives to the moribund courses of the past, if only students would hunt them out. The education system should give students much more help and guidance to make informed choices on their university course, rather than driving them all towards the same limited goals defined for them by politicians and academics.

The   extent   of   students'   acceptance   of   blatantly unacceptable situations was sometimes inexplicable. What, for example, was going on in the minds of the undergraduates who dutifully turned up for a class each week, before one of their number thought to mention to the departmental secretary that the lecturer responsible for it had not been seen for five weeks? It transpired that the member of staff was at home suffering from stress, but he hadn't thought to tell anyone and no-one in the department had noticed that he wasn't around.

The students' lack of initiative on this occasion was a sad reflection on the passivity that our education system is breeding in our young people. The failure of staff to notice anything untoward seems equally strange, until one considers how university departments function. They are not small readily-identified units as in a school or college, but large groupings of individuals and research teams who most of the time work independently of each other. They are administrative units consisting of people loosely connected by sharing the same subject interest.

The head of department role in some traditional universities is actually a temporary post, an additional responsibility held for perhaps four years. The holder isn't necessarily the most senior or influential member of the department and may not be one of its professorial staff. University departments enjoy considerable autonomy, but their power often rests with those who are least involved in their day-to-day administration. Heads of department aren't normally hyperactive in establishing and maintaining principles of good teaching practice, observing and monitoring the work of individuals in their department, and keeping a close eye on everything that's going on. Students aren't always aware who the head of their department is, and tend to think of the senior administrator or secretary in the departmental office as the person who sorts out most student problems - which is often not far from the truth.

The lack of basic management processes and procedures in the older universities means that teaching quality depends heavily on individual integrity and professionalism. A researcher who has little interest in, or commitment to, the teaching role can get away with malpractice that would result in dismissal in most other professions. Some of the staff who were referred to me for individual advice seemed to require character training more than professional development. One senior member of staff, a head of department in a large faculty, had, without informing his faculty head, undertaken to deliver a weekly lecture in a neighbouring university. Apparently he needed the money to help pay for his children's private education. However, the timing of this additional lecturing commitment overlapped with one of his lecture slots in his own university. His strategy for dealing with this problem was to terminate one lecture half an hour early or to start the other half an hour late. He alternated the groups that were short-changed each week. It didn't appear to occur to him that he was letting his students down in order to obtain special treatment for his own offspring.

One of the most perennial problems in higher education is the inadequacy of university student care systems. A recurring theme in feedback discussions with students is the need for more individual help and encouragement. Even those who cope well with their work would generally like more interest taken in them and a closer working relationship with staff. The following comments were transcribed immediately after an interview with a graduate looking back on her university experience:

"The teaching style meant that you had no contact with staff. You just sat in a lecture hall and listened. Sometimes staff lectured for two hours non-stop. Anyone with any knowledge of how to teach knows the futility of that strategy. I was taught by some fifteen different people. Only two, possibly three, knew my name. I don't know how anyone could ever write a reference for me. I didn't know who my personal tutor was. I think they changed every year. I was a self-sufficient person, but if staff had been more friendly or accessible there were minor problems that I'd have liked to share with someone. I had a lot of pressures in my life while I was at university. I'd have liked someone to know about these, someone to appreciate my achievement in managing to keep going."

Psychologists have long stressed the important role that a sense of belonging has in determining human well-being, and this is clearly a crucial factor for university students. A three-year research programme (2008-11), initiated and funded by the Paul Hamlyn Foundation and the Higher Education Funding Council for England (HEFCE), concluded that this was the most important factor influencing student success in their studies: "It is the human side of higher education that comes first - finding friends, feeling confident and, above all, feeling part of your course of study and the institution - that is the necessary starting point for academic success."

Of the different ways in which students gained a sense of belonging - friendship groups, the social life of the union, a particular extra-curricular activity, their course of study - it was feeling part of their course that was seen as most significant. They wanted to be fully engaged in the life and activities of their classes and for their contribution to be accepted and valued by staff and fellow students. They emphasised the importance of learning methods that developed their personal autonomy, and staff who encouraged and supported them as individuals. The final Report produced by the Paul Hamlyn Foundation and the HEFCE included a number of case studies highlighting initiatives in twenty-two universities designed to improve students' engagement with their courses.

It is extremely difficult to establish a rapport between staff and students on lecture-based courses. Yet, even in an age when there are far more effective ways for students to access the information and ideas that they need, the lecture often remains the basic method of tuition, particularly in the research-based universities. Lecturing is, of course, far less costly than small-group teaching, which makes it very attractive to management. For many staff, it seems a natural corollary to their years of immersion in a specialist area of study. They have, of course, to develop the ability to communicate their knowledge but, if that can be achieved, lecturing becomes a manageable routine alongside the demands of their research.

The same isn't true of teaching in the sense of managing the learning process through seminars, practical work and teamwork. This involves constant contact with students, engaging in two-way communication, responding to students' ideas, strengths and problems, listening and learning in order to adjust and vary what one is doing to keep everyone interested and involved. This kind of teaching calls for wider knowledge and a broader understanding of a subject than that needed for lecturing, because the interchange between teacher and students throws up unforeseen topics, problems and challenges. It requires flexibility, imagination and a wide range of people skills. It's a daunting prospect for a new entrant to the teaching profession, even after a year's training, professional guidance and lengthy work placements. For newly-appointed university lecturers with no such preparation it often proves too big a challenge.

An essential task for the newcomer to teaching is to establish basic routines from the outset. Untrained and unpractised lecturers are inclined to underestimate the importance of this. I observed a number of lectures which for the first five to ten minutes were constantly interrupted by late arrivals and in which the general level of audience concentration throughout left a great deal to be desired. On one of these occasions, the lecture concluded with the setting of a preparatory task for the following week the instructions for which were imparted against a hubbub of noise as students packed away and headed for the door.

No-one ever talks about discipline problems in HE but the young female engineering lecturer trying to stop rowdy chauvinists batting inflated condoms around the lecture theatre is in need of support. There's an understandable reluctance among new lecturers to play the school ma'am, but the most successful university teachers aren't afraid to employ strong-arm tactics if necessary. There was a department at Surrey University whose staff enjoyed a particularly good relationship with their students, despite being martinets over routine. One hungover student had a rude awakening one morning when his lecturer appeared in his hostel and tipped him unceremoniously out of bed. Harry Judge, Director of the Oxford Department of Educational Studies, was a charismatic and entertaining lecturer who expected his audience of postgraduates to be ready and waiting for him. Latecomers were informed by a notice on the door that the lecture had started and they were to go away.

Nearly all schoolteachers have made a positive career decision to teach: it's their chosen profession. That's not true of university lecturers, most of whom have decided to continue with their scholarship by undertaking research. Teaching is an additional responsibility that comes with their research role, and which may or may not be welcome. Untrained and inexperienced, they often don't know what to expect of their teaching commitment. They may, of course, turn out to be what we call 'born teachers', meaning that they have the personality and social skills that naturally equip them to motivate and inspire others. Others work at it and, through trial and error and practice, master the teaching side of their job. But academia is the natural home for scholars, many of whom have concentrated single-mindedly on their studies throughout school, college and university, and found this purpose in life to be congenial and rewarding. In the rarefied hothouse of a research university, their work narrows and intensifies so that they spend long hours in concentrated study, cut off from the more varied lives that most of us have. The absent-minded professor who is hopelessly out of touch with the world, socially inept, and completely unable to communicate his great knowledge is, of course, a caricature, but, like most caricatures, it has elements of truth in it.

Mary Lawson's delightful novel *Crow Lake* features a young university lecturer whose dedication to scholarship deeply affects her relationships with those close to her. She sums up her regrets at the end of the book:

"Great Grandmother Morrison, I accept that the fault is largely mine, but I do hold you partly to blame. It is you, with your love of learning, who set the standard against which I have judged everyone around me, all of my life. I have pursued your dream single-mindedly; I have become familiar with books and ideas you never even imagined, and somehow, in the process of acquiring all that knowledge, I have managed to learn nothing at all."

It's not difficult to find scholars who, although they may not recognise it, have ended up in that situation. By its very nature, scholarship is a lonely and self-centred occupation which has few points of contact with other people's lives. It is not therefore surprising if some academics emerge from their prolonged periods of isolation somewhat short of the people skills and understanding of human behaviour that is so important in a teacher. Research and teaching clearly have important points of contact, but the lifestyles of those who practise them are very different - so different that the combining of the two roles almost requires the teacher/researcher to be a dual personality.

Beneath universities' veneer of self-sufficiency, there is a recognition of this situation and the challenge that it poses. It was my experience that, once staff strongly opposed to the idea of training for the teaching role had got a mandatory rant out of the way, they'd usually enter into a reasonable conversation about teaching principles, and perhaps even attend an occasional workshop or agree to a departmental inset day. Occasionally well-established lecturers would come along for some advice.

A senior lecturer who obviously cared about his lecturing came to me for some help with a special assignment, a memorial lecture that he had agreed to give in New Zealand in honour of his father, a distinguished academic. The address would summarise his father's research findings and suggest ways in which his work might be taken forward. We adjourned to a lecture theatre where he began reading his carefully-prepared speech. The opening paragraphs were domestic reminiscences of his 'dad', which sat rather uneasily within the context of a read paper. I raised the possibility of this part of his speech being delivered less formally, that is, being spoken rather than read. I suggested that, if he employed speech rhythms and made eye-contact with his audience, he'd probably find that what he said would have more immediacy and impact. The improvement was marked and I was encouraged to advocate his continuing in the same way, which he did for a short time to promising effect. He naturally lost some fluency, but accepted the point that the gain in audience contact would more than compensate. He appeared a willing convert to the concept of lecturing by speaking, rather than by reading, and departed to redraft his paper as a series of headings that would serve as prompts for a speech.

Some weeks later he came to report on the New Zealand trip, which apparently had been a great success. The country's academic élite had mustered in numbers for the presentation and my colleague felt that he had acquitted himself well. He was generous in his appreciation of the help that I'd given him. "'No problems, then," I said, "with the changed format." Embarrassed silence. "Well," he replied, " In the end, I decided to read it."

We've all been there: planned a more adventurous way of doing something, but then got cold feet and reverted to the safety of a trusted but inferior strategy. The problem for experienced staff who want to respond positively to the call for an improvement in university teaching is that their methods have become habitual and, whilst they may be able to see ways of adjusting them slightly, contemplating a complete change of approach is a daunting prospect. One of the ways in which an effort is often made to move with the times is to attempt to get an oral response from students in lectures. Lecturers may, for example, try to ascertain how much their students already know about an aspect of the lecture topic. They ask a few basic test questions. No response. Change of tactic. "Have you encountered this before?" Silence. "Did any of you cover this topic at school?" Another silence. "Surely some of you did this on your A level course?" Apparently not.

Few students will readily contribute to a question and answer session in a lecture theatre with 60 or 80 people present, particularly if they're accustomed to a passive role as listener and note-taker. The occasional token attempt to obtain an oral contribution from a lecture audience is rarely successful, and, even if there's a response, what purpose does it achieve? Only a small percentage of students can contribute, so it's not an effective means of obtaining feedback on the level of understanding of the audience as a whole. And, with a large audience, students cannot be engaged in any meaningful way.

If lecturers wish to obtain meaningful feedback from an audience on their understanding of what they're being told in a lecture, then the technology for doing that has been available for thirty years. Lecturers can link up with all members of their audience, set questions on the course content and receive an instant analysis of the answers that shows not only the general level of understanding but those aspects of the material that have created the most difficulty. They are also able to obtain profiles of individual students and so identify those who are having major problems. If, on the other hand, lecturers genuinely believe in involving students fully in the learning process they need, as a department, to shift the emphasis away from lecturing to small-group teaching. That is of course a big decision and its effect on the quality of learning won't show immediately. Students have to get used to discussion as a way of learning. Members of staff, too, take time to develop the skills and confidence needed to make the transition from lecturer to teacher.

Chapter 9

Winds of Change

"No school, college, university or education system can in the end be better than the quality of its teaching force."

Roy Blatchford and Rebecca Clark,
Self-Improving Schools, 2016.

We are nearly all able to recall an inspirational teacher who made a major impact on our lives. My choice would be Professor Geoffrey Tillotson, who was head of the English Department at Birkbeck College when I was an undergraduate. Tillotson was a very dry, laconic character, in many ways a typical scholar, lacking the charismatic features that one tends to associate with outstanding teachers. He was an expert in eighteenth century poetic diction, not the most spellbinding component of our course. He often read poetry to us , in a quiet and wholly non-declamatory way. His understanding of a poem's meaning was crystal clear and conveyed with precise attention to structure, punctuation, rhyme and metre. The listener had the impression of being in direct contact with the poet.

Whatever we were engaged in - listening to a lecture, participating in a seminar, reading a text, writing a timed essay - Tillotson was totally committed to getting us to think for ourselves. His approach was a revelation to me, and to many of my fellow students equally accustomed to routine passive learning. He ran critical appreciation classes with groups of seven or eight students. Copies of an unseen poem would be passed round and we'd read it for a while before someone was asked to comment on it - 'anything that you notice, for example the number of lines - whatever you like.' We then went round the group brainstorming, each person making a fresh observation or building on what a previous speaker had said. When everyone had had a turn, we went round again and, of course, as we ran out of obvious things to say we had to work harder in our analysis of the poem. All contributions were accepted with courtesy: if an answer lacked substance or credibility, it was open to the group to qualify or develop it. Tillotson kept in the background and didn't pass judgement on people's comments, so you weren't vying with each other to gain praise for an erudite contribution, or holding back for fear of being 'wrong' or feeling inadequate. We were encouraged to speak freely and to respond to each other's ideas. We worked together to understand the poem, progressing from describing simply what we saw on the printed page to a critical analysis of the poet's intentions and methods, and so to an appreciation of the poem's effectiveness and impact on us. Tillotson was well ahead of his time with his Harkness methods.

Professor Tillotson was a great believer in looking for the essential truths. His advice on essay writing was to avoid the temptation to use the question as a starting point to say whatever one knew on the subject, 'going round in ever-widening circles and getting further and further away from what you are actually being asked to do'. The task, he explained, was the reverse of this - to get right inside the question, searching for its precise meaning, considering each facet and implication. It was a form of problem-solving: to come up with a direct personal answer to the question.

Tillotson's aim of full student engagement was evident from the start of the course. A few moments into his first lecture, he paused and surveyed his audience with a pained expression on his face. 'There are people writing,' he announced with studied incredulity. 'Please don't write while I'm speaking. You can't experience a lecture if you're busy scribbling.' I found this request very disconcerting at first: I realised that I'd never actually thought in a considered way about what a lecturer was saying: I had always been too busy trying to record as much of the content of the lecture as I could. And, without making notes, how could you retain the pearls of wisdom gathered in the lecture theatre in order to hand them back in a few years' time in the examination room? Tillotson, of course, had an answer to that problem.

It had been established from the outset that our involvement in lectures naturally included asking questions and expressing opinions. One of the more mature students stood up one day and referred to an assertion made by the Cambridge professor F R Leavis, the most influential, and self-important, literary scholar and critic of the day. Tillotson's by now familiar pained expression creased his face. "F R Leavis," he repeated, very slowly and thoughtfully, as if searching back into the inner recesses of his mind for some clue that would enable him to place the person named. "Is his opinion relevant? Is it more significant than your own, Mr Levy? Why, your name is almost the same as his."

Mr Levy had broken a golden rule: we were forbidden to read the critics. We had personally to analyse, criticise and evaluate the works that we read and give a personal response to them. As part of this process, we came to understand that other people's opinions, no matter how scholarly, were not necessarily more pertinent than our own, simply because they appeared in print. What mattered was how the literary works affected us, not what someone else thought about them. The authority of the printed word is often unjustified, a point driven home by a seminar in which we looked at the discrepancies and shortcomings of the much-vaunted Oxford English Dictionary, an exercise that fortuitously led to my discovering the unsung but superior merits of the Chambers equivalent.

The requirement to make our own judgement of the literature we studied was another culture shock. Although in the past I'd obviously formed opinions on the books I'd read, I don't think it had ever occurred to me that these might be acceptable as scholarly literary criticism. My essays had been a clumsy fusion of what I'd been told in class and the views of various critics, whose authority I'd simply taken for granted. Sometimes I would acknowledge sources, but most of the time I plagiarised unashamedly, stringing together extracts from different writers without even attempting to put them into my own words. No-one ever questioned this lamentable practice and at Borough Road Teachers' Training College it had earned me consistently high marks.

Birkbeck gave me a totally new perspective on the education process. I learnt more about the study of literature in one term than I'd gained from the whole of my previous 15 years' experience of formal education. Such is the power of great teachers to bring light to the darkest corners of the education system. As a staff trainer, I was naturally always on the lookout for successful practitioners. Academics in the Tillotson mould were invaluable allies in the drive for improved learning and teaching and I was quick to recruit them to assist with the staff development courses for which I was responsible. Most of my helpers were lower in the hierarchy than Tillotson had been and I quickly became aware that it was sometimes appreciated if their involvement in the process of training staff in the teaching role wasn't given too high a profile - for fear it came to the notice of their department's professorial grandees and reduced their chances of promotion.

This reprehensible situation in which successful university lecturers feel it is expedient to keep quiet about a commitment to their teaching role is at long last being exposed and stamped out. There is an interesting climate change taking place in the university world that is encouraging staff who have long been concerned at the poor quality of much university teaching to speak out and align themselves with a range of national initiatives to improve students' experiences. At the moment it's a mild breeze rippling through the system, but it's seeping even into the corridors of power in some of the research-based universities. It has raised an unlikely optimism among reformers about the future of university teaching and learning.

There have been a number of significant developments post-Dearing that have fanned this wind of change. The

ILTHE was duly established in 2002 in response to the Dearing Report's recommendation that there should be a national body responsible for overseeing and accrediting universities' in-house programmes of initial staff-training and continuing professional development. Two years later this role was taken over by the Higher Education Academy (HEA), which was formed to centralise the work of several different bodies concerned with learning and teaching in HE. Universities were strongly resistant to the idea of a standard programme of training and staff development, arguing, not entirely without justification, that each institution had unique features and therefore needed to design its own programme in accordance with its particular situation and contribution to student learning. The HEA has had to accept this and tolerates a wide range of approaches to the challenge of responding to Dearing. All schemes, however, are expected to meet a national set of benchmarks to establish the ongoing quality of their programmes which goes by the unwieldy title of the UK Professional Standards Framework for Teaching and Supporting Learning in Higher Education (UKPSF).

Within this flexible approach to training academics for their teaching role, there are two main routes that staff can take to qualification. All universities now offer courses leading to some form of post-graduate certificate in teaching and learning. Experienced staff can apply for an HEA fellowship based on an application recording their teaching experience and a self-assessment of its quality. There is an associate fellowship available for those who undertake only a limited amount of teaching and a senior fellowship for those who can demonstrate not only a sustained record of effectiveness in their own teaching, but also a leadership or management role with respect to specific aspects of teaching and learning provision. Highly-experienced academics who have made a sustained and effective impact on learning and teaching at a strategic level can apply for a principal fellowship. Thus a university that genuinely accepts the need to improve its commitment to the learning and teaching process has a means of involving staff at all levels of its hierarchy. The initial teacher-training certificate and the various categories of fellowship are awarded internally, via processes accredited by the Higher Education Academy. The HEA also invites direct applications for a competitive 'National Fellowship' from those who are at the forefront of the current pedagogical reforms. Fifty of these are awarded each year to staff who have made an outstanding strategic-level contribution to their university's efforts to enhance students' learning experience.

The traditional autonomy of universities inevitably means that there is a wide variation of response to the initiatives set in motion by the Dearing Report. Those universities that made an early start on some form of obligatory in-service training for newly-appointed lecturers now have nearly all their younger staff nominally qualified. In addition, a few of these institutions have as many as 40%-50% of their experienced staff holding one of the HEA fellowships. This level of progress is a tribute to the energy and commitment of staff who have used the external pressures for change to bring about long-overdue reforms within their institutions. Ultimately it is the professionals on the ground who determine the rate of change.

The figures for staff involvement in some form of professional development don't tell the whole story of an institution's commitment to change. Now that the debate about the learning experience of HE students is out in the open, reformers have been able to chip away at some of the out-dated attitudes and procedures that have traditionally maintained the inferior status of the teaching role in higher education. Chief of these are the criteria for promotion, which in the past have blatantly ignored teaching prowess. One cannot overestimate the importance of providing tangible rewards for good teaching. If you want to find out how serious a university is about its teaching role, then look at its promotion criteria. Is the requirement for successful teaching unequivocal or open to different interpretations? Are successful researchers still being promoted, regardless of the quality of their teaching? Can a member of staff move up the hierarchy on the strength of outstanding teaching alone?

Promising as they are, recent learning and teaching developments in HE have to be seen in perspective: they constitute a modest start on the reforms recommended by the Dearing Committee. There is no comparison between the on-the-job training for new entrants to university teaching and the initial training of schoolteachers, with its study and observation of good practice, lengthy work placements and individual mentoring. Nearly all universities now require their probationers to undergo some form of training for their teaching role, but a small number of the more refractory Russell Group are still holding out against this. Probationary courses elsewhere vary greatly in their credibility and value. Some involve a meaningful programme of seminars, assignments and background reading that amounts to a substantial time commitment, perhaps a total of several weeks spread over a two or three-year period. At the other end of the spectrum, the requirement is minimal and falls well short of the time that experienced schoolteachers and other fully trained professionals are expected to spend each year participating in ongoing staff development activities and keeping abreast of new developments.

An HEA fellowship is an important statement requiring experienced staff to reflect on their teaching and to undertake a personal assessment of its quality, but it doesn't involve a course of training or systematic and independent evaluation of an applicant's work . The early fellows have inevitably been people who feel good about their teaching and who can readily demonstrate their good practice. They are noticeably the outgoing personalities, the naturally effective communicators, people who have perhaps had some experience of the world outside academia. And, of course, they support the initiatives their institution is taking to raise the status of teaching and the quality of student learning. As one go-ahead staff developer observed, reflecting on her university's excellent progress: "We've plucked all the low-hanging fruit; the next stage is going to be much more difficult." Stubborn resistance to change is endemic in academia and nearly every university has an obdurate core of staff who really want to be left alone to get on with their research. Some of the Russell Group are still dominated by such hardliners who have yet to accept the concept of training for the teaching role.

A number of the universities leading the way with learning and teaching initiatives have reached a hiatus with regard to promotion criteria: having established a clear route for successful teachers to be promoted to middle-tier posts, reformers are now faced with the bigger task of opening up the way to a professorship. Here the criteria remain heavily weighted in favour of research reputation. Further progress depends on the extent to which senior members of an institution are committed to change. The same is true of appointment criteria: unless the head of department wants to be sure that successful candidates will prove to be good teachers, interviews will continue the traditional practice of concentrating on research potential. We are, for example, a long way from observing applicants for a lecturing post in front of a class. That innovation must presumably wait until university teaching is regarded as a true profession for which new entrants undertake thorough initial training.

There is one aspect of the Dearing legacy that has impinged on every HE establishment. The learning and teaching terminology, to which many traditionalists initially took such exception, has now become common currency. 'High quality learning' has become part of the marketing jargon used in every glossy prospectus, adding to the difficulty schools and university applicants have in distinguishing between rhetoric and reality. A 2015 Higher Education Green Paper, *Fulfilling our Potential: Teaching Excellence, Social Mobility and Student Choice*, has addressed this problem, proposing a Teaching Excellence Framework designed "to improve the quality of HE learning" and "give prospective students more information about the teaching they will receive on courses."

It will be a big step forward if every university department is required to state precisely how its staffing practices and teaching methods justify any claims it makes regarding the excellence of its teaching. Presumably a good starting point will be to state the percentage of staff who hold a teaching qualification or HEA fellowship, and to indicate any particular interests and strengths that the department or its individual members have with regard to learning and teaching. Some universities award prizes to their outstanding teachers and these will of course be mentioned, as will any holders of an HEA National Fellowship. Then each department will need to give a clear indication of the processes it uses to promote independence in its students. It will inform students of the particular specialist and transferable skills that the staff hope to develop during the course. Then students need to know the options they will have within the course and the opportunities there will be for them to pursue personal interests, projects, investigations.

If a department is completely open in revealing what the learning experience is like for its students, it will answer other leading questions. What percentage of time, for example, is devoted to active learning - practical assignments and projects, group activities, discussion, fieldwork, work experience? What is the staff/student ratio in these various learning situations? Is the teaching entirely by academics, or is it supplemented by professionals with relevant expertise from outside the university? What is the balance between theory and application? How much of the course is devoted to the subject's historical development and how much to its current relevance? For what careers do the department's courses prove particularly useful? What connections and cross references are made between the specialist subject and other areas of human knowledge and experience? If the lecture is still employed as a teaching method, how has it been adapted to ensure effective student participation? Do the methods of assessment allow for variations in different students' strengths and aptitudes? And, of course, most important of all, how do staff ensure that their students are fully integrated into the department and receive the individual support that they all need?

Some departments will relish the opportunity to set out their wares in this honest and informative way. Others will find it a very threatening experience. But the 2015 HE Green Paper contained a much bigger time-bomb that has taken some time to register fully across the sector. The intention is to introduce strong incentives for universities to achieve not just good but *excellent* or *outstanding* ratings for the quality of their students' learning experience. All institutions will have their teaching assessed against the new Teaching Excellence Framework. The intention is that this assessment will be mandatory and that the outcome will determine whether or not a university will be allowed to raise its fees in line with inflation! Wow! The implications of that seemingly simple statement are very interesting, for this exercise would, if implemented, produce a very different ranking of universities to the traditional pecking order based on research reputation. Realistically, is there any likelihood of the powerful Russell Group accepting a measure that might well classify some of its members as second class, and unworthy of an increase in the fees they charge? All the signs are that the scheme will go ahead, but probably with 'excellence criteria' so diluted that most universities will have little difficulty in meeting them.

The research-based universities have already suffered a minor irritation in the maintenance of their prestigious status. In 2005 the HEFCE launched a National Student Survey (NSS) designed to obtain students' opinions on their degree courses. The current version, administered by Ipsos Mori, focuses on 23 multiple-choice questions about the learning and teaching experience. Students are contacted mid-way through their final year and so those surveyed are largely satisfied customers: no attempt is made to contact the 20% of students who won't complete their course, either because they dropped out or transferred to another HE institution. The annual results are analysed and published by the press and numerous consumer magazines in the form of league tables that enable comparisons to be made between institutions. The media tend to focus on interpretations of student replies to questions about overall satisfaction. The top positions in these league tables usually go to small institutions offering distinct vocational courses. The Courtauld Institute of Art and the Brighton and Sussex Medical School, for example, regularly occupy high positions. Keele and other campus universities are also highly placed, as is the independent Buckingham University. None of the 24 Russell Group universities has featured in the 10 top positions in the last two years. This has clearly rankled and added to the pressures to change their attitude towards learning and teaching.

The seriousness with which universities respond to the annual NSS results - regardless of their validity and relevance - indicates the power of league tables to intensify competition. That is their over-riding purpose - to give free rein to market forces, as a means of driving up standards. Consumer satisfaction questionnaires have become a ubiquitous feature of modern life: nearly all the organisations that provide a service for us, from restaurants to garages, patio cleaners to refuse collectors, eagerly seek our opinion on whether we're a satisfied customer.

A few days ago I had a minor operation to remove a skin cancer. In the recovery room with my cup of tea and biscuit I was invited to fill in the consumer feedback form and indicate, on a four or five point scale, whether I'd recommend the department in which I'd spent the morning. I wasn't feeling that brilliant at the time and don't recall the precise wording of the categories, but it was in the 'definitely, probably, probably not, definitely not' vein. Everyone I'd encountered had seemed friendly and competent, so naturally I ticked the 'definitely satisfied' box. Even if my impressions hadn't been entirely favourable, I'd have probably given the same response: I'm a big supporter of the National Health service and admire the way its staff cope with the enormous pressure they're under. Of course, it was a pointless question I'd been asked: I won't know for another four weeks whether the op has been successful and, anyway, I have no experience of any other hospital's ENT department for purposes of comparison - any more than students have experience of other universities when asked in the National Student Survey whether their university experience has been satisfactory. Satisfactory compared with what? Measured against what benchmarks or standards? How can one possibly sum up three years' complex experiences in a single wishy-washy word like 'satisfactory'? These glib, closed-question, consumer-satisfaction questionnaires are an extremely superficial and mechanistic attempt to measure human reaction and, as such, one of life's daily irritants. Professor Lee Harvey, a highly-regarded expert in HE research, strongly criticised the National Student Survey in *Times Higher Education,* describing the questionnaire as 'bland' and 'methodologically worthless', 'a hopelessly inadequate improvement tool'. He was the Higher Education Academy's Director of Research and Development at the time and he lost his job following his criticisms: the Establishment doesn't take kindly to whistle-blowers.

Regardless of the well-publicised inadequacies of the NSS questionnaire, universities are unable to ignore an exercise that influences public opinion of their worth. Initially, some made no attempt to encourage their students to respond to the questionnaire, but they have now all fallen into line and recognised the need to respond to the NSS initiative. Although the pace is frustratingly slow, significant changes are clearly taking place in HE, and the NSS has contributed to the trend for universities to think more about their provision, to attach greater importance to student opinion, and to respond to the various external and internal pressures to improve the quality of their students' learning experience. As its advocates point out, no matter how ineffective it may be as a measuring tool, the NSS has fulfilled its intention, that of intensifying the competition between HE institutions for recognition and status. Everyone now feels compelled to take the annual NSS contest seriously and to prepare its participants accordingly.

The aim of the game is, firstly, to get students to take part and, secondly, to encourage them to tick the right boxes. Considerable time, effort and money go into this exercise. Poster campaigns explain to students how important their survey responses are to their university's reputation, and therefore, of course, to the credibility and status of the students' degree certificates. Vouchers or raffle tickets are provided for those who answer the questionnaire and some institutions hold dummy runs of the survey to iron out any student dissatisfaction before the test itself. Accounts of some of the cruder and more blatant attempts to manipulate student responses have, inevitably, found their way into the media, including a recording of one lecturer telling students to raise their scores for, if their university comes bottom, "no-one is going to want to employ you, because they'll think your degree is shit."

Universities have nearly all learnt the most effective ways of encouraging a positive student response to the NSS questionnaire and have therefore become uniformly successful in presenting a good image. As a result, there is remarkably little variation in levels of satisfaction across the sector. Thus the league tables actually obscure rather than reveal the very significant variations in the quality of students' HE experience. In 2015, for example, 42 of the universities near the top of the general satisfaction table were separated by just two percentage points, a clear demonstration of just how useless the results are in providing a means of comparing intrinsically very different institutions. Ironically, though, the awareness that the slightest dip in their results can see them plunge 50 places in the league tables puts universities under constant pressure to hone their strategies for obtaining high student scores.

It is essential that universities obtain meaningful student feedback on their HE experience and the manifest failure of the NSS exercise to achieve that goal emphasises the importance of institutions establishing their own systems. In contrast to the NSS, feedback needs to be ongoing, sharply focused and, most importantly, formative rather than judgemental and punitive. If students see that their views are respected and that they can actually influence decisions, they will identify strongly with the institution and engage in a meaningful partnership with staff to improve the quality of their learning.

I experienced a forcible illustration of full student engagement with the feedback process whilst working for the University of New York in its Bloomsbury outpost. Two cohorts of NYU students come to the UK each year to study in London for three months and to be taught by staff from this country. In accordance with the American system, they follow a modular programme with a wide range of options, many of which are topical, and relevant to their temporary environment. They include modules in *A History of London, London's Architecture, British Cinema, Multi-national Britain, Europe Since 1945, Renaissance Art in London.* Americans value general education far more than we do and their universities have no hang-ups over students studying modules that are not directly related to their main specialism.

My assignment was to obtain detailed feedback from students on each three-month course, to analyse the data gathered, and then to lead a staff training day at which the conclusions from the student evaluations were discussed and appropriate action agreed. All students completed an extensive questionnaire, consisting of closed and open-ended questions on the key aspects of their learning experience in London. There were specific questions on how intellectually challenging the course was, how successful staff were in interesting students and getting them involved, and on staff accessibility.

Key points to emerge over a series of these feedback exercises were that students found their studies most stimulating and rewarding when they involved a range of learning situations, including opportunities for student interaction, practical work and out-of-class activities. Variety was a recurrent theme, including variety in the way that teachers used their voice and presented their material. The attitude of the teacher to both course and students was all-important: 'it's the teacher that makes the course'. The most successful teachers were thought to be those who were well-organised, enthusiastic and, most importantly, able to achieve the course objectives with a lightness of touch: 'I learned without realising it'; 'there was a wonderful balance between fun and information'; 'he leads without controlling or intimidating, and that's important'.

The less specialist, more interdisciplinary approach to study in American schools and universities resulted in some interesting nuances in student expectations. American students are very aware of the role of structure in the teaching process. They expect to see the relationship between the different elements of a course, a class session or a lecture/presentation. Whilst they value variety, they expect different learning activities to be integrated into a balanced and coherent whole. They look for the connections between theory and practice, classwork and fieldwork, lectures and reading/written assignments, and between learning and assessment. The NYU students were quick to criticise staff if they hadn't briefed them sufficiently on off-site activities or didn't appear to recognise the importance of follow-up sessions that pointed up the lessons to be learnt from fieldwork. There was a perceived need for clearer statements of agendas, policies and objectives. Structure and good organisation were thought to be especially important in class discussion. Students liked an interactive classroom, but the more astute appreciated that merely providing an opportunity for students to participate is not sufficient in itself. Discussion has to be focused and purposeful. The challenge for the teacher is to lead without manipulating or inhibiting students.

In tandem with the student feedback exercise, staff too completed an evaluation of each three-month course, assessing what had gone well and less well, and indicating features that they would seek to improve next time round. Again, I had to analyse these evaluations and produce a report for staff development days. One way of doing this was to draw up parallel lists of student and staff conclusions, which produced a form of contract that outlined the two-way obligations and expectations of the teacher/student partnership. In general, the match between the two sides of the contract was encouraging, but once again the specialist/interdisciplinary difference between the American and UK approaches to education was clear. The emphasis on structure and the need to make connections between different parts of a course, features to which students frequently drew attention, were noticeably absent from the UK teachers' self-assessments.

At the start of term an induction day was normally held for each new student intake and attended by all staff. I was allowed to change the emphasis of this day to introduce the staff/student contract feature of the course. In mixed groups of students and staff, we discussed people's hopes and aspirations for the coming three months: students described what they wanted from their teachers; staff voiced their expectations of those whom they'd be teaching. The students were asked to assume the key responsibilities for the day, facilitating discussion, recording the main points that emerged and reporting back to a plenary session. Volunteers for these various responsibilities were briefed on their roles before the induction day began. Promises were wrung from staff not to dominate discussion, but to play an unobtrusive role in helping the chairperson to create the right conditions for profitable discussion. One of the ulterior purposes of the induction day was to demonstrate to staff the student potential for active involvement in the learning process and its evaluation. These were American youngsters much more accustomed to that role than UK students are. Moreover, their initiative and self-confidence in responding to the opportunity to study for a short period in another country suggested that they would have an above-average contribution to make to their courses. It would have been a missed opportunity not to take full advantage of this situation.

I enjoyed my contact with the NYU students and found their lively and wholehearted response to each semester's evaluation exercise very refreshing. They were accustomed to completing detailed surveys on all aspects of the education that they received and were frank and direct in their comments on staff - sometimes disconcertingly so. I learnt that to an American an asshole is an asshole. But if weaknesses were spelt out in no uncertain terms, so too were the qualities of the teachers whom they admired, and sometimes disarmingly recommended for a pay rise. In the American system, student opinion counts when decisions are taken to promote or fire staff.

The following are responses to a request in the feedback questionnaire for "responsible and constructive comments you may have about this professor, this course, and/or the course material". They highlight a recurring theme: the desire to be challenged, extended, enthused - even excited - by their teachers.

(1) Module: Representations of Women

"To be fair to the professor, our class got off on the wrong foot. Many of our classes had to be re-scheduled and that was no-one's fault. But some of the class responded badly to that and showed little interest in the course.

Still, I think an improvement is required from the professor as well. I didn't come out of the class with any sense of 'representations of women'. The choice of books was more than adequate, but we didn't acquire any sense of the critical dialogue that has arisen round this question.

I didn't feel that my written assignments were challenging. Normally in literature classes I am expected to demonstrate a thorough knowledge of the texts we are studying. I didn't really feel that I had to grapple with any difficult problems when working on written assignments... they were just too easy.

The professor focused too much on objective questions in class discussions. It is degrading to have to be pointed to an answer - to waste time re-iterating what is written in the text. The mid-term test was inane. It was really insulting to have to take an objective test in a collegiate class. We ought to be showing our <u>understanding</u> of the text and giving our <u>opinion</u> on it, not just recalling facts.

I encourage the professor to be more assertive when lecturing and to expect more from her students. Excite us. And push us to go further."

(2) Module: London Theatre

"I think Nesta is brilliant. I'm so excited about the theatre now - so much so that I leave every class absolutely exhilarated, nearly breathless. I didn't give a fig before about plays. Nesta is a great conductor of enthusiasm, a great facilitator of discussion and debate. The scope of the class is brilliant. I now have the vocabulary to talk about the theatre - I didn't before. We saw a whole range of theatre, that was good too. The written assignments are enjoyable (Good Lord!). Nesta challenges me, encourages me. Fantastic. I understand why theatre is so important now - and I will continue to see it, to write about it, to talk about it in the future. Epiphany. What more could one ask for in a class?"

New York University's Nesta and Birkbeck's Geoffrey Tillotson taught the same subject, but were clearly totally different characters, one an irresistible enthusiast, the other a scholarly literary critic who gave his students the understanding and confidence to develop their own analytical skills. Good teachers have much in common, but don't conform to a precise blue print. There was an elderly lady, always addressed as Mrs Ford, who taught one of the lower streams in the tough secondary modern school in which I began my teaching career. She was a small, rotund, grandmotherly lady who must have seemed very elderly to her pupils. She was totally unassuming - quiet, gentle, placid. I never heard her raise her voice. Passing her classroom, you got a picture of calm and peaceful industry. Somewhere else on her corridor you might well have found the antithesis - a teacher shouting to be heard above the classroom mayhem. There are many different ways of motivating, challenging and inspiring children and students, nurturing their natural curiosity, giving them ownership of the learning situation, and providing opportunities for them to find their passion.

Chapter 10

Twenty-First Century Priorities

"In no country is the strife between the new and the old educations more vehement - the education that deals with mind as spirit and that which deals with it as matter. In no country are there greater anomalies - greater differences not merely in the means, but in the ends of education...it runs through the whole system. "

Thomas Wyse, 1837.

During a year's fellowship at Keble College Oxford, I met three chemistry dons who were eloquent in their condemnation of a policy that provided them with a stream of students who were apparently extremely uninteresting and boring to teach - knowledgeable chemists, but 'dull dogs' in every other respect. This wasn't merely a passing observation: the staff concerned were really taxed by the situation and had instituted a system of regular assignments to try to remedy it. At the end of each term they set their students an extended essay, to be completed during the vacation. There was always a choice of topics, ranging widely across the arts, politics, the environment, the economy, international affairs - anything, in fact, except chemistry. I got the impression that the 'dull dogs' were too set in the specialist mould to be very receptive to this belated attempt to improve their general education. My new colleagues invited me, a non-scientist, to join them in their interviewing of their next cohort of Oxford chemistry applicants to see if, between us, we could choose a more interesting bunch of students for their following year's teaching. I'm not sure that we succeeded.

Looking back at that experience, I cannot help feeling that my chemistry friends would have greatly approved of the Salter chemistry course had it been around at the time. Salters chemists wouldn't necessarily have been any better educated in a general sense, but they would at least have been more interesting chemists, able to talk with some understanding about the application of their subject to the world around them.

Our highly specialised approach to sixth-form and undergraduate learning is extremely effective in producing 'dull dogs', young men and women with little interest in, or experience of, the world outside their narrow field of study. The UK secondary school system involves a process of gradually closing off areas of human experience and knowledge that children are conditioned to believe are less important. By the age of thirteen or fourteen, students are having to give thought to the very limited learning experience that they'll be subjected to in the sixth-form. Decisions on this crucial matter are influenced by a host of factors, many of which are superficial, short-term or largely irrelevant - strengths or weaknesses of current teachers, exam results achieved via a specific assessment mechanism applied at one brief moment in time, the enjoyment or dislike of aspects of a syllabus that will not necessarily feature much at a later stage of study, the status of different options. In theory, the students with the greatest freedom in deciding on their sixth-form programme of study are those who have been consistently high achievers in most or all of their subjects. Paradoxically though, many of these students have a particularly limited choice: they are steered away from practical and vocational subjects and expected to take a traditional grouping of high status academic options.

Students are remarkably unquestioning in their acceptance of the current restrictions imposed on their study programmes, but their pleasure and appreciation are obvious when an institution defies the system and allows more freedom of choice. Many of the open-access or comprehensive sixth-form colleges that burgeoned in the 1970s have made a point of allowing their students to take a combination of courses that reflects their personal interests and strengths, regardless of the politicians' and academics' ordering of priorities; admissions tutors will, of course, point out implications of students' choices, but not unduly pressurise them to fit into traditional subject combinations which they aren't keen to take. This flexibility has been one of the great advantages of the sixth-form colleges and was an important part of the original argument for their existence: their huge intake enables them to provide a timetable that accommodates a great range of study programmes to meet individual needs, something that simply hadn't been possible in most school sixth-forms.

This liberal attitude to the sixth-form curriculum is becoming increasingly difficult to maintain. The failure of both the Coalition and 2015 Conservative Government to protect post-16 education from the repeated rounds of cuts in the funding of public services has had disastrous consequences for the comprehensive college curriculum and, as always in these situations, it is the more imaginative policies that suffer most. Reducing funding is a standard way in which politicians are able to narrow educational objectives. The ever-increasing prioritising of traditional A levels - the Russell Group's 'facilitating subjects' - has put the colleges' liberal approach to sixth-form study firmly on the back foot. A 2016 Royal Society of Arts (RSA) Report on educational deprivation, *Educating the Failing 40%*, draws attention to ways in which students' choice of post-sixteen course can be restricted by the accident of where they live. One would expect such a report to acknowledge the success of the comprehensive sixth-form colleges in ensuring the widest possible choice of A levels for students. But the Report isn't actually interested in breadth: it's really assessing the extent to which students are getting the right preparation for admission to the Russell Group universities. Thus its reference to sixth-form college education implies failure rather than success:

"We can see that students who do well at GCSE are less likely to do facilitating subjects at A level if they are in an area where they transfer to a sixth-form college from school for post-sixteen education."

In a society indoctrinated to believe that academic success is the most important aspiration for young people, parents are bound to feel some unease at the suggestion that their local college is falling short of its duty to get its students into a 'good' university. The media, of course, senses a story here, and sets about stirring conflict by encouraging the opposition to the colleges to put the boot in:

"Denis Oliver, head-teacher of Holmes Chapel Comprehensive, an 11-18 school in Cheshire, told the *Times Educational Supplement* (TES) that facilitating subjects were the most popular A levels chosen by his sixth-formers. 'We've got a culture of high aspirations and parents are very keen for their children to aim high and go to university,' he said."

A spokesperson for the colleges is given the opportunity to explain why focusing on the facilitating subjects was not the best way to meet students' needs: "It's arbitrary and , for many students, those subjects are not right in getting them where they need to be and they may not be suited to them." Some sixth-forms were offering an 'impoverished curriculum' with as few as 10 A levels to choose from. "We offer a much broader range because we think that's the right thing to do."

Thus the battle lines are drawn up.

The comprehensive colleges find themselves somewhat out of tune with the times. The comprehensive principle is, of course, in regression and the 'college concept' is also being challenged as the best way to cater for the 16-18 age group. The comprehensive colleges came into existence during a period when it was obvious that many teenagers had outgrown school and needed a halfway house between its paternalism and petty restrictions and the freedoms and responsibilities of adulthood. They were a more self-assertive and questioning group than their modern counterparts, sometimes a bit bolshie and difficult, but more interesting and lively. Today's sixth-formers are passive and compliant by comparison, and less critical of school routines. Also schools have learnt to provide their senior students with a more adult culture for their sixth-form years. These factors haven't escaped the notice of those who would like to see a return to the school sixth-form, and preferably the grammar school version. As a result, the sixth-form is making a comeback.

Although the academic sixth-form colleges, with their massive cohorts on the Russell Group conveyor belt, are meat and drink to the grammar school lobby, there is little appreciation of the achievements of the comprehensive colleges, or indeed support for their continuation. A return to the school sixth-form was seen as an intrinsic part of the academy movement: Andrew Adonis, architect of that development, was adamant that secondary school academies should have a sixth-form. With the rapid proliferation of academies, that target has proved unachievable. However, the government's desire to bring back sixth-forms remains firm and has indeed been strengthened by the drive to increase the number of A level students following specialist academic programmes, a process that is always going to be more successful in a school sixth-form than in a college that temptingly offers a wide range of other relevant options. The hold that this combined political and academic objective has over the education system is a major threat to the comprehensive colleges and the significant improvements they have made to 16-18 education. The success of the colleges encouraged their pioneers to believe that they would eventually become the norm for 16-18 education; many who work in them now fear that their days may be numbered. It's a familiar story of education reform: success eventually provokes a backlash from those who have a vested interest in maintaining the status quo.

Despite the obvious 21st century need for a much more broadly-educated and multi-skilled workforce, we cling doggedly to the old highly-specialised education system. You need to work in a university to appreciate the absurd lengths that academia will go to preserve the purist tradition. In one of my university appointments, I met up with one of my ex-students who had a senior lecturer post in the medical physics department. Alan had studied natural sciences at Cambridge but, soon after leaving university, became interested in medical research. Partly to help determine the direction of his own career, he worked on a project to establish research-funding priorities in biomedical engineering. During this enquiry, data became available from the first ever major epidemiological study of urinary incontinence, which showed that incontinence was a medical condition affecting some 3·5m UK adults. The project also revealed that the products available to help people suffering from this condition were inadequate and unsatisfactory. Furthermore, the incontinence technology section of the Directory of Current UK Research that Alan compiled had not a single entry. He became convinced that, given that there was often no fully satisfactory cure for incontinence, designing effective ways of enabling sufferers to manage their lives more successfully would be a thoroughly worthwhile project.

Supported by leading urologists and a generous grant from the Department of Health, Alan established a collaboration with two other researchers - one a geriatrician, the other a nurse - which continues to this day. Together they have conducted and sustained a multi-disciplinary research programme aimed at improving the quality of life of people with intractable incontinence. In furthering this goal, Alan has engaged in a wide range of projects encompassing the whole gamut of physical and life sciences and medical technology. He has over 250 scientific and clinical publications and conference papers to his name, lectures world-wide and chairs and helps organise the international conferences run by the two bodies that represent this branch of medical technology world-wide. He has co-authored numerous international standards for incontinence products.

Early in his career, Alan became aware that his approach to medical research was very different to the norm. The standard procedure is for researchers to focus on a very precisely-defined aspect of a traditional subject, probing ever more deeply as the study progresses. By contrast, Alan's work was essentially outward-looking: he was engaged in a collaborative effort to solve a problem that entailed research spanning traditional subject areas. He became aware that he was something of a passenger when his department had to provide details of its research programmes, as his projects didn't fit neatly into the specified categories. Nor did they sit comfortably with the standard criteria for promotion, which depended on the number and quality of scholarly articles written for the specialist journal relating to a particular specialism. Alan had an impeccable record of publication in terms of both quality and quantity, except for one thing - his 250+ articles were spread over numerous journals in a wide range of traditional subject areas representing the various branches of his multi-disciplinary approach. The university promotions procedure couldn't cope readily with this aberration and it was clear that, to obtain the professorship that his research clearly merited, Alan would have to change tack and conform to the traditional focus on a particular subject. There was no way that Alan was going to do this: he was committed to an important and highly successful collaborative and cross-curricular research project and that was how he intended to go on pursuing his career. He was happy to settle for academic obscurity within his university, no doubt secure in the knowledge of the international community's high regard for the value of his work.

There's a postscript to this disturbing example of prejudice against interdisciplinary study and research. Twenty years later, during which time his international reputation had grown substantially, Alan was encouraged to apply for promotion to reader, the level of post immediately below that of professor. However, several of Alan's external referees made it clear that the promotion should be to a professorship and the impact of his work outside academia was at last acknowledged by his university. Alan received his university's retrospective recognition of the quality of his research shortly before he was eligible to retire.

When I arrived to take up a post as Head of English at Maidstone Grammar School, I was pleased to find that the teaching responsibilities were very fairly distributed throughout the department. There was a single anomaly: one member of staff who was never given a share in the teaching of the sixth-form A level classes. I enquired the reason for this and was told by the deputy head that the teacher in question only had a joint honours degree: he'd studied English at Cambridge, but unfortunately combined it with history. I made the required change of policy unobtrusively, but thought what a good case one could have presented for all teachers of English literature to have a solid grounding in history; how much better students' understanding of the literature of the past would be if it could always be set authoritatively within its historical setting.

Generalist teachers have always been undervalued in secondary schools and are invariably at a disadvantage in the competition for promotion. The status of the subject specialist has steadily risen in recent years and, in the present climate, few sixth-formers who contemplate teaching as a career are likely to consider any form of interdisciplinary degree as a route to that end. The trend is very much in the other direction - towards the situation that prevailed in the grammar schools seventy years ago, when a single honours degree was the sole qualification required for teaching. No training was deemed necessary to manage the arid routines that prevailed at that time.

On their arrival at the Department of Education, newly-appointed ministers and secretaries of state are accustomed to declare their hand straight away, the more provocatively the better. Nick Gibb, Minister of Education for Schools in 2016, came to the Department with a reputation as an unequivocal advocate of old-fashioned methods of schooling, with rigid pupil discipline top of his agenda. His first broadside, however, was on another subject. He is said to have announced to his colleagues at his first staff meeting that he "would rather have a physics graduate from Oxbridge without a PGCE teaching in a school than a physics graduate with a PGCE from one of the rubbish universities". Presumably this would have been a statement of support for the Teach First initiative.

The Teach First scheme was launched in 2002 and based on a US equivalent, Teach for America. It was pioneered in this country by a private American consultancy firm, McKinsey and Company, for which William Hague worked before he entered politics. The initiative was funded by a powerful Canary Wharf Group of businessmen and was seen by all the major political parties as a way of 'raising standards' in inner London secondary schools. It has subsequently been expanded to include many other deprived areas. The plan, drawn up by one of the McKinsey consultants, is aimed at encouraging newly-qualified graduates to try their hand at teaching before pursuing another career, hence the name, Teach First. Successful applicants are given an induction course in the summer after graduation. They are then asked to commit themselves to two years' teaching in a disadvantaged school, usually one with multiple problems - many children from poor families, low exam pass rates and difficulties in recruiting and retaining staff. The graduates are paid by the school from the outset and work on a timetable equivalent to 90% of the workload expected of a newly-qualified teacher (NQT). If successful, they are awarded a PGCE at the end of the year and serve their second year as NQTs. From very modest beginnings the scheme has grown steadily and been extended to include the primary sector. In 2015, according to High Fliers Research Limited, it was the largest graduate employer in the country, recruiting in the region of 2,000 graduates each year.

Teach First has proved very popular with graduates. Many of those intending to teach have been attracted by the prospect of going straight from graduation into paid employment, instead of adding another £9,000 to their student loan by undergoing the normal training. Others, contemplating a gap-year, like the idea of an unusually well-paid form of community service that will also help them develop skills that will prove useful in their intended careers elsewhere. The opportunity is confined to academic highfliers - only those with a first or upper-second honours are eligible - and encourages its recruits to think of themselves as potential leaders and pacesetters, either in education or elsewhere. Apparently some have gone on after their two years of teaching to be "central to developing new thinking, approaches and ideas outside of the classroom, with over 50 working in government and policy", no doubt some of them as advisers to Nick Gibb and his colleagues at the Department of Education. Teach First applicants must offer a standard national curriculum subject: thus someone hoping to teach in a secondary school whose qualification is in a discredited subject, such as art, drama, sociology, politics, environmental studies, will not be accepted.

Teach First's close association with big businesses and their deferred entry schemes has led to suggestions that it operates as a recruitment agency for business. Critics refer to the scheme as 'Teach first, then get a better job', but the organisation points out that an impressive 50% or more of its recruits commit themselves to teaching after their initial two years. Teach First is, of course, a direct challenge to the principle that teachers need to be trained *before* they start work, as well as being mentored and supported in the early years in post. The General Teaching Council for Scotland rejected invitations to take part for this reason. Another criticism is that the recruits tend to be solidly middle-class and there have been complaints that some arrive in the schools with an inflated view of what they have to offer deprived communities, and a poor understanding of the fact that they are, themselves, in a learning situation. Teach First strenuously denies this, but has probably been unwise in laying too much emphasis on its heavy recruitment from prestigious universities: according to the organisation, 10% of Oxbridge graduates apply to join Teacher First when they leave university. Furthermore its publicity and self-congratulatory progress reports don't win over sceptics, and the organisation would be well-advised to moderate some of its eulogies on the brilliance of its young academic high fliers. Its suggestion, for example, that "the presence of Teach First teachers ...raises the teaching standards of those who teach alongside them in the same department" is an insult to trained and experienced teachers.

The Teach First scheme has been very successful in its aim to raise awareness of the desperate plight of many of our inner city schools and in encouraging young people with a social conscience to help do something about it. The big disappointment is that it is yet another initiative that re-enforces traditional and out-dated educational priorities. The élitist approach to recruitment sets the tone for the whole enterprise, which focuses on all the familiar academic and political objectives - specialisation; academic subjects; improving exam results and league table positions; the need for nearly all pupils to follow a course geared to Russell Group university requirements; intensive grooming of high fliers for Oxbridge, and so on.

Teach First could have been very different. It has an interesting dimension to its recruitment in that it accepts applications from young graduate professionals seeking a career change. These applicants are, like the other recruits, untrained, but they at least have the advantage of having had some experience of a working environment. Such people are a great asset to a school, with their broader, more balanced view of the world that many of their pupils will enter when they leave school. How refreshing it would have been had Teach First been Teach Next, an initiative to bring experienced men and women into teaching, some making a career change, others on secondment from their normal employment. What an impact that would make on a disadvantaged school, particularly if the recruits were drawn from all forms of employment and not just the graduate professions. They wouldn't all have to be classroom teachers. The public schools employ huge teams of professional athletes and sportsmen and women to support their PE staff. A Teach Next scheme, with the generous funding enjoyed by Teach First, could have brought a refreshing new dimension to the learning experience of older teenagers.

Something has to be done to break the hold academia has over our schools. Unlike Nick Gibb, I've always believed that teachers should be trained for what is a highly complex and demanding job. But if alternatives have to be considered to address the serious problems of understaffing, then let it be a scheme that brings people in who can relate to a diverse comprehensive community and reflect the wide range of interests, aptitudes and aspirations of its children. A staffroom packed with middle-class upwardly-mobile youngsters for whom academic work has posed few problems is always going to struggle to understand children from an entirely different background.

The aim of giving all children the opportunity to achieve academic success is a thoroughly laudable one. But for this objective to drive the whole curriculum and be a never-ending focus of effort and resources is to deny the infinite variety of human aspiration and potential. Primary schools are having to spend an inordinate amount of time drilling children to pass government-imposed tests to prove that they have reached standard age-related expectations, expectations that are constantly being raised. This is an artificial political exercise in window dressing that has little to do with giving children a better education. In the secondary school, the academic focus becomes even more intense with the concentration on the Russell Group's 'facilitating subjects' and sidelining of creative and vocational options. Many of the problems of inner city schools are exacerbated by the constant pressure they are under to improve 'academic standards'. In the present climate, staff and children in many of these schools live every day with the label of failure and if, by virtue of some superhuman effort or external intervention, they are able to move off the bottom of the league table, they are immediately replaced by some other candidate for public vilification. It's a spiral of misery from which disadvantaged schools as a group simply cannot escape. Reverence for the concept of academic purity permeates our education system. In any pairing of alternatives, the academic and theoretical approach to learning is afforded higher status than the applied and practical; the narrow in-depth study is always considered superior to the more broadly-based and general; the obscure and difficult route to knowledge gains more respect than the straightforward and more accessible. One of the tasks of the educationist is to challenge this false and pernicious tradition at every opportunity.

The scholarly music critic is giving a pre-concert talk to a small group of enthusiasts. He is extolling the virtues of Dvorak's seventh symphony. In passing, he indulges in a few disparaging comments on the ninth ('From the New World') - lovely tunes, but.... A sycophantic aspirant to pundit status chimes in from the audience and endorses the academic scepticism: "The New World's always being played on Classic FM." The clinching argument: it's readily accessible and popular, and therefore clearly not out of the top drawer. Why do we tolerate this sort of academic snobbery, classifying human interests, tastes, achievements as high or lowbrow, classic or popular, worthy or worthless?

Yehudi Menuhin proved his academic credentials beyond any doubt, but had no time for élitist attitudes in the arts. He believed that music was for everyone and that it had the power to change people's lives. Motivated by a desire to take music out of the concert hall, he travelled widely and forged links with musicians in many different countries and cultures. He embraced all kinds of music, in the belief that they were of equal value. He gave memorable joint performances with

Stéphane Grappelli, ex-busker and jazz violinist, and with Ravi Shankar, a sitar player with whom he recorded a Grammy award-winning album, *West Meets East.* With Ian Stoutzker, generous patron of the Arts, Yehudi Menuhin founded what became the largest outreach music project in Europe which brings music to children with special needs, to hospice patients, residents in old people's homes and others who rarely have the opportunity to hear and see live performance. He took great delight in other people's music-making of all kinds and, on a tour of South Africa during apartheid, incurred the displeasure of the government by going out to the townships and sharing in the joy of the communities' dancing and music. Those who met Yehudi Menuhin were invariably struck by his humility and genuine interest in them as people. He was an educator whose inspirational impact on people wasn't confined to the world of music.

We seem to have lost sight of education as a process that embraces everyone. At one time the grooming of an academic élite for Oxbridge was the prerogative of the public schools and those state grammar schools that sought to emulate them. Now every state school and college in the country is expected to give the highest priority to preparing their students, if not for Oxbridge, then for one of the other prestigious Russell Group universities. School and college prospectuses vie with each other to impress prospective applicants and their parents by outlining the extra time they devote to preparing 'gifted and talented' students for the academic distinction that is their birthright. Leading the way in this marketing exercise are those sixth-form colleges that have concentrated on cultivating their academic reputation, rather than developing the wide-ranging opportunities afforded by their comprehensive status. They are still nominally open-access and they do offer alternatives to A level studies, but, in creaming off the students with the best GCSE results from a wide and unspecified catchment area, they are inevitably heavily weighted towards A level work.

This situation tends to be self-perpetuating as the academic-factory image deters less academically-inclined students from seeking a place. These 'grammar-school' colleges leave no-one in any doubt of their commitment to getting their 'gifted and talented' students to the top of the tree:

"Students can expect to be encouraged to apply for the most competitive course at the most prestigious universities (for example, the College is the third largest state provider to Oxford and Cambridge universities)....Specialist programmes, including mock interviews, are available for students who will face these as part of the selection process, for example if they are applying to study medicine or to Oxbridge. "

These colleges are not content with Oxbridge success for their students: they want them to secure a place on one of the most keenly-contested courses. Kudos becomes an end in itself - for the student and, more particularly, for the institution. Musically-inclined students go on to 'conservatoires' rather than music colleges. I asked an ex-student of one of these colleges about his experience. "It was fine," he said, then added, "but I was an A student. I wouldn't have liked to have been a C student." If life wasn't too good for A level students destined to miss out on the top grades what, I wondered, was it like for the lower echelons, those not aiming at university, for example? I tracked one down.

Elizabeth was a self-assured, articulate young woman quite at ease talking to a stranger about her college experience. She got good GCSEs and took four AS level courses that would lead to A levels in art and psychology, which she felt she'd enjoy, and English language and business studies, which she chose for their relevance to the workplace. She viewed her two years at college as a preparation for employment and was quite sure she didn't wish to go to university: "I'm the sort of person who learns by doing things and I had no desire to sit in a lecture room all day listening to some old professor talking."

At the end of her first year, Elizabeth dropped business studies and psychology and replaced them with a Chartered Institute of Legal Executives (City and Guilds) course (CILEX), which introduced students to the litigation process, general legal principles and the law office structure. The course sought to develop skills and knowledge required by the members of a team providing support to legal executives, solicitors and barristers. Elizabeth appeared to have done her homework and explained that the experience and training gained with a legal firm could lead to a chartered legal executive qualification equivalent to an honours degree.

Throughout her time at college, Elizabeth was very aware of not fitting in with the culture of her college. Because of her very respectable GCSE results, the staff tried to get her to alter her decision not to go to university. Also, all her friends were intending to apply for higher education and she felt a strong pull to go with the flow. She'd clearly given the matter considerable thought, but had decided that the attraction of university social life, which seemed uppermost in her friends' minds, wasn't sufficient to make her change her mind. The other aspect of higher education that influenced many of her friends was the assumption that it would lead to a better job. Again, Elizabeth had done her homework and she wasn't at all convinced by this argument: "It used to be special to go to university but, now that so many go, it doesn't mean so much. I know of several graduates who haven't found a job."

The time at the beginning of her second year when everyone was considering their university options was particularly difficult for Elizabeth. She remembered feeling very isolated. Everyone was busy getting advice, filling in the Universities' and Colleges' Admissions Service (UCAS) forms and writing their personal statements. Tutor periods were used for these activities and were therefore a waste of time for someone not taking part in the procedure. Her tutor tried to persuade her to fill in the forms, but she resisted. She'd have liked some careers advice at this point in her course, but all the time was taken up with advising university applicants.

Elizabeth experienced another wobble when she went with her boyfriend to look round the University of the West of England (UWE), in which he was interested. She liked the look of some of the practical courses, and the students they met talked very well of their teachers, some of whom apparently had a teaching qualification. UWE didn't match her unfavourable image of a university and she had doubts about her decision. But then she later visited a friend studying at a traditional university and didn't like the environment or atmosphere at all. She wouldn't, she said, have liked living in 'the slum conditions' which her friend was experiencing.

One of Elizabeth's positive experiences in her time at sixth-form college was the interest that her City and Guilds course tutor took in her: she supported her in her aspirations and was instrumental in getting her some appropriate work experience. Even so, when she joined a law firm straight after leaving college, Elizabeth felt unprepared for the world of work in a general sense. She was very ignorant of many of the basic routines and expectations. The first few weeks were hard and not helped by the fact that her friends were out partying every night before their university courses began. She is now very settled and fully confident that she made the right decision. She feels she's been fortunate in finding a firm that clearly believes in the merits of the experience route to promotion and qualification. She's well-paid and has already had a salary increase. She feels valued by the firm, who have given her the chance to work directly with some of their clients, particularly with one or two younger people who have responded well to discussing problems with someone of a similar age-group. She also appreciates the support she's received from her parents, who have always respected her career decision.

The education system has become far too directive and unresponsive to the interests, aspirations and desires of young people.   The inferior status of vocational courses causes immense frustration, but so too does the excessively specialised nature of the academic curriculum. Very many more sixth-formers would choose to study joint honours courses and other interdisciplinary options if it were not for the stigma attached to these alternatives to the single subject honours degree.   Because of the inferior status of joint degrees, some university departments have lower admission requirements for these courses, which of course adds to their 'second best' image. A considerable number of students study for joint degrees and they clearly enjoy the experience.

A survey commissioned by the English Centre of the HEA in 2011 found that approximately a fifth of undergraduates reading English at university were doing so as part of a joint degree. Students taking part in the survey were interviewed for their reactions to their courses. Most had made a positive choice to enrol for a joint degree: they hadn't wanted to confine their university studies to one subject and appreciated having two different perspectives on learning and meeting a wider range of people.   The most frequently mentioned benefit of joint courses was the way in which one study fed into the other: "There's so much overlap.   Each subject enhances the other." Most students had been able to make useful connections between their two subjects. A number had deliberately chosen a pairing that enabled them to balance a traditional academic study with a vocational course. Some felt that, with employers increasingly looking for multi-skills, graduates who could demonstrate some breadth and versatility could be at an advantage. Joint honours students had shown initiative in breaking the mould of undergraduate study and had, it was thought, something different to offer.

The HEA English Centre's survey revealed students' concern at the lower status of joint degrees. One student who had been turned down by both Oxford and Cambridge said that her school had told her that she'd put herself at a disadvantage in expressing interest in a joint degree. This experience was not unusual: students mentioned having encountered prejudice from teachers, parents and contemporaries. They felt that there was a general assumption in society that, if you were a joint honours student you were doing less work, or less difficult work, than a single honours student. Some critics obviously equated breadth with superficiality. Yet joint honours students took their modules from single honours courses and studied precisely the same number. In fact, because the modules were chosen from two different disciplines, the course was probably more demanding, because "you're constantly changing your thinking and style". This applied also to written work: you had to be adaptable, otherwise you could find yourself being marked down in one subject for doing something that was a requirement in the other.

A number of students admitted that, when they were asked about their course, they tended to mention just one of their two subjects. In this situation they chose to mention the higher status or 'academic show-off' subject, keeping quiet about, for example, film or cultural studies. Some students went as far as choosing their dissertation from the more highly-regarded subject, even when their preference was actually for the lower status subject. When students were studying two 'respectable' subjects, they appeared less concerned about mentioning that they were following a joint course: some had found that people were actually impressed when they mentioned they were studying English and History or English and Philosophy. The indication was that the prejudice against non-academic subjects was greater than that against the joint-degree concept.

There was strong criticism of university departments' failure to liaise over administrative arrangements for joint honours students. Timetables were drawn up to enable single honours students to have a good choice of options, but joint honours students had to structure "the timetable for one subject round the timetable of the other". This inevitably meant that choice of modules was restricted for joint-honours students: "There are so many fantastic modules that you get in single honours that you are not allowed to do in joint honours." There was also a lack of liaison over the scheduling of lectures, exams and essay deadlines, so that joint-honours students were constantly encountering clashes or having to cope with situations where competing demands couldn't be met. One student complained of having a two-hour lecture in one subject, immediately followed by a two-hour lecture in the other; the four-hour commitment straddled the lunch-hour and there was no time between the two sessions to get anything to eat. Staff could be very unsympathetic and unaccommodating over clashes between the deadlines imposed by different departments. Many of the respondents felt that tutors often made no allowance in lectures and seminars for the presence of joint honours students. This is a familiar complaint. I once had the opportunity to discuss the Oxford human sciences course with a group of students: they were taking modules from several different degree courses and mentioned that one of their tutors had told them he was happy for them to attend the lectures he gave his single honours students, provided they sat at the back and didn't ask any questions.

There was a very significant omission in students' responses to the HEA English Centre's survey: there was no mention whatsoever of their universities' having made any attempt to integrate the components of their joint degrees. Students had been able to make useful links between their subjects, but this was something they had done for themselves. Their courses were run by single-subject specialists and there wasn't the faintest hint of an interdisciplinary approach. The idea of departments working together to integrate specialist subjects is quite alien to academia. Staff are extremely protective of their specialism and rarely show much interest in the work of other departments.

Academia's tightly compartmentalised approach to learning is deeply embedded in our secondary school system, although it is not quite as all-pervasive there as it is in higher education. The usual secondary school method of moderating subject-department autonomy is to establish a faculty system which seeks to develop students' understanding of the connections and transferences between related subjects. Strong leadership is required for this to be successful. Schools need to appoint faculty heads with a genuine commitment to integration and their teams should contain as many broadly-educated and multi-skilled staff as possible - people with wide interests and interesting backgrounds; generalists, able and prepared to teach more than one subject; teachers who also have work experience outside teaching.

Schools that commit themselves to this approach are, of course, swimming against the tide. The present trend is in the opposite direction - for more and more emphasis on academic purity and specialist teaching, and a corresponding decline in opportunities for other kinds of learning experience. Nothing better illustrates this trend than the changes taking place in our primary schools, which are being required to adopt the secondary school specialist approach to teaching in order to make an earlier start on academic grooming. Topic-based, interdisciplinary learning experiences are at the heart of primary school education and rightly so: if the specialised, compartmentalised approach is really the right one for the twentieth-first century, let's at least give children a view of the world as a whole before they're forced to start considering which fragments of it are worth studying.

Current educational priorities suggest a bleak future for generalists of all kinds - those who favour maintaining a broad education for as long as possible before children have to specialise, members of the networks that exist to promote holistic and inter-disciplinary approaches to the curriculum , faculties looking constantly for opportunities to integrate subjects, teachers who habitually draw on different areas of human knowledge and experience to inform their teaching and students' learning of a specialist subject. But the politicians and academic purists won't have it all their own way; as they close off one opportunity another will rise to take its place. Even if we eventually arrive at Andrew Adonis's utopia of a teaching profession in which everyone, including infant school teachers, is an academic specialist qualified to Ph D level, there will still be educationists among them who are prepared to question the priorities they are told to observe. But let us hope that a backlash to the present arid and pernicious ideology will have occurred long before Adonis's dream has been realised.

One of my sixth-form college colleagues had had a bad day. She was one of several senior tutors who co-ordinated the work of the personal tutors responsible for student welfare, and her responsibilities included the induction of new students - interviewing them, discussing their options and working out their timetables to provide them with the combination of exam subjects and general studies options that they wished to study. Even in a very large college with an extremely flexible timetable, this could at times be a difficult exercise. On this particular day she was bemoaning the administrative problems we created for ourselves by providing each student with a broad learning experience whilst, at the same time, trying to meet everyone's first choice of options. She was a classicist and suggested it would be a lot easier if we simply required all students to study Latin, which would give them an excellent general education within the confines of a single specialist subject. I don't think she was entirely serious, but I could see where she was coming from.

Specialist and general education aren't completely incompatible: breadth can be a feature of *how* you teach as well as *what* you teach. Imaginative teachers who combine their specialist knowledge with an understanding of other subjects and a general interest in the world around them can explore the breadth of a subject as well as its depth. They can use their specialism to raise awareness and understanding of other areas of human knowledge and experience of which it is just a part. This works both ways: students' understanding and appreciation of a specialist subject can only be enhanced when it is placed in a wider context where its relevance and application are evident.

There is, however, one snag. Secondary school teachers will tell you that, in the present climate, they don't even have time to deal with many intrinsic aspects of their specialist subject, let alone explore its connections with other areas of study. Their focus is firmly on the exam and the narrow range of skills and material required for their students to get good grades. One of the key roles of a teacher is to respond to children's natural curiosity and interest in learning, to answer students' questions, follow up their suggestions, explore with them unforeseen - but nevertheless relevant - avenues of enquiry that arise in a lesson. Many teachers currently feel they must ignore such opportunities, for fear time will be 'wasted' on matters that are not strictly related to the requirements of the exam.

Students contribute to this pressure by their own concern that everything they do is geared to exam success. Tony Little tells of an occasion when he was headmaster of Eton and observing a year 8 poetry lesson in a local comprehensive school. The teacher clearly had a good rapport with the class and the lesson was going well. They were reading a poem and had reached the line 'And the heart sings for freedom'. At this point a pupil put her hand up and asked the teacher if she could tell them the assessment objectives of the poem A contrived story? Ask any secondary school teachers for their examples of the way in which the system is making children neurotic about exams.

The pupil in Tony Little's illustration was 13 and three whole years away from her GCSE exam. But the preoccupation with assessment extends right down to Years 7 and 8, and even into the primary school. Equally depressing is that students take their exam fixation with them into higher education. Professor Brian Cox, the BBC's *Wonders of the Universe* presenter, deplores his students' blinkered approach to human knowledge:

"I'll be teaching my first years about relativity and they'll keep asking, 'Is this in the end-of-year exams?' I say, 'I'm not telling you. I'm teaching you to be a physicist, not to pass exams.' They are supposed to be learning about nature. If they go to work for BAE Systems on the ejector seat of a Eurofighter, at some point someone's going to say, 'Is that safe, that ejector seat?"

The only sector with the power to do anything about this absurd situation is in fact higher education. Ironically, the universities which have been such a strong ally to the government in imposing a restrictive curriculum on secondary schools have themselves an enviable freedom to determine the content of their courses and their assessment methods as they like. Admittedly, many of them take little advantage of this situation, but some do: an increasing number of courses give students broader and more varied learning and assessment experiences than is customary in a traditional degree course.

One of the most popular and well-established of all university studies is the English BA honours course. The traditional emphasis is insular, literary and historical. Few modern authors or works by foreign authors writing in English find their way onto the syllabus. Any language component has normally been confined to Anglo-Saxon and Middle English: there has been no place for a study of the language that we use today. The current Nottingham University English BA programme clearly demonstrates the difference between this tradition and a thoroughly modern equivalent. The Nottingham course aims to 'develop an enquiring mindset', 'a firm and substantial understanding of literature and language', and a range of skills that will make students eminently employable. Students have a broad and varied initial programme that gives them a basic introduction to all areas of English language and literature, ranging from Old English to practical drama and modern theatre, literary time periods and genres to themes in contemporary novels or poetry. For their final year, students put together their own programme from a wide range of modules on offer. They can range widely over the different aspects of language and literature to which they have been introduced or focus on aspects that particularly interest them. There can be a heavy bias towards the historical development of language or literature or to the contemporary scene. Students are able to undertake voluntary work or a research project in a professional environment associated with their studies; they can take a module from another honours degree subject or, like New York University students, spend a semester at a foreign university. They can also select modules according to their preferred styles of learning and methods of assessment. Thus, for example, a student might choose a programme of modules that is entirely exam-assessed or coursework-based, or a mixture of the two, thus playing to their particular strengths. The freshness and variety of approach contrast significantly with the narrowness and repetitiveness of the traditional A level English experience. Students speak very highly of the Nottingham course and particularly its responsiveness to their interests, aptitudes and career aspirations.

The greatest contrast between traditional and modern approaches in the HE sector is to be found in university medical courses. Medical degrees have always had high status and a reputation for being difficult and inaccessible except to outstanding academic students; hence the policy of the sixth-form college which, over-conscious of its academic reputation, advises its high-fliers to put Medicine top of their aspirations. The subject has stood out as a model of academic purity and has bred more than its fair share of prima donna professors, very aware of their own importance, who in turn have produced a particular type of hospital consultant and surgeon who is singularly remote from his (rarely 'her') staff and patients.

The traditional university medical course is a clear example of academia's desire to separate theory and practice and to focus on the former. Thus students spend their first three years learning the academic information on which medical theories have been based; they range widely over different scientific disciplines, but do not at this stage look at specific practical applications in any detail. The course is lecture-based, with tutorials and a heavy essay requirement. After three years, students begin their practical experience with the academics' contribution assuming a subsidiary role.

Over a period of some 50 years, universities have been gradually modifying this approach. It has been an agonisingly slow process of toe-dipping into reform, but most universities now adopt an integrated approach to Medicine in which scientific knowledge is delivered alongside clinical training. The theory still comes first, but students have an opportunity to see how to apply it in a clinical setting. It is a modest recognition of the way in which human beings learn and of the need for medical practitioners to have people skills as well as scientific knowledge. As the Royal Society of Medicine explains in its advice to sixth-formers contemplating applying for a medical course: "Integrated courses are quite similar to traditional courses but have one major point of difference: you will start some clinical work from day one."

The good news is that some universities have had the courage to commit themselves to a total policy change, focusing on the practice of Medicine and using the academic material to supplement, not drive, the course. On these courses students work in small groups, learning about selected medical situations or case studies in a clinical setting. Students observe professionals at work, share their reactions and summarise what they have learnt. They become actively involved in simulation exercises and work placements. Courses of this kind are referred to as Problem-Based Learning (PBL) or Case-Based Learning (CBL) courses, although they usually involve a wide range of learning and teaching methods. The emphasis is on learning about the real-life situations and challenges that professional medics encounter, rather than on amassing a body of scientific knowledge.

Molly sent me a very detailed description of her first year on her University of Exeter medical course, which was structured in two-week case units each of which involved sessions in life-sciences, clinical skills and problem-solving, plus lectures and a work-placement:

"The thing that I'm most grateful for with the course is how varied it is. I am never bored or too settled into routine. It keeps me engaged and provides different ways of consolidating what I've learnt, so that I can find a method that suits me. The style of learning, with lots of group sessions, means the cohort mixes very quickly, which provides a good supportive network from very early on. I've talked to friends who only know faces on their university course and for much of the time don't have people they can consult or talk with. We have much more free time than we'd get on some other courses and I appreciate this as it enables me to take responsibility for my own work.

A lot of people struggled with the problem-based learning sessions initially. It was disconcerting that groups had to define the agenda for themselves and I worried that we might miss bits out or cover unnecessary material. Looking back, I realise that we were learning all the time how to evaluate what is important in a problem and the facilitator's guidance ensured that important content wasn't missed.

The life-science-centre sessions run by practising medical staff are really valuable and I always go away from them having learnt something. The anatomy sessions involve us in feeling naked models who are paid to be guinea-pigs. We also examine each other, if it's appropriate! We get to know people on our course very fast! The life science sessions answer most of the questions that arise from our problem-based learning discussions and give us an understanding of the anatomy and physiology of each case unit. They're a knackering three hours!

The clinical skills sessions are the highlight of the week for most students. They are often really good fun. We have a chance to practise on very life-like models and pieces of equipment such as strap-on boobs for breast examination. I like meeting the doctors, nurses and medical specialists. They are real, normal, likeable people and, by working alongside them, I really feel that I get to know them. Once a fortnight one of the sessions involves a group of actors who act the part of patients in a doctor's surgery. Students have to play the role of the GP. One week it might be investigating an abdominal pain; another time the 'doctor' may be trying to obtain a smoking or alcohol history. Two students are in each room with an actor, one of whom carries out the consultation, the other observing and making notes. At the end of the consultation the actor, the student playing the GP role and the peer reviewer discuss what went well and the improvements that might be made another time. The whole session is filmed so that students can observe the consultancy afterwards.

The placements in local medical environments are an effective way of demonstrating the application of learning and I am very pleased to have been introduced to this experience early in the course. The medical school tries to engineer the placements to fit each case study, eg ultrasound for the conception study unit. They are often very interesting, particularly when we are involved in the work.

The formal lectures involve a great deal of factual material which is difficult to retain. I struggle to make any notes and often find it hard to concentrate and follow the session for an hour (often two when lectures are back to back). The general feeling is that the lectures are the least useful part of the course - much of the content will probably be out-of-date by the time we graduate and, as practising GPs, we'll need to have access to the latest developments in, for example, the drugs that we prescribe. The most useful things to come out of the lectures are the power point slides that are made available on line to students. There are also helpful follow-up sessions: each fortnight's lectures are linked to a three-hour life science session in which qualified young doctors cover the lecture content in more detail, supplying examples and leading hands-on student activities.

Assessment is ongoing and designed to help us judge the progress we are making and what we need to be doing to improve. Everyone is expected to meet the demands of the course and we are not competing for particular grades. Assessment is two-way and there are regular opportunities for students to give their reaction to the course and the ways in which it is delivered. Staff really do take notice of what we say and a number of adjustments have been made in response to students' comments. I'm very glad that I ended up with this style of course: I feel it offers us the opportunity to develop into exceptional people and exceptional doctors."

These two innovatory courses, Nottingham English and Exeter Medicine, are both initiatives taken by Russell Group universities. And there are an increasing number of such examples. They send out a very different message to the schools from that of the Group's Executive which promotes the myth that the best universities are those that focus on traditional courses, traditionally taught. Slowly the research-based universities are waking up to the fact that, far from offering inferior courses, Nick Gibbs' 'rubbish universities' are leading the way in providing imaginative and well-taught alternatives to the characteristic tired fare of the Russell Group, alternatives that students enjoy and which equip them for the world they live in. The reformers working to improve university students' learning experience are in a strong position, not only to break the hold that academic purists have long had on undergraduate study, but to weaken their pernicious influence on school curricula and pedagogy. They have the wind behind them and need to publicise their achievements in the schools and lend their strong support to their embattled secondary school colleagues.

Chapter 11

The Curse of Competition

"We have some of the best schools and teachers I've ever seen in the world, but they operate in a crazy system designed to create the maximum unhappiness."

Peter Mortimore,
Education under Siege, 2014.

Among its many astute observations on the human situation, the Plowden Committee of 50 years ago expressed the fear that the society of the future would "be much engrossed with the pursuit of material wealth, too hostile to minorities, too dominated by mass opinion and too uncertain of its values." Some members of the Committee presumably lived long enough to see their prognosis amply realised.

In the 21st century, success in life is measured in economic terms. The all-consuming focus of big business - to make the greatest possible profits - has become a model for society as a whole. Individual success is calibrated by income and purchasing power, people's status determined by the number and size of their material possessions. The media presents an endless stream of enviable lifestyles featuring material comforts once considered luxuries, but now apparently a 'must have' for anyone wanting to enjoy life. For those who commit themselves fully to working their way up the pecking order of economic success, the acquisitive desire becomes a craving that, like a drug addiction, cannot be satisfied: the more we have, the more we want - and, the more others have, the more we strive to emulate or overtake them. A bigger house, a better car, a more exotic holiday location; then a holiday home, preferential medical treatment, exclusive education for the children, cars for every member of the family, a sailing boat....   Meanwhile, the underclass, who can only watch this endless accruing of privileges and material goods by the moneyed classes, become increasingly disillusioned and embittered by the unfairness of life that condemns them to a constant struggle to provide the basic essentials.

Competition produces winners and losers.   The more intense the competition, the more divergent the contrasting experiences of success and failure. Success breeds success. Money makes money. And, as the gap widens between the haves and have-nots, it becomes harder and harder to break out of a pattern of failure. The determination and ruthlessness with which human beings now compete is evident in all walks of life, but nowhere more obviously than in sport.   The financial consequence of success and failure in competitive games is measured in millions of pounds. It was estimated that, in the final 2016 play-off game in which two highly-placed teams in the Football Championship competed for the last promotion place in the Premier League, the difference between winning and losing was £200m. That was for the club: the individual players on the winning side were of course rewarded with staggering gifts and pay increases. Sportsmen at the top of their profession, such as Gareth Bale, Lewis Hamilton and Rory McIlroy, earn twice as much in a day as the average person in this country earns in a year. The consequences of the immense financial incentives to win sporting contests is clear to see: the fear of losing, the strain on the players' faces in tight situations, the negative play and time-wasting to protect a lead, the petulant outbursts of anger when things go wrong, the furious rounding on umpires and referees at close decisions, the delirious celebrations by the winners and the abject despair of the losers. Winning is everything. Playing attractively or providing entertainment for spectators is a desirable extra, but not the main objective. How often does one hear the football manager admit - "It wasn't pretty, but we got the points, and that's all that matters"? Most fans adopt the same attitude: they're desperate for their team to win and they maintain a constant stream of abuse at anything that looks like frustrating that desire - the opposition, the referee, mistakes by one of their team.

The drama of the win/lose contrast is shamelessly exploited by the media. Every winner's clenched fist, whirling shirt and backward somersault is caught by the camera, every bowed loser's misery and tears likewise recorded. A favourite shot is of the coach trying to console the inconsolable: the player whose crucial error was the only difference in quality between the two teams. Such a fine line between success and failure, joy and despair. This voyeurism isn't confined to sport: some of the endless TV shows in which members of the public compete for money prizes or celebrity status employ aggressive hosts or judges to heighten the tension by denigrating and ridiculing the efforts of weaker contestants. The disappointment and discomfort of the losers are as much a highlight of the 'entertainment' as the ecstatic reactions of the winners.

Cricket, once considered the most gentlemanly and civilised of games, has in recent years experienced the phenomenon of 'sledging', a practice used particularly in international matches whereby players seek to gain advantage by verbally abusing their opponents. The aim is to weaken players' concentration, thereby inducing error. Young players at the beginning of their career and those struggling for form or known to be prone to anxiety are prime targets. The practice has spread to tennis: in the middle of a hotly-contested match, Stan Wawrinka was informed by his opponent that his girlfriend was having sex with another tennis player. The apparent desire to see people discomforted or made miserable is a particularly unpleasant feature of society today. A popular sporting headline is one that draws attention to a team's 'thrashing' or 'hammering' by their opponents. In the collision sport of rugby, commentators report enthusiastically on 'a great hit', that is a tackle that not merely stops an opponent's run, but flattens him so that he doesn't get up from the ground and will probably take no further part in the match. More than one captain of recent England cricket sides has declared that his team's aim is to humiliate their opponents. Winning is no longer sufficient: the desire is to crush the opposition so that their confidence and self-belief suffer long-term damage. Again, spectators share this attitude: in football, the relegation of local rivals is almost as pleasurable as their own team's winning of the league.

The 2014 Ofsted report on the need for state schools to give more attention to the grooming of élite sportsmen and women accords well with the politicians' commitment to competition as the means of raising standards. The clearest indication of the present government's approach is to be found in UK Sport's policy on investment in sport. In recent years extremely generous resources have been made available to "athletes and sports with the greatest chance of succeeding in the world stage". The aim has been to "invest the right resources in the right athletes.....to enforce excellence and challenge underperformance." This single-minded focus on rewarding and nurturing an established sporting élite has been enormously successful in terms of our enhanced standing in the Olympic medal-winning table, and it would be unpopular amid the national euphoria that this has engendered to examine the price paid for lavishing vast sums on a handful of the country's most celebrated, and often already privileged, athletes, rather than, for example, helping clubs and schools badly in need of basic sporting facilities.

Our current education policy is driven by much the same principles as those underlying our investment in sport. The aim is to define as early as possible the winners and losers in our society. The school curriculum focuses on the traditional narrow academic route to professional and white-collar careers. Children are all driven to climb the ladder to that specific image of success and, as the pace-setters emerge, they are held up as examples that the rest must strive to emulate. As children pass through the system, they become labelled as successful or unsuccessful scholars. Gradually they accept these classifications and begin to perform in accordance with expectations of their success or failure. The gulf grows between the winners and losers, and different categories of success and failure are established. Outstanding performers are quickly identified, given special support and groomed for academic distinction. These are our potential leaders, destined for academic and professional careers and management roles in business and industry. The pressure all children are under to outdo each other is particularly intense for these high-fliers who are expected to aim for places on the most keenly contested courses at the most prestigious universities. Meanwhile, at the other end of the spectrum, those being prepared for their future forelock-tugging role in society are having to come to terms with their repeated failure. Ofsted calls it "preparing them for the setbacks that life will inevitably throw at them."

The politicians who have established this convenient system have neither experience nor understanding of what life is like for the losers that it produces - and for the parents who try to protect their 'failing' sons and daughters from the misery being inflicted on them at school. Here is one parent's attempt on social media to enlighten them:

"Dear Government,

This year, you have planned that children will leave junior school with a statement that they either meet, or do not meet age-related expectations. This means that seven years of primary education are summed up with an equivalent of pass or fail.

I have a few problems with this.

Firstly, you have, by your own admission, 'raised standards'. Unfortunately, this does not mean that you have invested millions into our crumbling buildings or raised the pay of hardworking and dedicated teachers and support staff. It does not even mean that the children are being given a higher standard of education than previously. 'Raising Standards' just means that you have increased the threshold for the equivalent of a 'pass mark'. Under the new system, the teachers have to teach 10 or 11 year old children work they would not have previously done until secondary. Teachers have to get their pupils to meet age-related expectations which are significantly more challenging than they have previously been. We have the same children as last year: the same learning difficulties, the same social and emotional challenges, and yet teachers are expected to magically up their game and increase what these children learn. I feel the implication from this is that teachers have not done a good enough job in the past, and if only they tried harder they would be able to get so much more from the children. Anyone who has any knowledge of the education system knows this is not the case. Teachers are committed and dedicated to getting the best possible results from every child in their class. They are already at breaking point. You cannot expect them to work harder than they already do.

My other problem is a personal one. As a parent of a child who has medical and educational needs, I know that under the new SATs he is very unlikely to reach age-related expectations. But how am I going to tell him when he is sobbing because he has 'failed', that in fact he has exceeded HIS age-related expectations? How can I convince him that to me he is not a failure, but a shining example of success? He is the most tenacious, hardworking and brave child I know. He always tries his best and wants to succeed. No matter what, telling him he has not met 'age-related expectations' will be telling him he is a failure. When he started school, we were unsure whether he would be able to remain in mainstream education at all. The school, his teachers and the support staff have worked very hard to make sure that he has progressed and it is a credit to the school that he has made as much progress as he has. However, the fact stands that, no matter how hard he works this year, it is very unlikely he will meet age-related expectations.

Is this really fair? Can we really judge our children against a standardized norm? Do we want a generation who grow up to feel they are failures already at the age of 11?

What does it matter if a child cannot name the 'preposition' or 'determiner' in a sentence? What matters is whether he loves books and has got a love of language. It matters that he is creative and imaginative. These are not the standards by which children are judged in the new SATs. Similarly, in today's society it does not matter if you can do long division. I have certainly managed to get through a university degree and have never mastered this skill. We no longer teach our children to be inquisitive and to love learning for its own sake. It is now just an exercise in exam technique.

It is not my child's fault that he was born in the school year that all the goalposts change. It is not his fault that the new tests are judging him against standards that he will struggle to reach. In Government, you do not see the child who burst into tears tonight at the thought that he would not be able to 'make the grade'. I strongly believe that these SATs tests will have a profound effect on some children's self esteem and maybe destroy their love of learning. Do you want a generation of disaffected children? Do you want children to be reluctant to learn as no matter how hard they try they will always be found wanting? If the answer is no, I would ask you to reconsider this new change to the education system, and instead concentrate on 'raising the standards' of education in its true sense: a love of learning and the joy of achievement.

Yours faithfully,

Lucy Hoggan (A Voter)."

Lucy received over 5,000 responses from parents who not only knew what she was talking about, but were prepared to stand up and be counted. Sadly, such cries from the heart have no effect on the government: children like Lucy's son are dispensable in the drive for raising academic standards, regrettable casualties of the system, but a price considered worth paying for a higher place in the world league tables of academic success. These are the priorities of a society losing its soul and compassion, a society in which the pursuit of material wealth is all important, in which the dignity and well-being of the individual are of little importance. It is no wonder that an increasing number of parents are opting out of the system and educating their children at home: but, of course, that is not an option that most families can contemplate.

The focus on the perceived needs of one section of the community at the expense of another is utterly reprehensible. It is also ineffective: the whole raising-academic-standards policy is a shop window exercise that is undermining the education of all our children, the achievers as well as the non-achievers. David Cameron considered it expedient shortly before the 2015 election to replace Michael Gove as Secretary of State for Education with someone less abrasive and contemptuous of informed opinion. Nicky Morgan's task was to repeat Gove's mantra without causing so much offence. This she did quite successfully, but without giving the impression that she understood what she was talking about. The following letter to the *Guardian* shows just how ill-conceived some of the government's current policies are. It focuses on the policy of introducing young children to academic university routines that should have no place in schools, secondary or primary:

"As a lecturer to English language university students on analysing English grammar, I was both surprised and horrified to see that the same ability to label grammatical categories and parts of speech, such as determiners and subordinating conjunctions, is expected of ten-year-olds in their English SATs tests.

Education Secretary Nicky Morgan defends the government position on this by saying that children need to know the basics. However, it seems she has failed to grasp the basic fact that labelling language is not the same as using it effectively - just as labelling the parts of the engine does not enable you to drive effectively - and that this knowledge does not contribute to the very necessary basic English language skill of being able to express oneself effectively, both orally and in writing.

Training children for the new tests is resulting not only in a reduction in teaching time devoted to developing their oral and writing skills, but also in a reduction in both creativity and enthusiasm for language development in these children."

We're no longer educating children: we're drilling them in a limited number of skills associated with high academic achievement, in order to create the impression of progress. In the process we're stunting children's growth and potential and wasting our most precious asset. One of the biggest culture shocks that I experienced during my teaching career was when I moved into the academic hothouse of a grammar school from a secondary modern school with no tradition of homework or preparing pupils for examinations. At Maidstone Grammar School I became form master of the top stream in the fifth year (current year 11). The school was highly selective and had six streams in the fifth year. My 'A' stream charges had been drawn from the very top band of 11+ successes. However, it quickly became evident that this crème de la crème form had its own hierarchy of achievement and habitual winners and losers. Most were aiming for Oxbridge and all were manifestly capable of A level study, but a number had no intention of entering the sixth-form. After five years of being ensconced near the bottom of the form in the interminable class orders produced by their teachers, they were conditioned to regarding themselves as failures. Counselling had little effect: the spark had gone out of these highfliers and they just wanted to get away from an environment in which they were unhappy.

This is what happens in intensely competitive situations: winning breeds a confidence and self-esteem denied the habitual loser. And it happens at all levels of the success/ failure spectrum. Each form or class in a school is a microcosm of the whole cohort and produces its own winners and losers. Contrary to the government's claims, competition doesn't lead to everyone doing better: it results in an ever-widening gap between those who reap the rewards of success and those who repeatedly experience the disappointment of failure.

The top football clubs in the English premier league adopt a policy of building a large squad of outstanding players who have to compete each week for a place in the team. The theory is that the fierce competition to gain a regular place raises the level of the team's performance, but there is a heavy price to pay in terms of individual casualties. Some of the club's internationally-acclaimed players find themselves spending longer sitting on the substitutes' bench each week than actually playing. In theory, the manager of the team can rotate his players so that every member of the squad gets opportunities to play. However, in reality the intense pressure to win means that his primary aim is inevitably to field the best possible side for almost every game; thus he picks the in-form players, those who have most impressed on the training ground. Gradually, as the season progresses, some players establish themselves as indispensable team members, thereby reducing the number of places for which the other squad members are competing. All members of the squad have an outstanding record of success at the highest level, but nevertheless the system turns some of them into inadequates who lose form and thus play only bit-parts for most of the season. They move on to other clubs where, with a different manager, some regain their confidence and become winners again, but for others the experience of rejection may well be repeated.

It is the same in education: intense competition can quickly turn winners into losers. Some of the most neurotic and unhappy children in our schools are those who are constantly in fear of not living up to their 'gifted and talented' label. The educational process involves constant trial and error, being prepared to try out new ideas and then to learn from one's mistakes and unproductive approaches. The present system's heavy emphasis on perfection inhibits children's creativity and freedom to experiment: too much is at stake to risk getting things wrong. Children tend to clam up in this situation and never reveal their capabilities. Mark Rylance tells a very moving story of how, as a young boy, he was constantly corrected and criticised for speaking badly and not making himself understood. At one stage of his life he reacted by becoming totally withdrawn and hardly spoke for a year.

The most disastrous use of competitive sport as a model for our education system has been the introduction of football-style league tables that pit schools against each other in a fierce competition to meet the government's all-important criterion of educational success - the achievement of good test and exam results. These tables rank schools according to their pupils' achievements in very traditional methods of assessment and are seized on by the media with headline acclamations of the winners and castigation of the losers. The 'naming and shaming' of 'failing' schools is an essential part of government policy, the theory being that disgraced schools will redouble their efforts to get out of the bottom half of the league table. If only it were as simple as that.

Many of the general public readily accept the government's extremely limited view of what constitutes a good education and view the tables as an accurate judgement of a school's overall quality. There is a slightly less invidious measurement, still based on the narrow criterion of test results, but showing the extent to which schools improve their pupils' academic level of achievement. 'Value-added' tables are largely ignored by the media and hardly impinge on the general public. The crude exam results tables take no account of the enormous differences that exist between schools with respect to catchment area, facilities and resources, staff recruitment or any other factor that has a bearing on exam performance. This inevitably means that many dedicated and successful teachers find themselves labelled failures because of circumstances beyond their control: they know full well that, no matter how hard they work, their pupils will not be able to emulate the achievements of the 'comprehensive grammar' schools secure in the upper reaches of the table - any more than League 2 football teams can compete with the rich and powerful clubs occupying the top positions in the premier league.

The effect of the education league tables is to increase the reputation of the 'good' schools and the poor image of the 'bad' - regardless of their particular circumstances. The consequences are obvious: the 'good' schools are praised by the government and media, and sought after by parents, teachers, sponsors and employers; the 'bad' schools become pariahs, losing middle-class pupils, receiving less funding because of falling rolls, finding it increasingly difficult to recruit staff, and generally lacking support. Parental response to the league tables is particularly significant: a 2015 survey, undertaken by Opinium Research for Santander Bank, claimed that as many as one in four UK families have moved house or bought a second property in order get within the catchment area of a desirable school. Some parents use mail-drop addresses in order to appear closer to sought-after schools than they actually are. Tony Blair's vision of parental choice of school has become a reality for many middle-class families and seriously undermined the comprehensive principle.

Intense competition brings out the worst in people: the desire to win becomes paramount and there is a temptation to consider any means of achieving that aim. This is nothing new. 'Sportsmanship' was always an ideal more than a reality, but the fact that the word has virtually dropped out of use is indicative of a deterioration in the way in which we now compete. The quality desired in today's competitors is a ruthless determination to win. Thus those chosen to lead our international sports teams are more often or not hard men who aren't averse to racist abuse or a head butt or two on the football field or a sly bit of eye-gouging in the rugby scrum. Dirty play is not merely condoned but encouraged: during the 2016 European Championships, Roy Keane spoke openly on TV of instructions given to his Irish team to 'take opponents out' of the game. It's depressing to see the way in which the market forces policies of successive governments have encouraged some leaders in education to adopt comparable underhand methods to keep ahead in the league table game.

All UK comprehensive schools are expected to abide by an admissions code designed to ensure that they do not select on grounds of ability or social class, but there are numerous ploys that schools can adopt if they wish to ignore this principle. Faith schools are, for example, notorious for the complexity of their admissions criteria, which create multiple opportunities for parents to make spurious claims concerning their religious beliefs, and for the school's leadership, if they are so inclined, to pursue a policy of selection and discrimination. The London Oratory School, the Roman Catholic school to which Tony Blair and Nick Clegg chose to send their children, was given a sharp reprimand in 2015 by the government's watchdog, the Office of the Schools Adjudicator, for cheating over admissions: the school was found to have broken admissions rules in over 100 different ways. The school appealed against an injunction 'to rewrite its admissions policy to lessen the degree of discrimination on all fronts'. The Secretary of State's response to this conflict was to propose a curb on objections to school admissions arrangements by organisations such as the British Humanist Association (BHA) and the Fair Admissions Campaign (FAC) who continually draw attention to the malpractices of faith schools. This attempt to silence the whistle-blowers was, however, strongly opposed, particularly in the House of Lords, and the government was eventually forced to admit that the overwhelming majority of the BHA and FAC accusations were well-founded. The London Oratory School eventually withdrew its appeal and agreed to comply with the instruction to change its policies. However, the Government has subsequently abandoned attempts to require schools to play fair over admissions and the implementation of the September 2016 Green Paper would ensure that faith and free schools would be released from any such obligations.

When Sir Tim Brighouse was appointed Commissioner of London Schools in 2002 with a brief to improve the very low levels of academic achievement in many of the capital's secondary schools, he found that schools were even then 'playing fast and loose with admissions systems', exploiting loopholes in order to improve the quality of their own intake at the expense of their competitors. The intense competition between London schools was proving extremely destructive. Thus an essential strategy of the highly successful London Challenge initiative that Tim Brighouse put in place was to establish a framework for schools to work together, supporting each other and sharing best practice through a range of joint activities, programmes and publications. Schools had to learn a new language of shared values and purpose, and adopt unfamiliar processes of communication and co-operation. This was not easy for people unpractised in working in teams or solving problems through consultation and compromise. Such invaluable experiences are a very low priority in an education system obsessed with training children to outdo each other.

Another area of the education system where cheating is common is in the administration of the primary school SATs. Teachers are under intense pressure to ensure that their school does well in the league tables, but caring staff find it very distressing to see the anxiety and strain that these tests induce in many young children. It is thus not altogether surprising that some schools find devious ways of helping their pupils to produce correct answers. These ploys include coaching pupils on the test content in advance, giving help to pupils during the tests, altering finished scripts, and leaving useful wall displays uncovered in rooms used for the tests. The Standards and Testing Agency received over 500 reported instances of malpractice in 2013, a tip of an iceberg that suggests the whole exercise was probably invalid. In an earlier year, the school at the top of the SATs league table was found guilty of serious cheating and had to write to parents to inform them that none of the school's results were accurate.

Sir Anthony Seldon, Vice-Chancellor of Buckingham University and previously Master of Wellington College, has been a persistent critic of the way our society worships at 'the high altar of academic qualifications'. In an article in 2015, he claimed that our schools have been subjected to 'a hideous lie': that 'they only exist to get people exam passes, and that what can't be examined or tested is inappropriate and a waste of public money.' This 'pernicious philosophy' he said 'had been allowed to rip the heart out of schools'. Seldon has a penchant for dramatic observations on education and, at the time that he wrote this, I rather assumed that it was merely a colourful way of indicating how the focus on preparing students for assessment - and one limited form of assessment - has skewed the whole curriculum and significantly narrowed young people's learning experience. I now suspect that he was implying more than this. 'Ripping the heart out' is an apt metaphor for what is currently happening in our schools. Faced with the incessant pressure to improve their school's test and exam results, the character of teachers is changing, along with the new priorities. The ideals and aspirations that brought them into the profession are being eroded and their desire to work with young people to build a fairer and more just society is being stifled by the pressure to focus single-mindedly on the politicians' arid agenda.

A few weeks ago I experienced one of those uplifting moments that remind one of people's essential generosity and goodness. Upon returning to an underground car-park from some late afternoon shopping, my wife and I couldn't get our car to start. We were going on from our shopping expedition to see one of our grandchildren playing the lead in the final night of his school's production of *Crazy for You* but, by the time we'd established that there was something more seriously wrong than a flat battery, we had more or less resigned ourselves to missing the show. However, approached by a young couple who asked if they could be of any help, we said we'd appreciate a lift to a taxi rank. Apprised of our situation, they quickly offered to take us to the theatre 15 miles away and brushed aside our protests at the inconvenience that this would cause them. They were going out for the evening and had to ring to say they'd be late at their destination as a result of the considerable detour entailed in helping us.

As we chatted on the journey, it emerged that one of our good Samaritans had recently attended a comprehensive college that I knew by reputation. I asked about her sixth-form experience and she plunged into a very full description:

"I became disillusioned with my sixth-form college. The courses were good, but I felt the teachers weren't interested in me as a person. They wanted me to fit in with their plans, rather than support me in what I wanted to do. They only seemed interested in ensuring that students got the best possible exam results to add to the College's academic reputation. I had this feeling right from the start - before I started, when I went for my interview to discuss my A level options.

I wanted to study English, Psychology, Business Studies and Drama. I'd got good GCSE results and knew I could succeed on an academic programme, but I wanted to study a fun subject as well. Drama was an obvious choice. I'd been in a very good Youth Theatre for five years and took part in the All-England Drama Festival. We also performed in Paris.

I wasn't thinking of a career in drama, but it just seemed a good idea to have a break from academic work.

My best GCSE results had been in English, maths and languages and the tutor who interviewed me tried very hard to get me, firstly, to specialise in languages, and then to include maths in my choice of subjects. I was quite sure I didn't want to study either languages or maths and stuck to my choice of subjects. But, as soon as I got to college, I was put under pressure to drop drama and take four academic subjects. In the end I gave in and started the maths course, instead of drama. I came to enjoy the maths, but was still resentful that I'd not been able to study what I wanted. I also found the four academic subjects took up all my time. I worked hard and had no break, no life outside my studies.

Part way through my first year my grandfather had a heart attack and died. We're a very close family and I'd seen my grandfather almost every day of my life - he lived close by and I was always calling in. I found his death very upsetting. I couldn't concentrate and started missing lessons. I went to College but just sat in the library. My mother contacted the College to explain why I had not been attending classes and she was asked by my maths teacher to come in with me to discuss the situation. By the time this happened, I'd started going to classes again, but my teacher was very aggressive, saying that my absence was 'not acceptable'. My mother again explained about my grandfather's death and its effect on me. The teacher showed no understanding and seemed unwilling to accept my mother's explanation, saying, 'That might be so'. Those were her exact words - 'That might be so'. She was extremely rude - I'd never experienced anyone so rude. My mother was very upset at the suggestion that she'd lied. When she got home she took a photo-copy of the death certificate and sent it to the maths teacher. She never received an apology.

I'd only missed six days - not a particularly long time - and when I took my mock AS levels I did better than most students. There was no sign that my absence had affected my work. During the grieving for my grandfather, which went on for a long time, I got good support from my friends, but no teacher ever asked me how I was. My personal tutor, who also taught me for English, never said anything. My work in English hadn't been affected by my absence, so she may not have noticed that I'd missed some lessons. I was still having a bad time, just going through the motions, going to college, attending lessons, returning home, studying all evening. I worried about my work and the upset with my maths teacher had left me thinking that I might get kicked out because of what had happened. I became very secluded and, towards the end of the spring term, was diagnosed as suffering from anxiety.

In my AS levels in June I did well, coming in the top 5% of the year. During the summer holidays I thought a lot about what I was going to do. My mother didn't want me to return to the College and I considered transferring somewhere else. But my first year experience had set up in my mind the fact that college was really only for people who wanted to go to university. I'd never wanted to. I knew people who'd been to university and wished they hadn't. I'd intended to start work after A levels and so I decided to look for a job and not take A levels. "

Colleges with an intense focus on academic results will inevitably produce casualties of this kind, but this particular ex-student had attended a genuine comprehensive college which I knew had an excellent reputation for putting students at the centre of the educational process, responding to their needs and caring for them as individuals. Its prospectus stresses the college's diverse community and its commitment to celebrating difference. To hear of attitudes so far removed from these aspirations was an alarming indication of how corrosive the power of the counter ideology has become. I found myself looking for excuses for the college, hoping that what I'd heard wasn't true. Perhaps the mother had handled the interview badly and antagonised the teacher, or maybe there was a hidden agenda of some kind. Yet so much of the detail of the account rang true. The pressure to succumb to the Russell Group's preference for students to study an exclusively traditional academic combination of A levels and the grind and monotony of spending every available moment striving to do better than other students - these are increasingly common student experiences. The variety of opportunities that life offers the 16-18 age group make it one of the most exciting and potentially rewarding stages of young people's development. To impose a work ethic of such intensity that students feel that at this stage of their life they must put all their personal interests aside in order to concentrate on their specialist academic studies demonstrates just how far we have moved towards the kind of control over young people's lives normally associated with a totalitarian state. The principle of present sacrifice for future rewards runs through the whole of our educational system and is the cause of lost opportunities and much unnecessary unhappiness.

The 1989 United Nations Convention on the Rights of the Child stressed the need for children to have space for leisure, play and relaxation and to be given opportunities to take a full part in recreational and cultural activities. We still pay lip-service to that idea, but the lives of many schoolchildren are now dominated by the work ethic that has spread throughout the system. I recall an occasion during my time as a grammar school head when a parents' meeting was enlivened by a debate on the merits and demerits of homework and a number of those present argued strongly that homework interfered with the many more worthwhile activities that their sons and daughters wished to engage in out of school. I had a lot of sympathy for that view, but was engaged in getting rid of a number of other grammar school sacred cows at the time and thought it unwise to add another to the list. I've often wondered how the parents would have divided on the homework issue, had I put it to the test. Letchworth, the first garden city and home of a well-known progressive school, had more than its fair share of liberal thinkers: I might well have got away with a 'no homework' policy. I regret not trying. Such a reform would, of course, be unthinkable now. The grammar school homework system has spread throughout the secondary sector and is now making heavy inroads into primary schools.

There has been considerable research into the usefulness or otherwise of homework - as I know to my cost, for I was required to review it all at one stage of my career. Some researchers claim that students benefit from doing homework; others that they don't. Most studies are inconclusive. As with much research, some of the conclusions reached seem to relate more closely to the researcher's prejudices and premises than to the evidence gathered during the research process. My own contribution to the received wisdom on this subject entailed a study of the attitudes towards homework held by pupils in some of the comprehensive schools from which students transferred to the sixth-form college that I was leading at the time. Eight hundred and forty-six pupils from three different schools completed an extensive questionnaire on their homework experience. The responses were remarkably uniform, showing no significant variation between schools, age-groups or the two sexes.

Researchers are prone to discovering the obvious, and my first finding was that children didn't like homework. So no ground-breaking revelations there. But the difference between children's attitude towards school and towards homework was interesting: over half said they enjoyed school, but a mere 2% admitted to the same feeling about homework. A significant number rushed their homework, or did it on the way to school, or copied others' work. Some simply didn't do it, offering an imaginative range of excuses. The majority completed their homework, but did so in obedience to the system - to satisfy teachers and parents, and to avoid getting into trouble. They rarely seemed to be motivated by a genuine interest in the set tasks or by seeing any purpose or intrinsic value in extending their school work into the evenings and weekends. There was virtually no evidence of a developing expertise in the organisation and management of their homework: the sixteen-year-olds appeared no more confident or competent in dealing with the homework situation than the younger pupils. There was a lot of frustration over the process and the time that had to be devoted to it, time that children would have liked to spend in other ways. As one of the youngest respondents commented: 'Well, homework's all right but, you know, there's a whole world out there.' Other problems that received frequent mention were: uncertainty over the instructions given, not having the right books or equipment, a sense of inadequacy when they were unable to complete assignments satisfactorily, and anxiety about getting into trouble. Children rarely mentioned the difficulties they experienced with homework to their teachers and were careful not to reveal the extent to which parents had helped them, or actually done the work for them.

Homework suffers badly from the assumption that 'more is better': if children work longer hours, they'll learn more and so get better exam results. Not true. It's the quality and effectiveness of what you do that matters, not the time you spend doing it. During my eighteen years as principal of a sixth-form college that reduced A level work to minority time, I never had reason to worry that students' exam results suffered as a result of their receiving significantly less instruction than in other institutions. Rather the reverse: with the reduction in staff/student contact time, teachers weren't able to talk their way through the syllabus: they had to develop students' understanding of how to learn for themselves, which not only served students well in their exams but prepared them for the independence expected of them when they left college for employment or higher education.

There is no doubt that we attach too much importance to the quantity of children's homework and not enough to its quality. The relationship between class-work and homework needs to be thoroughly overhauled. There are too many situations in which children receive information and instruction in class and then have to apply what they have learnt for homework. In the technological age, children have excellent opportunities for informing themselves on topics that have traditionally been taught didactically. They need, of course, to receive professional guidance on how to evaluate, select and make use of the information they gather, and this is the teacher's role. Homework used to be called 'prep' and we need to consider ways in which that concept is relevant today: children learning at home in preparation for class where they can apply their knowledge with the teacher available to provide advice, to answer questions and to ensure that children understand what they are doing. Some parents are, of course, willing and able to fulfil that role when the work is done at home, but many are not. Moreover, the quality of study is greatly enhanced by ordering learning experiences so that homework leads into class-work, rather than the other way round. The Brighton, Hove and Sussex Sixth-Form College promotes this approach, calling it 'flipped learning' because it reverses the traditional process.

Discussion is an obvious example of the benefits of using homework to prepare for class-work. Without preparation, many students are ill-equipped to participate in discussion and there is a tendency, particularly when a new topic is being introduced, for the process to become a question and answer session between the member of staff and a few generally-knowledgeable and confident children. If the whole class prepares for a discussion, everyone is in with a chance of contributing - or at least of understanding what people are talking about. The other advantage of using homework as preparation for what is going to be done in class is that teachers soon find out just how effectively children have carried out their homework tasks. And they're not having to mark exercises that may have been completed largely by parents.

The emphasis on homework quantity rather than quality simply reflects the whole education system, which is caught up in a frenzied work ethic of ever-increasing demands on children and teachers. Schools are so busy responding to the politicians' agenda that they often haven't time to think about the nature of the experience children are being offered. Anyone who did national service or was a regular soldier in the ranks will find this situation very familiar. The first thing you learnt in the army was total submission to the system: you had no identity as a person, only as a number. You were someone else's property - to be hounded with a barrage of instructions and directions from morning to night, ordered from one activity to another in quick succession. You became punch-drunk, an automaton with no mind of your own, going through the motions each day until you could crawl, utterly exhausted, into bed at night. A great deal of the time was spent on window dressing, painting boulders that marked pathways, 'squaring off' bedding so that sheets and blankets were folded identically, polishing the mess cans used as dishes, and so on. Much of the bullshit, such as the cultivation of a shining layer of polish on one's boots or the scrubbing of barrack room floorboards with toothbrushes, was utterly pointless, devised simply to demonstrate the power the non-commissioned officers had over the recruits. You were routinely abused by the sergeant-major whose avowed and successful aim was to make himself as loathsome and unpopular as possible.

I'm constantly impressed that so many teachers remain loyal to their principles and manage to overcome the problems that the system throws up. In recent years, the level of political control of education and the constant changes of personnel and variations of policy by different governments have made the professionals' task increasingly difficult. The plethora of shop-window tasks, accountability requirements, reporting and recording procedures has added enormously to staff workloads, and recent research shows that teachers undertake more unpaid overtime than the staff in any other occupation. A survey of 2000 teachers revealed a startling level of stress: 84% stated that they had suffered from mental health problems at some point over the previous two years.

The politicians are dismissive of claims that teachers are suffering from stress and low morale and actually see complaints of overwork as a vindication of their policies and a cause for self-congratulation. Sir Michael Wilshaw, the combative Chief Inspector of Schools from 2012 to 2016 made it clear that " if anyone says to you that staff morale is at an all-time low, you know you are doing something right". This is a line that the *Daily Mail* has adopted when defending Michael Gove from criticism from the teaching profession. During his reign, Michael Wilshaw pursued a vigorous and punitive crusade against perceived weak teachers, occasionally expressing his views in a way that implied that the profession as a whole was insufficiently committed and hard-working. Assertions, for example, that teachers don't know what stress is, and should stop moaning and get on with their job, caused immense resentment.

The adversarial stance adopted by Ofsted towards the teaching profession is a major factor in teachers' current low morale and the growing number leaving the profession. Teachers would like some respect for the work that they do, an inspection system that recognises the difficulties they face and the things they succeed in, as well as the areas that need to improve - and a service that provides tangible support and encouragement in rectifying weaknesses that have been identified. Bully-boy tactics can cow people, but they won't win support for your policies. Ofsted's confrontational approach breeds resentment, particularly in schools that know that, whatever they do, they're likely to remain in the lower reaches of the league table. But even the successful schools feel threatened by the current style of inspection. The head of one of my nearby infant schools tells me that she goes to work every day apprehensive that it will bring the news that the inspectors are to visit. She has no reason for thinking that the school is failing to maintain its 'outstanding' rating, yet the anxiety is there all the time. The government sees this as a healthy sign that its drive to make the teaching profession work harder is having the desired effect. But leadership jaundiced by anxiety harms teachers and eventually learners. The teaching profession views Ofsted as judgemental and punitive, devoid of any supportive role. When I obtained my first headship, one of the first letters I received congratulating me was from a member of the inspectorate, an English specialist who had been very helpful to me as a head of department. Chalk and cheese.

In the classroom, teachers are finding themselves getting further and further away from those whom they teach and thus becoming increasingly deskilled in dealing with children. The emphasis on a standard, externally-imposed body of knowledge, that has to be learnt for exam purposes, limits opportunities to tap into children's own agenda. There is less and less time to respond to their individual interests and views, to exploit their natural curiosity, and to answer their questions. And less time to get to know pupils as individuals, to listen to what they are doing outside school, and to support them when they are going through a difficult patch. Knowledge-based syllabuses grow in size and, in the struggle to cover the ground , teachers are conscious of sifting out everything from their lessons that isn't strictly relevant to the assessment process. They complain that they find themselves only ever talking to children about their exam work and potential results.

At a time when children are experiencing unprecedented pressure to work harder, the school care systems that help them cope with the stresses of growing up are being systematically eroded. GPs and mental health charities all report an alarming increase in stress -related disorders and illnesses in children, including those in our primary schools. The director of campaigns, policy and participation at the mental health charity, Young Minds, comments:

"We are sitting on a mental health time-bomb and the more we put young people under extreme pressure to achieve academically, the more we are storing up problems in adulthood that will cost us dearly in NHS and social care costs."

The financial cost of teachers' dwindling care role is already being felt by schools. One Hampshire 11-16 comprehensive in a very middle-class catchment area is spending £200,000 a year on non-teaching medical and counselling staff. We are moving from prevention to cure, having to accept that our system makes our children stressed and unhappy and trying to deal with the consequences. When teachers get a moment to reflect on their declining job satisfaction, the loss of meaningful contact with children is a significant factor. The work they want to do, and for which they trained, has changed significantly. It's not surprising that so many of them are deciding to leave the profession. By no means all of them are being replaced. There is currently a generally-recognised crisis of recruitment, partly concealed by the employment of a large number of part-time, temporary and unqualified teachers and by the heavy recruitment of teachers from abroad. The education system would, like the national health service, not survive without its immigrant employees. The most depressing feature of the teacher recruitment problem is the number of new entrants who give up after a few years. Peter Hyman, one-time strategist to Tony Blair and now an innovative head-teacher, comments:

"More than 40% of teachers leave within 5 years of starting. To see their enthusiasm on day one and witness the slow erosion of their heart and soul is desperately sad."

Chapter 12

Returning Education to the Learners and Teachers

"If we are to harness the energy of this brilliant generation of teachers, if we are to design schools that genuinely prepare children for life in the 21st century, and if we are to stop the haemorrhaging of talent from the teaching profession, then we need a revolution in the way we treat teachers, develop their potential and nurture their creativity."

> Peter Hyman, The Courage
> of our Convictions, 2016.

Most of us can identify turning points in our careers, fortuitous opportunities or changes of direction that made a significant difference to our lives. I've always considered myself extremely fortunate to have been given the opportunity to help promote a new approach to sixth-form education, in the form of the comprehensive 16-18 colleges pioneered by the Hampshire Education Authority. The excitement of working in collaboration with enthusiastic teachers and LEA officers to establish an entirely different kind of educational provision was a formative and very rewarding experience. It was an excellent example of what can be achieved by people united by a shared vision. The London Challenge initiative was another.

These of course were localised reforms. The Finnish education system provides a remarkable illustration of what can result from co-operation at a national level. In the last 40-50 years, Finland's and the UK's education systems have moved in opposite directions: Finland's from highly centralised control to local responsibility; the UK's from local authority responsibility to central government control. And the ways in which these changes were brought about were equally contrasting. Finland's reforms were carefully planned, with school principals, teachers and municipality representatives - all of them, significantly, with professional experience in education - engaged in an intensive collaborative exercise to agree and implement principles and policies. Also involved in the planning process were the teachers' national union (the OAJ), teacher educators and researchers from the universities, and various other stakeholders. The changes in the UK have been introduced piecemeal over a considerable period of time with governments of different persuasions steadily reducing the role of local education authorities and, in the process, largely ignoring the views of the teaching profession and educationists in general. In Finland the changes were widely supported. In the UK they have deepened the corrosive divisions in our society.

The Finnish education system is based on equity and inclusivity. It has been strongly influenced, as the Plowden Committee in this country was, by the teaching of the American reformer, John Dewey, who believed that the purpose of education was not to acquire a predetermined body of knowledge and set of skills, but to realise everyone's individual potential to the full. There are also clear indications of the influence of another American, Howard Gardner who, in his work *Frames of Mind: the Theory of Multiple Intelligences*, exploded the myth of a single intelligence.

Finnish schools are fully comprehensive and unstreamed. There is no strong tradition of élite institutions, state or private, and parents normally send their children to the neighbourhood schools. In a study of its member countries' education systems, the world Organisation for Economic Co-operation and Development (OECD) concluded that Finland achieved the highest level of equity between schools. The aim is to have a good school for every child and for all children to do well in the development of their individual potential. Children are not measured against some designated age-related norm and then classified as above or below average, successes or failures. There is no attempt to identify and groom an academic élite for exam success at the expense of other children's education. The Finns are very sceptical of the world-wide drive to produce exam successes that will give countries a high ranking in the PISA tables. They do not wish their schools to be judged solely, or mainly, on their results in public exams: they want their children to be educated, not drilled in a limited number of set routines. Consequently, their society is largely free of the frequent testing, the constant instruction and practice in exam techniques, and the widespread cramming by private tutors that are common in many education systems across the world. All schools provide a broad and balanced learning experience, not merely recognising, but celebrating, the diversity of their students and the range of their practical, artistic, vocational and academic interests and strengths. Non-academic courses don't have the inferior status that they have in this country and some 40% of students complete their education in vocational colleges. Whenever possible, children with special needs are retained in mainstream education and schools are accustomed to supplying extra support for students experiencing temporary difficulties, as well as those with ongoing problems.

Finnish schools take the health and welfare of their children very seriously. Their teachers would be horrified if they were to witness the distress and misery that we inflict upon even the youngest of our schoolchildren by the pressure we put schools and individual pupils under to outperform each other in public tests and exams. Finland honours the principle of the United Nations 1989 Convention on the Rights of the Child that children should have time and space to be children, and not have to study and work all the time. Thus Finnish schools have a shorter school day and set less homework than their UK equivalents. Teachers' involvement in pupils' appraisal reduces the anxiety that formal assessment systems tend to generate.

A new national framework for the Finnish curriculum was drawn up in 2014, since when municipalities and schools have been working together, to a deadline of autumn 2016, to revise each school's curriculum to ensure that it is up-to-date and relevant. National guidelines include a requirement for all teachers to promote 'transversal competences' such as 'thinking and learning to learn', 'managing daily life' and 'IT competence'. This applies both to class teachers of young children and subject teachers of older pupils, who must teach the transversal competences as well as the skills specific to their subject. There is also a strong focus on cross-curricular themes that are to be embedded in the working culture of schools - in subjects, extra-curricular clubs and societies and in special activities, such as excursions, camps and school festivals. These themes include, among others, cultural identity and internationalism, responsibility for the environment, media skills and communication, participatory citizenship and entrepreneurship and, perhaps most significantly, growth as a person.

As part of this commitment to general education, every municipality must ensure that each of its schools includes a major multi-disciplinary learning module in the curriculum for each year group. The aim of these modules is to help students to see the connections between the different subjects they study and to understand how the knowledge and skills they are acquiring can be applied to the world beyond school. As the Finnish National Board of Education's Head of Curriculum Development patiently explains to me, someone from a totally different educational culture, "They learn to collaborate and create knowledge together." The length and precise nature of each of these modules is decided by the municipalities, in collaboration with their schools. The modules are often topic studies or enquiry-based projects, but they also include initiatives such as artistic productions and community projects. These are essentially collaborative activities, with students and teachers working together to plan and implement the modules. Students learn to "take responsibility for their own studies, to create contacts with partners outside school, to use digital tools and environments in diverse ways." The government feels that the new multi-disciplinary initiative is making an invaluable contribution to the recent curricular reforms. "They seem to inspire teachers and help them to rethink teaching and learning approaches as well as the roles of teachers and students." The Helsinki municipality has agreed with its schools that they will include not one, but at least two such modules in each year.

The breadth of Finnish education is reflected in its assessment system. The Matriculation Examination seeks to measure students' general maturity, including their readiness for higher education. The focus of these exams is to test students' ability to cope with unexpected tasks. The standard form of assessment employed in most other countries concentrates on strictly objective tests that avoid open-ended questions which enable candidates to express a personal opinion. The Finnish exam adopts a totally different approach. Students are routinely asked to show that they can deal with issues relating to politics, war and violence, evolution, the environment, health, sex, ethics in sport, drugs, losing a job and popular music. Such issues invariably require a multi-disciplinary perspective and enable candidates to draw on their knowledge and understanding of different subjects.

Instead of sitting a national exam, students who follow vocational courses are assessed by their schools, in accordance with national guidelines designed to maintain equity between schools. The aim of the assessment is to develop a positive self-image and personal growth in students who have different strengths and competencies. Students are required to make a self-assessment of the knowledge, understanding and skills that they have gained from their course. They are then interviewed and assessed by their teachers.

One of the most significant of the many distinctive features of the Finnish education system is the trust and responsibility that it places in its teachers. Many young Finns regard teaching as the most prestigious of all professions - above medicine and law - and training to teach at primary level is one of the most sought-after university courses. The country has developed outstanding HE education courses which provide prospective teachers with an understanding of the underlying theories behind the country's education system. Students are trained not only to teach, but to diagnose, plan and evaluate. Finland's teachers are arguably the best trained and qualified in the world and they enter a profession that will provide purposeful professional development throughout their careers. They are paid slightly above the country's average salary level, but, more importantly, they are expected to exercise their professional expertise and judgement to the full - both independently and collectively in their schools. They are given considerable autonomy and control over the curriculum, teaching methods, student assessment, school improvement and community involvement. Responsibility and trust are put before accountability. The Finns call it 'teacher professionalism'. Throughout the world, young people enter the teaching profession fired with enthusiasm to work with children - to develop their potential to lead a rewarding life and to make a valuable contribution to their society. Finnish teachers are given the responsibility, the latitude, the support and the time to fulfil that mission.

Finland has a good record of achieving political consensus on important social and political issues. Even so, there was inevitably a sharp debate over the country's educational reforms. Strong concern was voiced at the wholesale rejection of education policies taken for granted in other countries. All the familiar extreme right-wing priorities were advocated - more teaching and testing; more competition between students and schools; more specialisation and parental choice; additional time devoted to increasing the performance of 'gifted and talented' students, and a greater awareness of the need to compete with other countries with regard to academic exam results. But the drive for a distinctive and different approach was maintained, and steadily gained support. The critical voices were dramatically silenced when the OECD published its first PISA educational standards league table, based on a series of tests given to 15 year-olds throughout the world. Finland's students were top of the OECD's thirty countries in all three subject areas examined - in reading, mathematics and science.

The educational world was amazed that a country that had rejected a market-forces approach to education could outperform every other OECD member in the league table game and even compete with those Asian countries outside the OECD that focus single-mindedly on drilling their children for exam success and use every trick in the game to ensure league table supremacy. Since 2001, Finland's league position has varied, but has always been high, and, in the most recent round of tests, it was again the most successful OECD country. Finland has reacted calmly to its fame and maintained its commitment to educational principles very different to those of most of its PISA competitors. The country has been inundated with visitors trying to discover the secret of its successful education system. One of those well-equipped to enlighten them is Pasi Sahlberg, former Director General of the Finnish Centre of International Mobility and adviser to the country's Ministry of Education and Culture. Dr Sahlberg has analysed education systems around the world and received numerous awards for his work on equity and excellence in education. He explains Finland's success in a few words:

"The Finnish recipe for good education is simple: Always ask yourself if the policy or reform you plan to initiate is going to be good for children or teachers. If you hesitate with the answer, don't do it."

UK politicians haven't been very prominent among the delegations visiting Finland to ask questions and observe what goes on in their schools. Hardly surprising, as the Finnish system blows a gaping hole in the arguments that have produced our country's education system. Our leaders tend to stick stubbornly to their preference for the totalitarian model of education which produces unquestioning conformists to the party line. McKinsey and Company, the American firm employed by the British government to pioneer the Teach First scheme, produced a report on successful education systems across the world that education reformers would find interesting. Finland wasn't even mentioned.

Of course no-one in their right mind would advocate trying to replicate the Finnish system in this country. A great deal can be learnt from the way other people do things, but ultimately an education system reflects the values and priorities of the particular society of which it is a part. British values and priorities are not Finnish values and priorities. Our country is materialistic, class-ridden and deeply-divided. It has lost any sense of shared values or understanding of how to work together to achieve a shared goal. The rhetoric is still there - respect for the individual and minorities, fair play and decency, tolerance and equality - but the reality is that a significant section of the community ignores these ideals in pursuit of its own selfish ends. The idea of UK politicians with professional experience of education sitting round a table with teachers, teacher-trainers and students, in a collaborative effort to devise a school curriculum based on the concept of nurturing each child's natural curiosity, interests and aptitudes - this is a fantasy as unrealistic as expecting the House of Commons to conduct its affairs in a civilised and decent manner.

There is no better indication of the appalling political double-talk that pervades the UK education system than the Government's September 2016 Green Paper, *Schools that Work for Everyone*. This policy document re-iterates the Prime Minister's pledge that her Government will be "dedicated to making Britain a country that works for everyone, not just the privileged few". And this principle is to be placed at the heart of our education system, ensuring that all children will be given the opportunity to achieve their potential. The Government, we are told, is committed to delivering diversity and 'real inclusivity' in schools. The rhetoric could have been lifted straight out of the Finnish blueprint for an equitable education system. But the similarity ends there. The proposals outlined are a ragbag of all the familiar British obsessions with academic priorities, examination success, élite institutions and Thatcherite market forces. The aim is not to do away with privilege, but simply to enable more children to benefit from it. Thus public schools will be required to offer more scholarships for state school children, more children will have a grammar school education and more of those from deprived home backgrounds will go to Russell Group universities. And all these institutions - public schools, grammars and traditional universities - will be expected to assume a patronising role helping the casualties of a divisive system to cope with the loss of their most academically-successful students. The whole document is a masterpiece of chicanery and second-hand-car salesmanship. And delivered with the confidence and authority of a logical argument.

Reasoned argument isn't a characteristic much associated with politicians. When Gove imposed his doctrinaire, one-size-fits-all national curriculum on schools in 2013 the *Independent published* a letter signed by academics from 100 British universities expressing deep concern at the new demands on teachers and children, demands that it was convinced would erode rather than raise education standards in the way that Gove claimed:

"Much of it (the new national curriculum) demands too much too soon. This will put pressure on teachers to rely on rote learning without understanding. Inappropriate demands will lead to failure and demoralisation. The learner is largely ignored. Little account is taken of children's potential interests and capacities, or that young children need to relate abstract ideas to their experience, lives and activity.

The new curriculum is extremely narrow. The mountains of detail for English, maths and science leave little space for other learning. Speaking and listening, drama and modern media have almost disappeared from English.

This curriculum betrays a serious distrust of teachers, in its amount of detailed instructions, and the Education Secretary has repeatedly ignored expert advice. Whatever the intention, the proposed curriculum will result in a 'dumbing down' of teaching and learning."

Michael Gove responded to this reasoned argument with a spectacular temper tantrum. Writing in his mentor's *Daily Mail on Sunday,* he poured out a stream of abuse against the 100 signatories of the *Independent* letter. They were Marxists, the 'new enemies of promise'. They were a 'set of politically-motivated individuals who have been actively trying to prevent millions of our poorest children getting the education they need.' These academics help 'run the university departments of education responsible for developing curricula and teacher-training courses'. They are part of 'the Blob'. In the past, Gove continues,

"The Blob tended to operate by stealth, using its influence to control the quangos and committees which shaped policy. But the Blob has broken cover in the letters pages of the broadsheets because the Government is taking it on. We have abolished the quangos they controlled. We have given a majority of secondary schools academy status so they are free from the influence of the Blob's allies in local government. We are moving teacher training away from university departments and into our best schools. And we are reforming our curriculum and exams to restore the rigour they abandoned."

During the coalition government, Nick Clegg made no secret of his opposition to the new national curriculum and the 'absurd' behaviour of its architect, Michael Gove. Speaking to journalists on his campaign bus during the run-up to the 2015 election, the Liberal Democrats' leader said he'd been told that

Michael Gove personally drew up lists of medieval monarchs that he wanted children to learn about in their history lessons. Clegg was quoted in the *Independent* as saying: "I'm afraid this happens in government. I've seen this where a secretary of state, it all slightly goes to their head, they think it's their personal fiefdom or their personal gift."

This is certainly a common characteristic of education secretaries. John Patten who held the office from 1992-4 was charged by Jonathan Dimbleby in a BBC interview with taking "a vast panoply of powers upon yourself which allows you ... to ride roughshod over contrary opinion and simply heed those who are compliant to your own assumptions and attitudes." Patten gave a distinctive twist to his self-importance by talking as if he had a direct line to God. His thesis appeared to be that loss of fear of the eternal consequences of goodness and badness encouraged criminality, indiscipline and bad behaviour in schools. Corporal punishment figured prominently in his ideology and, as a secretary of state, he matched Gove in heaping abuse on those whose educational ideals were different from his own. An early advocate of removing education from local education authority control, Patten launched an extraordinary attack on the newly-appointed Director of Education for Birmingham, the highly respected and charismatic educationist, Tim Brighouse, now Sir Tim Brighouse. At a party conference he called Brighouse 'a nutter' and spoke of his "fear for Birmingham, with this madman let loose, wandering the streets, frightening the children".

Tim Brighouse did in fact walk the streets of Birmingham after he had been appointed: he wanted to get the feel of the city which was home to the children whose education would be affected by his leadership of their schools. The first time I met Tim I walked a few city streets with him. He was Director of Education for Oxfordshire at the time, a post that he acquired at the age of 38. I had asked to meet him in connection with a book I was writing. I reported to the reception desk at the council offices and asked for directions to the education department. I was told that Mr Brighouse would come out to meet me, which he did. We shook hands and he said, "Would you like lunch, or shall we do an art gallery?" We walked through the Oxford streets, busy with August visitors, our short journey to the art gallery punctuated by three separate meetings with passers-by whom Tim obviously knew. Initially, I assumed these must be heads of his Oxfordshire schools but quickly realised, from the conversations, that they were classroom teachers. Their pleasure at seeing their Director of Education and being asked for an update on their work was palpable.

Directors of Education need to keep themselves well-briefed by their officers on the schools in their charge, so that, like good teachers with their pupils, they are aware of their individual circumstances, strengths and weaknesses. Tim Brighouse, however, has always set himself a much greater challenge - to get to know his schools and the people in them personally. He is essentially a people person. He inspires heads and their staff by his genuine interest in them, his obvious appreciation of their efforts, his understanding of the problems and difficulties they face, the supportive way he encourages people to improve their performance and the way he gets educationists working together in pursuit of shared goals. It's a management style that many politicians have clearly decided inappropriate in an education system controlled by market forces. It's a tribute to all those educationists, who like Tim Brighouse work tirelessly to keep a beleaguered profession thinking positively, that teachers have managed for so long to withstand the constant denigration and abuse that pours forth from the Murdoch press and its political supporters and lackeys.

Tim Brighouse is a warm and generous man, tolerant, understanding, able to see the other side of an argument. But Patten badly underestimated the inner confidence and resolution of the person he reviled. Without any great public display of indignation at the Education Secretary's defamation of his character, Tim sued him for libel. Patten settled out of court and had to issue an unreserved apology in which he admitted "that his remarks were false and without any justification whatsoever". Patten lost his job and disappeared from public notice and influence. The compensation for damages and the expenses that Patten had to pay, together with donations received in response to a national campaign to support the libel action, amounted to a considerable sum, which Tim donated to charity. The larger part of the money was used to found an organisation called the University of the First Age which supports teenage summer schools and topic-based 'super learning days'.

Ridicule and abuse are the standard response of politicians and their media allies to anyone who questions the Establishment's limited view of education. Regardless of the validity and quality of their work, liberal thinkers run a constant risk of being labelled '60s' progressives' or dangerous Marxists dedicated to destroying our society, a stigma they then carry to the grave - and indeed beyond. Andrew Adonis, in his account of how he and Tony Blair worked to dismantle the comprehensive school system, adds a sour postscript to the glowing tributes paid to Michael Marland, one of its outstanding architects, after his death from cancer in 2008. Adonis sneeringly dismisses Marland as 'a bow-tied guru of the comprehensive movement' who failed as a head.

Michael Marland wasn't a big man physically but he was an educational colossus, a man of great enthusiasm and energy who had an immense influence on British education, not only as a result of his lecturing, writing and contribution to national committees, but through his example as a dedicated and highly imaginative teacher and head. He led from the front and inspired others by what he did, as well as what he said. He believed passionately that education was a major force for good that had the power to enable people of different races, beliefs, social backgrounds and opinions to understand each other and work together to improve the quality of human relationships. He was a tireless champion of the importance of the arts and multilingual education and a pioneer of new approaches to classroom teaching, pastoral care and community education. His work on community relations extended far beyond the school gates.

I first heard of Michael Marland when, as a head of English, he replaced his school's standard journal of dry, self-congratulatory reports of the year with a creative magazine produced by students and featuring original articles, poems, photographs and artwork. I was just one of many English teachers who picked up on this new idea and ran with it. Some years later he asked me to contribute to a series of good practice books that he was editing for the publisher Heinemann and then to help him run annual courses for teachers at Churchill College, Cambridge. He was a perceptive and supportive editor and a brilliant course leader. I recall an occasion on one of his courses when a main speaker had badly disappointed with a key talk that went all round the subject but was sadly short of substance. We adjourned for tea and, when we returned, Michael said he'd had a few thoughts on the afternoon topic that he'd like to share with us. He then proceeded to deliver the lecture we'd hoped to hear from the visiting speaker - pertinent, challenging and, as Michael's talks always were, full of practical detail and sound common sense.

What always impressed me about Michael was his efficiency and effectiveness. He may have worn a bow tie, but it would have been very difficult to have found anyone less like the hard-line politicians' habitual caricature of a 60s' hippy 'progressive' whose airy-fairy theories destroyed class discipline and the essential rigour of learning. Michael had his feet firmly on the ground and his classic little manual, *The Craft of the Classroom* (1975), which has been a life-saver for generations of young teachers, states unequivocally that if any would-be teachers find the notion of 'control' repugnant they should re-consider their profession. Another highly influential book that reflected Michael's own practices was *Pastoral Care* (1974) in which he states, 'The central task of the school must be sensitive, warm, human, efficient, realistic and thorough.' I spent a day in one of Michael's schools and had the privilege of seeing an example of its care of children first hand. A difficult and unresponsive Year 9 or 10 boy had turned a corner during the week of my visit, having spent much of his time in the art studio engaged in a piece of artwork that had captured his imagination - only to have his newfound interest and more positive attitude to school snatched away from him by another pupil who had ruined what he was creating. He was completely distraught, unconsolable - destroyed, together with the piece of work that had given him a rare experience of pleasure and feeling of self-esteem. During my visit, I was able to see how Michael and his staff dealt with this very difficult situation and I was greatly moved by their compassion, patience and professional skill. I cannot say that I experienced an epiphany on that day, as the importance of the teacher's care role was already something to which I gave much thought. But there is no doubt that what I saw intensified my desire to ensure that pastoral care was always at the forefront of my concerns as a head and principal. This is perhaps the greatest gift of truly outstanding educationists - to strengthen the resolve of those who share their ideals and convictions and to help maintain their commitment to the things that really matter in working with young people.

One of the few things our divided British society is able to agree on is its disillusionment with our leading politicians. Most of the electorate don't listen to them, and many of those who do don't believe what they say. The popular image is of a group of people who profess to have the public interest at heart, but who will actually say and do almost anything to further their own interests and those of their close associates. No section of our community has more reason to hold that view than those working in education. Education involves a search for truth and consensus, and a striving for harmony in human relationships. The system in this country has been shaped by people whose ideas and behaviour suggest a diametrically opposite agenda. The blatant failure of successive ministers and their officers to examine evidence, consult, or listen to informed opinion before they make decisions; their constant tinkering with the system to establish their own political credibility; their overweening sense of their own importance and the dogmatic way in which they impose their personal ideologies; the small-minded readiness to resort to abuse and personal attacks the moment that anyone disagrees with them - these all ensure a thoroughly negative impact on the teaching profession.

The Cambridge Primary Review, sponsored by the Esmée Fairbairn Foundation and led by Professor Robin Alexander, published its final report in October 2009. It represented the findings of the most extensive review of primary school education undertaken since Plowden in 1967. Impressively thorough and wide-ranging in its research and consultation, this review was built on the latest findings on children's capabilities and the ways in which young people learn at different stages of their development. It reaffirmed the importance of respecting children's needs, views and experiences as laid down by the UN Convention on the Rights of the Child. Whilst the review report was obviously concerned with primary education, a number of its most important recommendations related to the education system as a whole. Pertinently, it called for an end to 'the discourses of derision' and stressed the need to ensure that the education debate showed 'respect for research evidence and professional experience', so that it 'exemplified rather than negated what education should be about'. It recommended that the present 'top-down control and prescription' should be replaced by 'professional empowerment', stating unequivocally that 'it is not for government, government agencies and local authorities to tell teachers how to teach'.

Predictably, the Report got the usual short-shift treatment. Sensationalist media headlines distorted the Review's findings, and it was to these headlines that the politicians responded:

"In our archive we have a record of all media coverage of the Review and all published government responses. There is a clear and direct relation between them. Government responded not to what we reported but to what the media said we reported."

The last 50 years have seen a steady stream of reviews of education that demonstrate why major changes to the system are so necessary. The reports that result from these exercises are an invaluable support to teachers in the absence of the national organisations, networks and LEA advisory and training services that successive governments have systematically closed down. They recognise and applaud the excellent work that teachers are doing, despite the enormous pressures they are under to abandon their principles and ideals and to conform to a damaging political agenda. They inspire new ideas and spawn initiatives in response to their recommendations. Some of them, like the Cambridge Primary Review, lead to some form of action group to take their recommendations forward, despite the inevitable government opposition. Sadly though, none of these studies, enquiries or consultative exercises achieves its fundamental aim: to persuade government of the urgent need to change direction. In that respect, the educationists involved in such initiatives are simply wasting their time and energy.

During my time as a sixth-form college principal, the College's senior management team supplied detailed evidence to four different national enquiries into the sixth-form curriculum. All were set up by governments seemingly aware of widespread concern over early specialisation in the secondary school and the narrowness of the sixth-form curriculum. Yet all were abortive. No serious attempt to broaden sixth-form students' experience can overcome the Establishment's absolute faith in the A level 'gold standard'.

Involvement in these exercises can be very time-consuming. Gordon Higginson showed me the evidence that his committee had read during their 1987-8 consultation exercise to find a way forward on the sixth-form curriculum: it ran the length of one wall of his study in Southampton University. Another of these repeated initiatives required an alternative sixth-form curriculum to be trialled in various schools and colleges in different parts of the country. Those taking part were asked to estimate how a new approach might work out in practice - the kind of problems that might arise over its administration and management and the ways in which it would change students' programmes of study. Queen Mary's College was one of the institutions involved and we had to interview the whole of an A level cohort, several hundred students, to explain the proposed system to them and ask them to decide on the choice of subjects that each would make if the proposals were a reality. We then designed a timetable to show how students' requested programmes could be delivered. This exercise involved busy staff in an immense amount of extra work for no additional remuneration. They accepted this philosophically, believing that they were engaged in a genuine consultative exercise. But such goodwill tends to run out when it becomes obvious that there is no likelihood of any of these 'consultations' actually influencing government decisions: they're simply window-dressing, strategies for keeping reformers quiet while the government gets on with implementing its political agenda. As for independent enquiries such as the Cambridge Primary Review, they're doomed from the start. One strongly suspects that education secretaries and their ministers don't read any reports produced by reviews of education, whether independent or government-initiated. If they do, it's certainly not with an open mind, for the standard blanket condemnation with which they're habitually dismissed negates any reasoned debate. It's not surprising that many educationists have come to the conclusion that some of those who wield power over them have little genuine interest in education at all.

Michael Gove's paranoid response to the academics' letter in the *Independent* provides an interesting insight into the political agenda that lies behind many of the policy decisions that have shaped our present form of education. It makes it clear, for example, that organisations like the Schools Council and the General Teaching Council were disbanded because they gave educationists a voice, or, as Gove puts it, they were run by 'The Blob'. These people are, apparently, motivated by a desire to prevent children receiving the education that they need. They have allies in local government who share their aims. That's why it's been so necessary to relieve the LEAs of their responsibility for education. But the worst members of 'The Blob', says Gove, are the academics who run university education departments and indoctrinate trainee teachers in Marxist ideas. The government intends to close these places down. The education departments have already been relieved of the responsibility they once had for helping to determine the school curriculum and exam system, and this has enabled the government to restore rigour to children's studies and to re-introduce traditional objective methods of assessment. The next step, Gove continues, is to get rid of these academic 'enemies of promise' altogether - by the simple expediency of dispensing with teacher-training and doing them out of a job. This sheds a whole new light on the Teach First initiative. Increasingly, new entrants to the profession will go straight into teaching from university, just as they do in higher education. Ideally, they will have followed an Oxbridge, lecture-based course in a traditional subject. They will thus have experienced seven to eight years of formal academic instruction - GCSE, A level and single-subject honours degree - untainted by any new-fangled educational ideas. The dream is of a teaching profession completely subservient to the government's political agenda.

Educationists pray that this will never come about: that those who really care about education and the kind of society we build for our children will survive whatever the politicians throw at them. Even prisoners and the inhabitants of concentration camps find ways of expressing themselves creatively. And it is still possible to find plenty of examples of good practice throughout the education system -

imaginative syllabuses, outstanding classroom practitioners and innovative whole school policies. But, as political control steadily tightens, it's getting harder and harder to hold on to fundamental educational principles. The pressures are relentless and come from different directions, not just the government itself - the Murdoch press and its readers, governors and school managers driven by the competitive urge, and children themselves, who are being indoctrinated to believe that test and examination success are the only things that matter in their school experience.

Day after day, classroom teachers look for ways of nurturing children's natural curiosity and creativity; encouraging their imagination and problem-solving; developing their independence, resilience and adaptability; helping to shape their character and moral values. But, increasingly, they are working in a culture that no longer prioritises these ideals, indeed often denigrates them. Most teachers are still passionate about their role, but the excitement has gone out of their job and their fighting spirit is becoming exhausted. In stark contrast to the media and political reaction to the Cambridge Primary Review, the public and professional response was overwhelmingly positive. The educationists responsible for the Review worked hard at their dissemination events to encourage the teaching profession to embrace their proposals, pointing out that many of them could be taken forward within the present set-up. The habitual response from heads and teachers was that, whilst they liked the ideas, they couldn't act on them without government permission. This is indicative of a depressing and dangerous resignation, an acceptance of political control and its pernicious consequences. Teachers are no longer educational pioneers: they have been reduced to rearguard action, just clinging on to the principles in which they believe, preventing them from being snuffed out altogether. They are the victims of a top down ideology, servants of a system which requires them to do only what they are told. Pasi Sahlberg's simple recipe for a successful education system - always put the children and their teachers at the forefront of your thinking - seems a hopelessly unattainable goal in this country. Yet if we don't fight for this ideal we are lost.

Everyone who knows and hates what is happening to our education system should now stand up to be counted. More voices have to be raised in support of good practice, and in opposition to every measure that undermines it. And those voices have to be louder. Let's take every opportunity to stress the educational, social and cultural benefits of our genuinely comprehensive schools. Good teaching and exciting courses, at all levels, should be widely publicised - by parents and students, as well as educationists. We need more parents to use social media, as Lucy Hoggan did, to explain the adverse effects government policies can have on children; more leading educationists, like Tim Brighouse, taking on the abusers and exposing their underhand methods; more groups like children's writers, designers, artists, musicians, dancers, actors publically denouncing the way in which creative subjects are being removed from the curriculum; more employers speaking out against the failure of the present system to develop the qualities that young people should be bringing into our businesses and industries. We want a much stronger drive to promote practical and vocational education and to prepare students for the many excellent HE courses that are now being offered as an antidote to the Russell Group's traditional adherence to academic purity. We must give meaningful support to those who train our teachers and put a stop to the nonsense about closing the education departments of universities.

There comes a time in all struggles to bring about change for the better when you have to take matters into your own hands. That moment has come for all who genuinely care about education. We have been on the back foot for long enough. There have been years of fragmented protest and lobbying from different sectors of education, separate teaching unions, parents' organisations and various protest groups seeking specific reforms. All to little effect. The Establishment has found it only too easy to keep these largely uncoordinated initiatives apart and play one off against another, thus negating their impact. We now have to unite in concerted and sustained action to return ownership of our children's education to where it belongs - the children and their teachers.

References

Chapter 1

Sir Ken Robinson, *Out of Our Minds*, Capstone Publishing Ltd, Chichester, 2011 (revised edition), p 7.

Pablo Picasso, quoted in *Peter's Quotations: Ideas for Our Time,* Laurence J.Peter, Bantam Books, New York, 1977, p 25.

Sir Peter Ustinov's Obituary, BBC News Online, 29th March, 2004.

Sir Richard Branson, *Times*, London, 11th September, 1998, p 19.

H G Wells, *The Outline of History* (published in instalments, 1919), Reprint Services Corporation, 1920.

Mark Carney, speech to Lloyds, Insurers, 29th September, 2015.

Pope Francis, encyclical, *On Care for our Common Home*, 5th April, 2015.

President Obama, speech to the Glacier Conference, *Global Leadership in the Arctic: Co-operation, Innovation, Engagement and Resilience*, Anchorage, Alaska, 31st August, 2015.

Sir Ken Robinson, Afterword, *Out of Our Minds*, Capstone Publishing Ltd, 2011, p 285.

Sir Martin Rees, *Our Final Century: A Scientist's Warning: How Terror, Error and Environmental Disaster Threaten Humankind's Future in this Century - on Earth and Beyond*, Heinemann, 2003.

Charles Darwin, *Origin of Species by Natural Selection*, 1815.

John Cridland, Education and Skills Survey, *Learning to Grow: What Employers Need to Learn from Education and Skills*, CBI/Pearson, June 2012.

Professor Michael Bassey, *Political Impact: from the Least State-Controlled to the Most in 24 Years*, Nottingham Trent University Website, 2013.

Barry Sherman, quoted in Professor Michael Bassey's *Political Impact : from the Least State-Controlled to the Most in 24 years*, 2013.

Gateway to Growth Report, *Central London Connections: Building Futures,* CBI/Pearson, 2014.

Stephen Isherwood, radio interview, May, 2015.

Daily Mail article quoting Judith Carlisle, Headmistress, Oxford High School, 1st August , 2014.

Buckton Vale Primary School, letter to Year 6 pupils, May, 2015.

Central Advisory Council Report ('Plowden Report'), *Children and Their Primary Schools*, DES, 1967.

United Nations' Convention on the Rights of the Child (UNCRC), UNICEF, 1989.

Chapter 2

William Lovett, *Importance of General Education and the Modes to be Pursued in the Different Schools*, 1840.

Chris Woodhead, A *Desolation of Learning; Is This the Education Our Children Deserve?* Rake, Sussex: Pencil Sharp, 2009, p 98.

Michael Gove, speech delivered to the Social Market Foundation, *A Progressive Betrayal*, February, 2013.

Sir Michael Wilshaw, speech to the Association of School and College Leaders (ASCL), March, 2014.

Barry Hines, *A Kestrel for a Knave*, Michael Joseph, 1968, p 72.

Charles Dickens, *Hard Times*, 1854, (Penguin, 1969, p.48).

Nick Gibb, BBC World at One interview, May, 2016.

Michael Morpurgo, speech to Wicked Young Writers' Award Ceremony, December, 2012.

Anthony Howard, *The Life of R A Butler*, Jonathan Cape, 1987.

Maurice Kogan, *The Politics of Education: Edward Boyle and Anthony Crosland in Conversation with Maurice Kogan*, Penguin, 1971.

Conversation with Estelle Morris, the Baroness Morris of Yardley, 16th July, 2015

Chapter 3

Melissa Benn, *School Wars*, Verso, 2011, p xvii.

Nuffield Foundation, *Nuffield Science Project*, 1962.

Sir Charles Snow, Rede Lecture: *The Two Cultures and the Scientific Revolution*, 1959.

Sir Cyril Burt, *Experimental Tests of General Intelligence*, British Journal of Psychology, 1909.

Tony Blair, Government Green Paper: *Schools - Building Success*, February, 2001.

Alastair Campbell, press briefing introducing Government Green Paper, *Schools: Building Success*, February, 2001.

Michael Gove, press interview preceding Conservative Party Conference, September 2008.

Chris Woodhead, *Class War*, Little, Brown, 2002, p 127.

Theresa May, speech on becoming Prime Minister, No. 10 Downing Street, 13th July, 2016.

Chapter 4

Sir Gordon Higginson, Foreword to Report on *Advancing A levels*, 1988.

Arthur Claydon CBE, *Maidstone Grammar School: A Record, 1549-1965*, Headley Brothers Ltd., 1965, p 21.

Andrew Adonis, *Education, Education, Education*, Biteback Publishing Ltd., London, 2012, p 225.

Khalil Gibran, poem in *The Prophet*, Alfred A. Knopf, New York, 1923, p 12.

Sir Frederick Kenyon, letter to T.F.Tout, Professor of History, University of Manchester, 1918, quoted by Sir Christopher Ball in *A Proper General Education*, 1984, p 82.

Sir Christopher Ball, paper - *A Proper General Education*, 1984, p 83.

Sir Gordon Higginson, Foreword, *Report on Advancing A levels*, HMSO, London, 1988.

H.C.Bradby, *Thomas Arnold's Rugby Reforms*, 1900.

Mike Baker, BBC News, 26th February, 2005.

Sir Charles Snow, Rede Lecture: *The Two Cultures and the Scientific Revolution*, 1959.

Jean Piaget, *The Origins of Intelligence in Children*, International Universities Press, New York, 1952.

Chapter 5

Sir Cyril Norwood, Head Master, Harrow, article in *The Spectator* quoted (p.75) in Nicholas Timmins' *The Five Giants: a Biography of the Welfare State*, Harper Collins, London, 2001.

Baroness Blackstone interview, *Guardian*, 12th July, 2005.

The Campaign for the University of Oxford, letter to alumni, January, 2015.

Winchester College prospectus, Anderson Norton Design, London, 2015.

Good Schools Guide, June 2013.

The Tatler Schools Guide, 2011.

Michael Gove, speech to independent school headteachers' conference, 10th May, 2012.

Patrick Wintour, article, *Private and State Schools to Co-Operate More or Face Penalties*, *Guardian*, 25th November, 2014.

Frances Ryan, article, *Forget Tristam Hunt's Tinkering: Private Schools Should Have Their Tax Breaks Stopped Altogether*, *New Statesman*, 25th November, 2014.

Sir Michael Wilshaw, Foreword to the Ofsted Report, *Going the Extra Mile: Excellence in Competitive School Sport*, HMSO, June 2014.

Marlborough College website, September, 2016.

Michael Wilshaw, speech to independent school headteachers, Wellington College, 2nd October, 2013.

Sir Anthony Seldon, *Guardian* interview, June 2012.

Chapter 6

Wally Olins, founder of Wolff-Olins Business Consultants, Sir Ken Robinson's *Out of Our Minds* (revised edition), Capstone Publishing Ltd., Chichester, 2011, p vi.

Report of Nick Gibb's opening remarks to staff after being appointed Schools Minister, May 2010, *Guardian*, 16th May, 2010.

Sir Tim Brighouse, interview with Peter Wilby, *Guardian*, April 2007.

Russell Group, promotion video, 2015.

Michael Gove, written statement to Parliament on reformed GCSE and A level content, 9th April, 2014.

BTEC Courses, Peter Symonds College, *Prospectus*, 2016.

David Willett, BBC radio programme, 12th January, 2016.

Ipsos Mori Report for the DfE, *The Effects of the English Baccalaureate*, HMSO, 5th October, 2012.

Schools Music Association, *Guardian* summary of public statement, 23rd September, 2012.

Creative Industries' Directors and Chief Executives letter to *The Times*, *The Arts in Schools*, 8th January, 2016.

Professor Lloyd Webber interview with Richard Jinman, *The Independent on Sunday*, 1st November, 2013.

Arts Council Report, *Drama in Schools*, 1st October, 2003.

DfE letter to Birmingham Repertory Theatre concerning the role of drama in schools, November, 2012.

Patricia Baldwin, *Guardian* article, 7th January, 2013.

Chapter 7

Jean Piaget, *The Origins of Intelligence in Children*, International Universities Press, New York, 1952.

Conversation with Julia King, the Baroness Brown of Cambridge, Vice-Chancellor of Aston University, 25th January, 2016.

Salters Horners A level Physics Course, feedback from teachers, 14th March, 2012.

Michael Gove, ITV Programme, *Daybreak*, 8th July, 2013.

Andreas Schleicher, Global Education Management Systems (GEMS) People Article, *Building Skills not Degrees*, 12th March, 2014.

Charles Dickens, *Hard Times*, 1854 (Penguin, 1969, p.48).

Andrew Adonis, account of visit to Durand Academy by *Times* journalist, Helen Rumbelow, *Education, Education, Education*, Biteback Publishing Ltd., London, 2012, p 225.

Pauline Gibbons, *Scaffolding Language, Scaffolding Learning: Teaching English Language Learners in the Mainstream Classroom* (2nd edition), Portsmouth NH:Heinemann, 2015, p 94.

Chapter 8

National Committee of Enquiry into Higher Education, *Higher Education in the Learning Society* ('Dearing Report') HMSO, London, 1997 para. 3.41.

HECFE/Paul Hamlyn Foundation, *Building Student Engagement and Belonging in Higher Education at a Time of Change: Summary of Findings and Recommendations* from the What Works: Student Retention and Success programme, 2012.

Mary Lawson, *Crow Lake*, Vintage Books, 2003, pp 321-322.

Chapter 9

Roy Blatchford and Rebecca Clark, editors, Introduction to *Self-Improving Schools: the Journey to Excellence*, National Education Trust, John Catt, Woodbridge, 2016, p 11.

Higher Education Green Paper, *Fulfilling our Potential: Teaching Excellence, Social Mobility and Student Choice*, HMSO, London, 2015.

Professor Lee Harvey, letter to the *Times Higher Education* magazine on the National Student Survey, 17th April, 2008.

Harriet Swain, *Guardian* article on the National Student Survey: *A Hotch-potch of Subjectivity*, 19th May,2013.

Chapter 10

Thomas Wyse, article in *Education Reform*, Central Society of Education, 1837.

Royal Society of Arts Report: *Educating the Failing 40%*, Open Public Services Network (OPSN), RSA, 25th March, 2016.

Times Educational Supplement article on RSA Report: *Educating the Failing 40%*, 25th March, 2016.

Report of Nick Gibb's opening remarks to staff after being appointed Schools Minister, May 2010, *Guardian*, 16th May, 2010.

Farnborough Sixth-Form College prospectus, 2015-2016.

Higher Education Academy Report: *The Experience of Joint Honours Students of English in UK Higher Education*, English Subject Centre (HEA), June 2011.

Tony Little, speaking at an Intelligence Squared debate in favour of the motion *Let's End the Tyranny of the Test: Relentless School Testing Demeans Education*, Emmanuel Centre, London, 1st October, 2015.

Brian Cox interview, *Radio Times*, 28th June, 2016.
English Department, University of Nottingham: video of staff and students talking about the BA Honours English Course, 2016.

Advice to students applying to university to read Medicine, Royal Society of Medicine, 2016.

Chapter 11

Peter Mortimore, *Education Under Siege*, Policy Press, Bristol, 2014.

Government Department for Culture, Media and Sport, *How UK Sport Funding Works*, HMSO, 13th August, 2012.

Ofsted Report, *Going the Extra Mile: Excellence in Competitive School Sport*, HMSO, London, 20th June, 2014.

Lucy Hoggan, open letter to the Government on the new SATs requirements, January, 2016.

Jill Cosh, letter to *The Guardian*, *Grammatical Tyranny*, May, 2016.

Mark Rylance, interview on the BBC's *One Show*, 22nd July, 2016.

Opinium Research/Satander Bank Survey, *Families Moving House to Secure School Places for their Children*, August, 2015.

Officer of the Schools' Adjudicator, *Admission Referral Decision about the London Oratory School, OSA*, London, 19th June, 2015.

Sir Tim Brighouse, *The Story of London Challenge*, edited by David Woods and Tim Brighouse, London Leadership Strategy, 2014.

Sir Anthony Seldon, article in the *Radio Times*, *Speak Up for Schools: Our Children Need Inspiring - not Testing*, 30th May-5th June, 2015.

Lucie Russell, Campaigns Director, Young Minds, quoted in *The Guardian*, 20th May, 2011.

Peter Hyman, *The Courage of Our Convictions, Self-Improving Schools: The Journey to Excellence*, National Education Trust, John Catt, Woodbridge, 2016.

Chapter 12

Peter Hyman, *The Courage of Our Convictions, Self-Improving Schools:*

The Journey to Excellence, National Education Trust, John Catt, Woodbridge, 2016, p.20.

Irmeli Halinen, Head of Curriculum Development, Finnish National Board of Education, private email, 30th June 2016.

Dr Pasi Sahlberg, *Finnish Lessons*, second edition, Teachers' College Press, New York, 2015, p xxiii.

Government Green Paper, *Schools that Work for Everyone,* HMSO, London, September, 2016.

Academics' letter to the *Independent, Gove Will Bury Pupils in Facts and Rules*, 19th March, 2013.

Michael Gove, article, *The Enemies of Promise, Mail on Sunday*, 23rd March, 2013.
Nick Clegg, quoted by the *Independent*, 7th April, 2015.

Jonathan Dimbleby television interview with John Patten, BBC I, 28th February, 1993.

John Patten, statement in the High Court, 22nd June, 1993, reported in the *Independent*, 23rd June, 1993.

Andrew Adonis, *Education, Education, Education*, Biteback Publishing Ltd., London, 2012, p 146.

Michael Marland, *The Craft of the Classroom*, Heinemann Educational Books, London, 1975, re-issued 2003.

Michael Marland, *Pastoral Care*, Heinemann Educational Books, London, 1974.

Report of the Cambridge Primary Review, sponsored by the Esmée Foundation, University Faculty of Education, Cambridge, October 2009, revised August 2010.

Professor Robin Alexander, *Evidence, Policy and the Reform of Primary Education: a Cautionary Tale, Forum*, Volume 56, No.3, Symposium Books Ltd, Oxford, 2014, p 362.

Acknowledgements

I'd like to thank everyone who has contributed in some way to this book:

- Jill, my ever-patient wife and astute critical friend; our children, whose views as parents and/or educationists have been invaluable;

- the grandchildren for their insightful and often entertaining observations on their various educational experiences;

- the students, parents and teachers who have been happy to talk education with me, to comment on key themes and, above all, encourage me in my writing - Alan Bennett, Tessa Blackstone, Tim Brighouse, Nuala Burgess, Alan Cottenden, Peter Cunningham, Dilly Fung, Eddie Grimble, Irmeli Halinen, Mark Henderson, Helen Higson, Lucy Hoggan, Julia King, Richard Lewney, Eugenia and Rod Lawrence, Tracey McCarley, Jane Machell, Julian Miles, Estelle Morris, Jon Nelson, David Read, Marcus Rutland, Anthony Seldon, Neil Smith, Gareth Thomas, Graham Virgo, Patricia Woodman.

I owe a particular debt to those friends, colleagues (and indeed strangers) who undertook to read (and in some instances proof-read) my manuscript, and who have subsequently recommended the book so warmly: Geoff Barton, Melissa Benn, Nick Dineen, Gwyn Evans, Evelyn Glennie, Chris Green, David Green, David Heaton, Rachel Macfarlane, Bob Moon, Mark Rylance, Chris Thompson, David Woods and Terry Wrigley.

Eric Macfarlane,
November, 2016.

Lightning Source UK Ltd.
Milton Keynes UK
UKOW02f2249041216
289159UK00004B/70/P